KU-512-563

DISCOVER SOUTHERN EUROPE

Reader's Digest

PUBLISHED BY THE READER'S DIGEST ASSOCIATION LIMITED

LONDON   NEW YORK   MONTREAL   SYDNEY

DISCOVER SOUTHERN EUROPE

Translated and edited by Toucan Books Limited, London
for Reader's Digest, London

Translated and adapted from the French
by Antony Mason

For Reader's Digest
Series Editor: Christine Noble
Editorial Assistant: Caroline Boucher
Production Controller: Byron Johnson

Reader's Digest General Books
Editorial Director: Cortina Butler
Art Director: Nick Clark

ISBN 0 276 42511 1

Discover the World: SOUTHERN EUROPE
was created and produced by Hubert Deveaux & Co, Paris
for Selection Reader's Digest S.A., Paris, and first published
in 1999 as *Regards sur le Monde: L'EUROPE DU SUD*

©1999 Selection Reader's Digest, S.A.
212 boulevard Saint-Germain, 75007, Paris

CONTENTS

INTRODUCING SOUTHERN EUROPE   5

Land and sea   6

A brief history   16

THE PLACE AND ITS PEOPLE   30

1 A TALENT FOR NATURAL COLOURS   32

The Cyclades: balcony on the Aegean   34

The heart of the Sardinian maquis   35

The fabled hills of Tuscany   36

The sierras of Aragón: a Wild West landscape   37

Mediterranean volcanoes: deceptive beauty   38

The Mediterranean: perilous, and in peril   40

Mountains, as Nature intended   42

The Algarve: colours and scents of Africa   44

Dalmatia: between rock and the deep blue sea   45

2 PEOPLE AND RESOURCES   46

The vine: a time-honoured heritage   48

Produce from the hothouse of Europe   50

Timeless olives   52

Marble: the white gold of the south   53

Fishing: a noble tradition in decline   54

From nomadic grazing to battery farming   55

Tides of exodus   56

Slovenia: defying the odds   58

Albania: anger and resignation   59

Sun, sea and tourism   60

3 LIVING IN SOUTHERN EUROPE — 62

The white villages of the south — 64

The shape of modern life — 65

A passion for religion — 66

The Basque region: tradition, autonomy and terrorism — 68

North versus south: divided Italy — 69

Living Mediterranean-style — 70

Italian television: fantasy and politics — 74

The thrill of the corrida — 75

A passion for football — 76

Mafia: organised crime — 77

The Belearic Islands: where all of Europe holidays — 78

The Balkans: letting the genie of nationalism out of the bottle — 80

Keeping the peace: putting the genie back in the bottle — 82

4 CITIES OF SOUTHERN EUROPE — 84

The Golden Age: Cordoba, Seville and Granada — 86

Madrid, and the art of good living — 88

Barcelona: Catalan capital — 89

The hills and villages of Lisbon — 90

Naples: living on the edge — 91

Venice, a city afloat — 92

Florence: Renaissance perfection — 94

Pompeii: snapshots of daily Roman life — 95

The Vatican: a tiny world capital — 96

Rome — 98

Layers of history — 99

The rich small cities of northern Italy — 104

Malta: sentinel of the southern Mediterranean — 106

Dubrovnik: pearl of the Adriatic — 107

Athens: the fount of Western civilisation — 108

Greece's sacred places — 109

Balkan capitals: finding their role — 110

5 CULTURE AND TRADITIONS — 112

Festival time — 114

Singing to the world — 116

Flamenco: dance with fire — 117

A passion for opera — 118

Writing: in pursuit of a formidable tradition — 119

European cinema: proud to be different — 120

A wealth of art — 122

The Venetian palette — 124

Portraits of Spain — 125

The grand palaces — 126

The stones of faith — 127

Mount Athos — 128

An archaeologist's dream — 129

6 LANDS OF INDUSTRY AND INVENTION — 130

Milan: the design capital, with a taste for luxury — 132

High fashion and the world of ready-to-wear — 133

From the Medicis to the Agnellis: a tradition of patrongage — 134

Greek shipowners: fabulous fortunes — 135

Around Italy by pasta — 136

Italian driving: second nature — 137

MAPS, FACTS AND FIGURES — 138

INDEX — 155

ACKNOWLEDGMENTS — 160

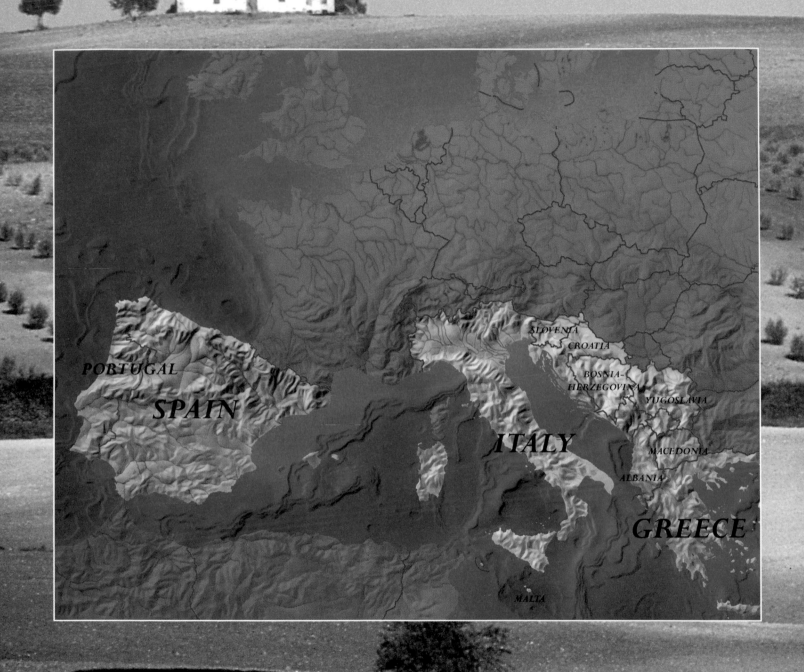

INTRODUCING
SOUTHERN EUROPE

Here are countries synonymous with the word Mediterranean, evoking the same images of sunbaked coasts, fragrant with the scent of pines and aromatic herbs, descending to azure seas. In these lands, age-old olive trees shoulder the dry summer heat like sentinels and the hinterland rises through plains of orange groves, vineyards, wheatfields and pasture to snow-capped peaks. This charmed and varied setting was the cradle of Western civilisation, and remains vibrant with a distinctively southern energy, pizzazz and relish for life.

Land and sea

Only the Strait of Gibraltar prevents the Mediterranean from being an inland sea. This tiny spout, 8 miles (13 km) across at its narrowest point, makes the sea virtually tideless, but a strong current flows through it to replace water lost by evaporation to the intense heat of the sun – so fierce that it has turned land just 300 miles (480 km) to the south into the Sahara Desert.

Parts of Spain are desert, a graphic reminder of the power of the southern sun. Summers are hot and mainly dry. Only certain kinds of plants can tolerate these conditions – plants such as oleander, olive and cypress trees, and vines. They can gather strength in the cool winters and during spring rains. The climate can be unforgiving and harsh on the inland plains, but by and large it is tolerable. In fact, to many people Southern Europe has the perfect climate, especially where there is shade, or cooling coastal breezes.

The hills and mountains provide refuge from the summer heat. Southern Europe is heavily contoured, reaching a crescendo along the northern borders in the high, snow-capped peaks of the Pyrenees and the Alps. Some parts of the mountain regions are so remote and wild that they bear little resemblance to the coasts, yet in the case of the Picos de Europe in northern Spain, the sea is only about 20 miles (32 km) away.

The mountains bear witness to the great heaving and folding of the Earth's crust that has taken place across the region in the past. The process continues. A faultline runs east–west through the centre of the Mediterranean region, an unsettling brooding presence that from time to time judders with an earthquake across Italy or Greece. Magma from this faultline wells up under Mount Etna and Mount Vesuvius, both still potentially lethal.

Aeons of interaction between land and sea has left the coastline ragged and fretted. Southern Europe consists essentially of three great peninsulas: Iberia, Italy and the Balkans. No part of Italy or Greece is more than 150 miles (240 km) from the coast. Ports lie in the protection of the countless indents that provide vital gates between the sea and the land. From earliest history, trade links spanned the self-contained world of the Mediterranean lands, and with the trade in goods came exchanges in technology, art, religion, mathematics and philosophy. The sea, trade and prosperity provided the essential propellants for the first civilisations of Southern Europe.

Sophisticated urban civilisations flourished in Greece, then in Italy, and then the Romans exported their version of civilisation across almost the entire continent of Europe and right around the Mediterranean Sea. The pattern was writ large again 1500 years later, when the Portuguese and Spanish – again by means of the sea – took their civilisations across the globe. Suddenly Southern Europe was linked by sea to the entire world, and ruled over much of it. But then Southern Europe rested on its laurels, remaining a largely agricultural economy until well into the 19th century, while Northern Europe took the initiative in colonial expansion and the Industrial Revolution.

The blend of history, climate and landscape has moulded Southern Europe into a vibrant quilt of nations. They do not see themselves as one, and are keener to point out their differences than what they have in common. But it is these differences that are the region's fascination. Each year, foreign visitors are lured by a variety of cuisines and landscapes, sun-drenched beaches, a rich archaeological legacy, art collections, traditions of hospitality, business opportunities – and the people's infectious desire to live life to the full.

Seen from space   A colour-enhanced satellite image echoes the English writer Lawrence Durrell's description of the Mediterranean as 'cobalt-blue'. It also highlights how Southern Europe is delicately poised between fertility and the desert rim of Africa.

Rocky reflections *Dozens of small, mirror-clear lakes like this one pepper the Cirque de Sobavedo, a scoop of rock high on the sides of the Vall d'Aran, a spectacular valley in Spain's central Pyrenees. On these high slopes, one of Europe's great rivers, the Garonne – known here as Garona – has its source: a tumbling torrent on its way to the plains of south-west France. A few miles to the south, the Pyrenees, that rugged chain of mountains that provide Spain's natural northern frontier, reach their highest point at Pico d'Aneto (11 170 ft/3404 m).*

Warm water *Swans on Lake Bled, northern Slovenia, can enjoy the benefits of water heated to 25°C (77°F) by hot springs. The lake, called Bledsko Jezero in Slovene, was formed by a glacier that scoured a path through the Julian Alps. With its combination of lake, woodlands and mountains, Bled became a fashionable resort at the turn of the 19th century, and maintains the tradition today, with golf and watersports in the summer, and skiing in winter.*

Magnet for writers *Lake Como lies in the foothills of the Italian Alps, about 22 miles (35 km) north of Milan. It is a famous summer retreat, cherished in the past by travellers and writers, including Wordsworth, Shelley, Byron and D.H. Lawrence. Despite the tranquil air of the elegant villas that line its shore, spring waters can send flood waters surging over the banks, and summer storms can whip the lake's surface to a fury.*

9

Cleft in Crete The Samaria Gorge runs for 11 miles (18 km) through the Greek island of Crete, making it the longest gorge in Europe. At the Iron Gates, its narrowest point, it is just 13 ft (4 m) wide.

Natural cathedral Over many thousands of years lime-bearing droplets of water have created a fantasy world in the Cueva de Nerja, the most spectacular caves of Andalucía in southern Spain.

Early art The caves of Altamira, in Cantabria, northern Spain, have some of the best preserved prehistoric paintings of Europe. These bison were painted on a cave ceiling about 16 000 years ago.

11

Window on myth   Locals call this arch
It Tieqa, 'the window'. It is one of many
dramatic sculptural shapes carved into the
rocky coastline of Gozo, the second largest island
of the Maltese archipelago, by the restless
churning of the Mediterranean Sea. Gozo is
thought to be the island of Ogygia in Greek
myth, where the shipwrecked Odysseus landed
and was held captive for seven years by the
goddess Calypso, who promised him eternal
youth and immortality.

Island of gold   Sifnos is one of a scattering of
Greek islands in the Cyclades group in the
central Aegean Sea, to the north of Crete. On
steep hillsides, the thin soil was garnered into
terraces, to yield onions, lettuce, almonds and
olives, as here in the valley of Kastro on the east
coast. Most of the Cyclades had to turn to the
sea to survive, creating a long tradition of
seamanship dating back over 4500 years. Sifnos,
however, had a gift that inspired the envy of all
Greece: gold mines. But in the 6th century BC
the mines became flooded by the sea – it was
said, as a punishment by the gods for trying to
cheat the Oracle of Delphi of its annual tribute
of the precious metal.

Break for grazing   Donkeys have played a vital
role across Southern Europe, particularly on the
islands of the Mediterranean, where roads were
sometimes little more than precipitous, winding
tracks, leading up from the coast to inland
villages and farms.

Bewitching heights *The Sierra dels Encantants (Enchanted Mountains) form part of the Parque Nacional d'Aigües Tortes, at the western extreme of the Catalan Pyrenees. This area of tarns and meandering streams is the most accessible part of the Pyrenees, cherished by holidaymakers as well as more serious walkers and climbers. But many of the peaks remain remote and untamed – the domain of eagles, lammergeiers and chamois (known here as izards).*

Snow and blossom *Pink and white almond blossom spangles the hillsides of the Sierra Nevada, refreshed by the spring rains. Sierra Nevada means 'snowy mountains', and the highest peaks remain snow-covered throughout the year, despite their location in the far south of Spain. During the scorching heat of the summer, the meltwater is vital for the ancient and ingenious irrigation systems used to sustain agriculture, particularly in the valleys around Granada, just to the north.*

Shades of blue *Much of Sardinia's coastline represents what is, for many people, the quintessential Mediterranean landscape. On the Capriccioli peninsula, sun-warmed rocks drop away to a sandy sea-floor, which shades the water azure, while farther out the depths are cobalt-blue.*

A brief history

On the face of it, the Mediterranean region might seem an unlikely setting for the birth of Western civilisation. Rimmed by sun-scorched, arid land, it presented a severe challenge to Europe's first farmers of nearly 10 000 years ago, who had to tease from it their crops of wheat, pasture for their sheep, and the fruits of olive trees and vines.

But these early settlers were driven by curiosity as well as hunger. While the land produced meagre dividends, the great blue expanses of sea that stretched out before it appeared to offer other opportunities. To cite a favourite expression of Classical times: Fortune favours the brave. If Aeolus, Greek god of the winds, so favoured them, propitious breezes would carry them to fishing grounds, or trading ports. But equally a tempest could blow, and claim victims for Poseidon, the god of the sea.

From myth to history

Myth and real events are inseparably entwined in the early history of the Mediterranean. The Greek god Poseidon sought the destruction of Odysseus on his epic voyage from the Trojan War to his home on the island of Ithaca, because the hero had blinded Poseidon's son, the one-eyed

giant Polyphemus. In a world constantly stretching the boundaries of knowledge, supernatural intervention may have seemed as real as the war itself – which was probably a genuine historical event around 1200 BC, played out by armies from Greece against a powerful ancient settlement, near the Aegean coast of modern Turkey. In the *Iliad*, the 8th-century BC Greek poet Homer tells the story of the Trojan War, and explores the meaning of heroism, the horror of battle, and the position of humans manipulated by the gods to their own ends. In his *Odyssey*, Odysseus's story, he reflects the fears, visions, beliefs, morality and driving passions of the Greek people. Complex, contemporary realities percolate through a fictional account of the distant, mythical past.

Worthy subject *A clay figurine made in the 7th-century BC in Boeotia, in east-central Greece, reflects the importance of agriculture.*

Minoans and Mycenaeans

Several thousand years of Mediterranean history had passed before Homer's day. The Greeks were building upon a heritage of civilisation founded by the kingdoms of Crete – later called the Minoans. And Crete itself was heir to a history of farming stretching back to 7000 BC, and trade

Homecoming *In this frieze, Odysseus, disguised as a beggar, returns to his wife Penelope.*

Seascape *A 16th-century BC fresco from Santorini shows the sophistication of Minoan shipbuilding.*

16

with Egypt and the eastern Mediterranean dating back to 3500 BC.

From about 1600 BC, the Minoan kings organised a successful agricultural and trading economy around lavishly decorated palaces. In about 1700 BC, the parallel Mycenaean civilisation developed on mainland Greece, and may have been responsible for the Minoans' sudden demise in around 1500 BC. The Mycenaeans disappeared with equal mystery in about 1200 BC, perhaps as a result of invasion by the Dorians, or as a consequence of a war with Troy. They left behind the remains of massive palaces. These were known to the Greeks who followed several centuries later, and they inspired myths of giants and heroes – the stuff of epic poems.

Victory roll   This silver coin celebrates the victory of Gelon, ruler of the Greek colony in Syracuse in Sicily, over invaders from Carthage in 480 BC.

Greek civilisation emerged in about the 8th century BC. Central to its success was the concept of the city-state, or *polis*, where citizens were placed at the centre of the decision-making process –the foundation of democracy. Prospering from successful agriculture and trade, as early as 750 BC the Greeks began to spread out across the Mediterranean and into the Black Sea, setting up trading posts that soon developed into towns and colonies. Expatriate residents took with them the ways of the homeland, exporting Greek culture far and wide. But generally the Greeks were not expansionist empire builders: the colonies made their own treaties with local people, and were more or less autonomous. The Greek presence in Asia Minor (modern Turkey), however, brought them into conflict with the Persian Empire. The Persian Wars of 499-494 BC ended with a Greek

The Greek World

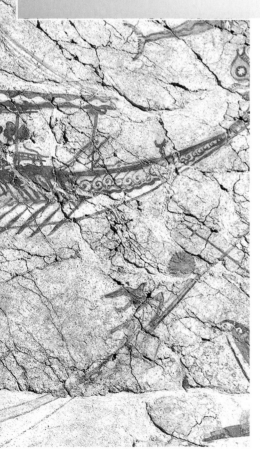

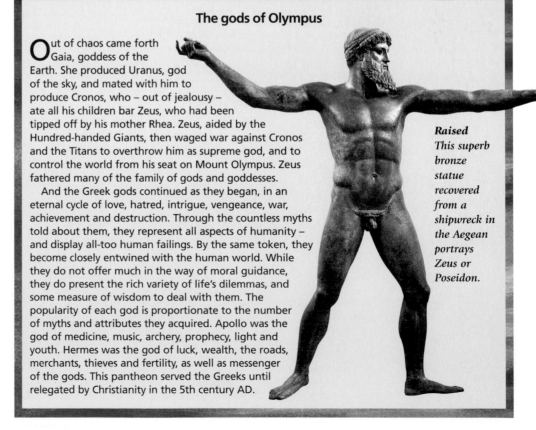

The gods of Olympus

Out of chaos came forth Gaia, goddess of the Earth. She produced Uranus, god of the sky, and mated with him to produce Cronos, who – out of jealousy – ate all his children bar Zeus, who had been tipped off by his mother Rhea. Zeus, aided by the Hundred-handed Giants, then waged war against Cronos and the Titans to overthrow him as supreme god, and to control the world from his seat on Mount Olympus. Zeus fathered many of the family of gods and goddesses.

And the Greek gods continued as they began, in an eternal cycle of love, hatred, intrigue, vengeance, war, achievement and destruction. Through the countless myths told about them, they represent all aspects of humanity – and display all-too human failings. By the same token, they become closely entwined with the human world. While they do not offer much in the way of moral guidance, they do present the rich variety of life's dilemmas, and some measure of wisdom to deal with them. The popularity of each god is proportionate to the number of myths and attributes they acquired. Apollo was the god of medicine, music, archery, prophecy, light and youth. Hermes was the god of luck, wealth, the roads, merchants, thieves and fertility, as well as messenger of the gods. This pantheon served the Greeks until relegated by Christianity in the 5th century AD.

Raised   This superb bronze statue recovered from a shipwreck in the Aegean portrays Zeus or Poseidon.

victory. The dominant Greek city was Athens, which now went through a Golden Age under Pericles (c.495-429 BC).

Countless familiar aspects of Western civilisation were forged in ancient Greece. The alphabet took shape, creating the building blocks of European literature. The tragedies of Aeschylus, Sophocles and Euripides, and the comedies of Aristophanes played to audiences of 15 000 at the great open-air theatres. Sportsmen pitted their skills against one another in the Olympic Games, said to have been founded in 776 BC. The proportions and harmony of Greek architecture provided inspiration through succeeding ages; their sculpture has rarely been surpassed. The enquiring spirit of Greek learning laid the foundations of science, mathematics, geometry, astronomy, medicine, philosophy and ethics.

The Hellenistic world

Athens was effectively the capital of the Greek world, politically and culturally, but its dominance was not universally

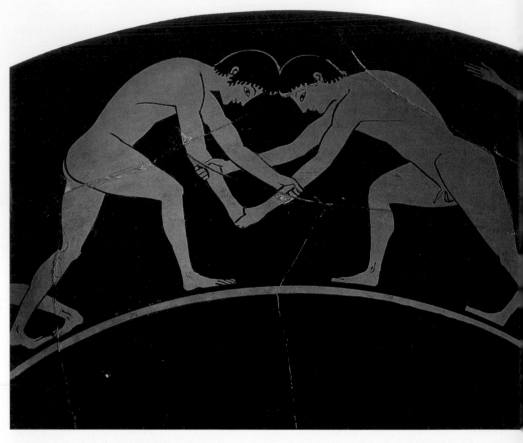

Study in red   Greek 'red-figure' pottery was invented in about 530 BC. The black was painted on, while the red is the natural colour of the clay.

Champions of Greek learning

Greek thought separated experience from religion and myth, and subjected history and the natural world to objective analysis. From this, philosophers were able to propose the best ways for humans to live in society and control their own destiny. Democracy was one of their most important legacies.

SOCRATES (c.469-399 BC)
Socrates is considered to be the father of Western philosophy. He sought to sow the seeds of doubt in debate, using a question-and-answer format to test assumptions. His main concerns were ethics, knowledge, virtue, justice and right conduct. He concluded that virtue is knowledge, and vice derives from ignorance, as no one does anything wrong knowingly.

PLATO (c.428-348 BC)
Socrates' philosophy was preserved mainly by his disciple Plato (left), who founded the Academy near Athens. Plato wrote a series of dialogues to explore concepts of politics, ethics, knowledge, the soul and the cosmos, and developed the concept of an ideal city-state, called the Republic, based on wisdom, rational thinking, justice and harmony.

PYTHAGORAS (c.580-500 BC)
Predating Socrates, the wisdom of Pythagoras was preserved by his followers. By conducting experiments in musical notes, they discovered the numerical relationships between them and concluded that numbers were the basis of all things – including abstract concepts such as justice.

HERODOTUS (c.484-423 BC)
Herodotus' account of the Persian Wars is regarded as the first work of modern narrative history. He used many of the elements of modern history-telling, placing the battles in the context of the causes, the political circumstances and military statistics.

THUCYDIDES (c.460-400 BC)
Thucydides wrote the history of the Peloponnesian Wars.

appreciated. Rivalry led to a 27 year war with Sparta. Helped by Persia, Sparta defeated Athens in 404 BC, but the wrangling between Athens, Sparta and Thebes rumbled on into the next century. This disarray permitted the rise of Macedonia to the north. In 346 BC, King Philip II took control of most of northern Greece, and in 338 BC he defeated the Athenians and Thebans at the Battle of Chaeronea. When he was assassinated two years later, he passed to his son Alexander a power base with which to take on the might of the Persian Empire. By his death at the early age of 32, in 323 BC, Alexander 'the Great' had carved out an empire stretching from Greece to India. It quickly fell apart, but the influence of Greek, or Hellenistic, culture had a lasting impact across the entire region.

The Iberians

Meanwhile, Greek influence had also spread to the other end of the Mediterranean. There were Greek colonies in Sicily, mainland Italy, southern France and Spain. Eastern and southern Spain had been dominated by the Iberians since the 6th-century BC. They made sumptuous jewellery in copper, silver and gold, and traded with the Greeks and Phoenicians.

The Phoenicians were the original great trading nation of the Mediterranean, emerging from ports in what is now Lebanon in about 1000 BC, and – like the Greeks – creating a network of depots and independent settlements. Their greatest foreign settlement was Carthage, in modern Tunisia. Founded in about 800 BC, by the 3rd century BC it dominated the western Mediterranean, and had close trading contacts with the Iberians. In 237 BC, the Carthagians created a province in south-eastern Spain, which in 221 BC came under the control of Hannibal.

Iberian beauty The 'Lady of Elche', found at Elche near Alicante in southern Spain, dates from the 5th to 4th century BC and shows how far the influence of Greek art had spread.

Study in black 'Black-figure' vase-painting preceded red-figure work, and was a speciality of Athens. Here Achilles battles to recover the body of his friend Patroclus, killed by Hector.

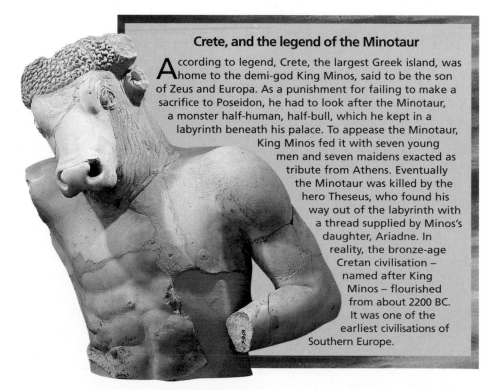

Crete, and the legend of the Minotaur

According to legend, Crete, the largest Greek island, was home to the demi-god King Minos, said to be the son of Zeus and Europa. As a punishment for failing to make a sacrifice to Poseidon, he had to look after the Minotaur, a monster half-human, half-bull, which he kept in a labyrinth beneath his palace. To appease the Minotaur, King Minos fed it with seven young men and seven maidens exacted as tribute from Athens. Eventually the Minotaur was killed by the hero Theseus, who found his way out of the labyrinth with a thread supplied by Minos's daughter, Ariadne. In reality, the bronze-age Cretan civilisation – named after King Minos – flourished from about 2200 BC. It was one of the earliest civilisations of Southern Europe.

The Etruscans and Romans

The Etruscans dominated the north of Italy between the 7th and 5th centuries BC. Gifted merchants and sailors, they traded their metalwork and gold wares with the Greek and Carthaginian settlements established in southern Italy and Sardinia. The Etruscan script remains an enigma, but their remarkable sculpture and painting speak of a society of great joie de vivre and humanity. Wheat from the Etruscan plains fed the emerging power of the region, the city of Rome, with which the Etruscans had a close and complex relationship. The fragility of the alliances between Etruscan cities, however, left them vulnerable to the Roman army when Rome began to expand.

By 264 BC Rome had conquered the whole of Italy and conflict with the Carthaginians was inevitable. In the First Punic War against Carthage, from 264 to 241 BC, Rome emerged victorious. In 218 BC Hannibal, the Carthaginian leader in

Nature's bounty   This lavish Etruscan tomb painting shows fishermen and bird hunters.

Spain, launched his ambitious plan to conquer Rome, setting out at the head of an army of 50 000 foot soldiers, 9000 horsemen and 37 elephants. A large portion of his force was made up of Iberians. Crossing the Alps, he launched a surprise attack on Italy, and came close to conquering it in a series of victories culminating at the Battle of Cannae in 216 BC. Although widely

supported by many disaffected Italian peoples, he failed to consolidate his control of the north, and was forced by Rome to withdraw to Carthage in 203 BC. He was finally defeated by the Romans at Zama in North Africa in 202 BC. Rome was now free to conquer Sicily, Sardinia, Spain, and then Greece. Then it looked north, and set about conquering the Celts, or Gauls, in France.

Band of gold   *A fine gold bracelet from the 7th century BC was among the Iberian treasures of El Carambolo, near Seville in southern Spain.*

Together even in death
Dining couples were depicted in clay on Etruscan tombs of the 6th century BC. Such studies are unusual for the era because of their touching realism and the status they give to the role of women.

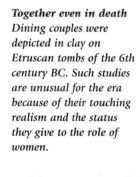

Rome: from Republic to Empire

From 511 BC, Rome had been ruled as a republic, but as it expanded and prospered through conquest, military leaders emerged who were able to exert political power, both in the provinces and at home. The tension between them and the civic authorities was

Bronze study *Legionaries were the agents of Roman expansionism.*

resolved only in the first century BC, when Julius Caesar, conqueror of the Gauls, seized power after a civil war and ruled as a dictator. His successor, Octavian, finished off his rivals – Mark Antony and the Egyptian queen Cleopatra – at the great sea battle of Actium (off north-west Greece) in 31 BC, so that he was left with undisputed power over the entire Roman world.

As Emperor Augustus (from 30 BC to AD14), Octavian reorganised the army and streamlined the political hierarchy of Rome into a pyramidal structure better suited to governing an empire, with the emperor as absolute ruler, ruling through the Senate. The emperor was in direct control of the imperial provinces, while others were run by a proconsul, appointed by the Senate.

Although blighted by internal strife in Rome, the empire continued to grow across North Africa and into Asia. Under Emperor Trajan (reigned 98-117) it reached its greatest extent. The 2nd century AD was a period of unprecedented stability and prosperity, permitting the spread of Roman engineering, learning, law and medicine. The dominance of the Romans diminished as the provinces developed, and in AD 212 the privilege of citizenship was extended throughout the empire.

Rome and Christianity

Augustus's successor, Emperor Tiberius (reigned AD 14-37), was in power when Christianity first appeared in the Roman Empire. Saint Peter the Apostle came to

The Roman Empire at the death of Trajan (AD 117)

Julius Caesar: military genius

Rome's shift from Republic to imperial power was largely the work of Julius Caesar (c.100-44 BC). A brilliant general, he subdued the Celtic tribes of Gaul, pushed the frontiers with the Germanic tribes beyond the Rhine, and made two expeditions to Britain. Concerned about his power, the senate demanded that he surrender command: instead he marched triumphantly on Rome in 49 BC, then defeated his rival, Pompey. He consolidated Roman expansion into Asia before returning to Rome in 45 BC, where he ruled as dictator. He was assassinated in a conspiracy led by Brutus and Cassius.

Feat of engineering *Segovia, in central Spain, has the tallest surviving Roman aqueduct, rising to 128 ft (39 m). It was built under Emperor Trajan, who was born in the Spanish province of Baetica.*

21

The long arm of Roman law

A central feature of Roman civilisation was its system of law. Although it changed over time, its evolution can be traced virtually from the foundation of Rome in 753 BC, and to the creation of the Twelve Tables of codified law in 450 BC. It remained part and parcel of Roman life everywhere until the eventual fall of the Eastern (Byzantine) empire in AD 1453. As Roman rule spread to foreign lands, a system of law called *jus gentium* (law of the nations) was devised to incorporate universal principles of law. It was also modified by *jus naturale* (natural law) based on reason and influenced by Greek models. This system gradually permeated all nations under Roman control. When the Roman Empire replaced the Republic after 27 BC, the emperors took control of law-making. This streamlined the system of introducing new law, but also made it more complex, demanding a new class of trained jurists. The system had reached a state of maturity by the early 4th century, and the process of codification was completed under Emperor Justinian I in the *Corpus juris civilis*, published in AD 535. European scholars resurrected the study of Roman law, notably at the University of Bologna in Italy after the late 11th century. It became the essential basis of law in many countries of the Western world.

The great split

At the same time, the power of Rome became diffused. Constantine underlined this process by making the Greek city of Byzantium his second capital, renaming it Constantinople (now Istanbul). The Roman Empire soon divided into two, the Western empire still based on Rome, and the Eastern empire based on Constantinople. The Western empire, weakened by its much-devolved government, now came under intense pressure from the 'barbarians', buffer-zone Germanic peoples, who in AD 376 were pushed across the River Danube and into the Roman Empire by the Huns. They were absorbed as mercenaries, but ran into conflict with the Roman authorities, seized power, and then swept across the empire.

Rome and apparently was martyred there. Christianity was seen as subversive because it promoted monotheism, which was sacrilege to the polytheistic Romans. Christianity spread first through Asia Minor and into the Greek mainland and islands. The Romans were more reluctant converts, and sufficiently worried about its attractions to carry out persecutions. These became intense under Diocletian (reigned AD 284-305) and Galerius (reigned 305-10), who attempted to erase Christianity from the empire. A crucial turning point came in AD 312, when Emperor Constantine permitted official tolerance of Christianity in a bid to unify his empire. By about AD 400, the majority of people within the Roman Empire were Christian.

Cyril and Methodius: apostles to the Slavs

In AD 863 the Byzantine government commissioned two brothers, Cyril and Methodius, to translate religious texts into Slavonic. Cyril adapted Greek to create the first Slavic alphabet, now called the Glagolitic, a process completed by Methodius after Cyril's death in AD 869. The use of Slavonic (as opposed to Latin) in church services caused controversy, but the practice was adopted by all Slavs who recognised the Eastern Orthodox Church after the East-West Schism of 1054. The liturgical language formed the foundation of Slavonic literature. Transcriptions by St Cyril also corresponded to the language spoken by Slavs of the north, and another alphabet, probably devised by his disciples, was adopted for Russian and named Cyrillic.

Convert Under Emperor Constantine, Christianity became a state religion.

Underground art Stucco catacomb paintings such as this at San Gennaro, Naples, are the earliest surviving examples of Christian art.

Literary saints Saints Cyril and Methodius, portrayed in a monastery fresco.

elevated emphasis on body

Byzantine mosaic   Roger II (reigned 1130-54) receives the crown of Sicily from Christ.

accumulated great power and insisted on the use of Latin, in Byzantium the Church was subordinate to the emperor and was permitted the use of local languages. The two traditions formally split in 1054, becoming the Roman Catholic Church and the Eastern Orthodox Church.

Balkan troubles

During the 'barbarian invasions', the Slavs spread into the Balkans. After an invasion in AD 746, they also settled in parts of Greece. Meanwhile, rival Slav kingdoms developed on the northern borderlands of the Byzantine Empire. Dynastic quarrels and ethnic squabbles plagued the region, leaving it vulnerable to Muslim conquest in the 12th century.

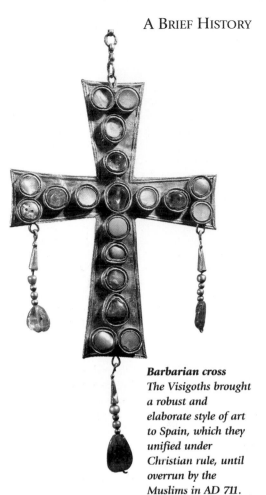

*Barbarian cross
The Visigoths brought a robust and elaborate style of art to Spain, which they unified under Christian rule, until overrun by the Muslims in AD 711.*

Takeover bid   A golden helmet decoration depicts an enthroned Lombard king. The Lombards were a German tribe from the Danube region who conquered northern Italy after AD 568.

Rome was sacked by the Visigoths under Alaric in AD 410. The last Western Roman emperor, Romulus Augustulus, was deposed by the German Odoacer in AD 476, and Italy was overrun by the Ostrogoths in AD 490. The Visigoths and the Sueves occupied Spain. Despite the label 'barbarian', in many ways they were direct heirs to the Roman tradition: they were mainly Christian and used Latin as the language of government.

Meanwhile, the Eastern empire held firm. With Greek as the main language, it developed along a different path, and evolved into what is now called the Byzantine Empire. Under Emperor Justinian I (reigned AD 527-65), it recaptured much of the old Roman Empire, including Italy. In the 8th century it faced a new threat from the east: the rapid and dynamic emergence of the Arab Islamic empire, which swept across North Africa and into Asia Minor. The Byzantine Empire managed to hold it off at the gates of Constantinople.

The Christians of Europe had by now divided into two camps: those led by the Pope in Rome, and those led by the patriarch in Constantinople. While the Pope

The history of our alphabet

The Greek alphabet originated with the Phoenicians, and the first two letters were alpha and beta – the origin of the term 'alphabet'. Because it was based on sounds, not ideas or pictures, writing could respond to the flexibility of the spoken word, and this allowed all kinds of literature to flourish. The Romans adopted the Greek method of writing and made improvements. It spread across the Roman Empire and was preserved into the Middle Ages by Church scribes, who invented small-letter versions of the capital letters. Being a rendition of sounds, the Roman alphabet could be used to transcribe any language, and was adopted across most of Europe as Latin gave way to the use of local languages in writing. The Latin style of lettering was well-suited to printing in the 15th century, and our form of writing is still referred to as Roman.

Words and pictures   An illuminated Greek manuscript of the 11th century BC.

Arab influence *Moorish Spain was noted for the exquisite designs of its ceramics.*

Royal palace *The Alhambra at Granada, Spain, built in the 13-14th centuries, is a masterpiece of architectural grace and harmony.*

Al-Andalus

In AD 711 Islamic Arab forces led by Tariq ibn Ziyad began the conquest of Spain, crossing from North Africa to Gibraltar. They swiftly overran the Visigoths, and were soon pressing into France, to be turned back eventually by the Franks at Poitiers in AD 732. By AD 756 they had consolidated their control over Spain, which they called al-Andalus (Andalucía), ruling it from their capital at Córdoba. Growing rich from their agriculture and urban industries producing leather, silk and woollen cloth, Moorish Spain became one of the most prosperous regions of Europe, with a sophisticated and tolerant society in which Jews and Christians could partake. Even when ruled as a centralised Islamic state as the Caliphate of Córdoba (AD 912-1031), only about half the inhabitants were Muslim. After the Caliphate, Moorish Spain fissured into a large number of small kingdoms, based around the cities. Córdoba, Seville, Toledo, Saragossa and Granada played host to some of the great minds of the Arab world.

In the 13th century, under pressure from the Pope, the expanding Christian kingdoms of northern Spain united and launched a concerted effort to retake Moorish Spain – the 'Reconquista.' By 1235 Muslim possessions had been pared down to the kingdom of Granada. The Moors were simultaneously ejected from Portugal, but they hung on to Granada until 1492.

Culture clash *An illustration of an epic poem, attributed to Alfonso X (called 'The Wise'), king of Castile and Leon (reigned 1252-84), depicts a battle with Muslim forces during the Reconquista.*

Marco Polo and the splendours of the East

During the 13th century trade across Asia was disrupted by the Mongol empire, which had spread westwards as far as the Black Sea. In the 1260s, two Venetian traders, Maffeo and Niccolò Polo, tried to skirt the Mongols, and found themselves drawn all the way to China, where they were treated honourably by the great emperor, Kublai Khan. It was an unprecedented journey, to a land known to Europe only by vague myths. They returned to Venice in 1269, and then, with the blessing of the Pope, mounted a second expedition, this time taking with them Niccolò's 17-year-old son Marco. Marco spent more than 15 years touring the East before finally returning in 1295.

Point of departure   A 15th-century depiction of St Mark's Square in Venice.

The Crusades

The Reconquista formed part of a larger campaign, orchestrated by the Pope in Rome, to regain territory from the Muslims. A series of Crusades was launched to retake the Holy Land and protect pilgrimage routes. From all over Christendom, nobles and knights volunteered, as a means of gaining spiritual salvation. There were nine Crusades in all: the first took place in 1095-9, the last in 1291.

While the Crusades brought some measure of unity to Christian princes in the West, the Byzantine Empire fell into prolonged decay, and was gradually reduced to a small domain around Constantinople by the encircling Muslim Ottoman Empire, founded in the late 13th century. After the decisive Ottoman victory over the Christians at Kosovo in 1389 Greece, Macedonia, Albania, Serbia and Croatia fell under its control; Constantinople held out against the Ottomans until 1453.

It was against the threat of Turkish expansion that the old Crusader military-religious orders of knights occupied and held a number of strategically vital posts in the Mediterranean. The Knights Hospitallers occupied the Greek island of Rhodes from 1310 to 1522; other Knights of St John were given control of Malta in 1530.

Venice: at the crossroads

Every year, in a splendid ceremony, the Doge (leader) of the independent republic of Venice re-enacted the symbolic marriage ceremony that bonded his lagoon-based city to the sea. Venice's fleets served the Crusaders, and established a virtual monopoly of trade at the frontiers of the Islamic world, in the eastern Mediterranean. As the Byzantine Empire collapsed, Venice rose to fill the vacuum, and played a leading role in the sack of Constantinople in 1204. Traded goods included Middle Eastern cotton, the valuable Asian spices used in medicines and food preservation, and incense. Venice itself produced luxury goods made from silk, leather, gold and silver. Its ally and sometime rival on the other side of Italy was Genoa, another independent republic, which controlled much of the trade in the Black Sea.

The rise of the Ottoman Empire posed a threat to the trading nations. At the Battle of Lepanto in 1571 an alliance of Venice, Genoa and Spain put an end to Ottoman expansion in the Mediterranean. But by this time, Venice and Genoa were being eclipsed: Europe had discovered the world beyond the Mediterranean.

Muslim Spain

Christian kingdoms (Portugal, Castile, Aragón)

Muslim lands at the start of the 11th century

Bay of Biscay

Douro

Ebro

Toledo

Tagus

CALIPHATE OF CÓRDOBA

Córdoba

Mediterranean Sea

Atlantic Ocean

North Africa

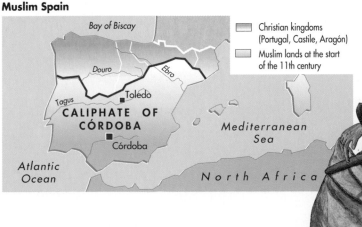

Spice trade   A cinnamon seller, from a 15th-century treatise on plants.

Discovering the world

A number of developments combined in the 15th century to enable pioneer navigators to leave their known shores. Portuguese shipbuilders developed the caravel, the perfect small sailing ship for exploration. Sailors also now had the compass, hourglass, astrolabe, backstaff (an early form of sextant) and star charts to assist navigation. They were also encouraged by the promise of profits from trade, by royal courts in quest of territory, and by scholars and map-makers in search of knowledge.

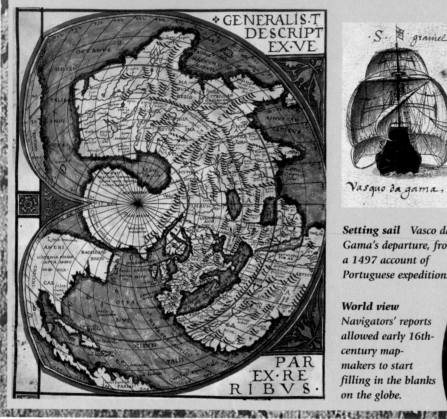

Setting sail Vasco da Gama's departure, from a 1497 account of Portuguese expeditions.

World view Navigators' reports allowed early 16th-century map-makers to start filling in the blanks on the globe.

Pioneer Vasco da Gama was the first European navigator to reach India.

The world outside

The spirit of adventure excited by the Crusades led to a new, more ambitious project of overseas exploration and colonisation. There was still some crusading zeal in this mission: Muslims controlled not only the spice trade at the eastern end of the Mediterranean, but also the trade in gold across the Sahara from West Africa. Christian explorers wanted to outflank them, and also to win converts to their faith. The Portuguese began by sailing down the west coast of Africa, hoping eventually to locate the source of the spices. In 1488 Bartolomeu Dias rounded the Cape of Good Hope. Ten years later, Vasco da Gama followed the same route, and then sailed into the Indian Ocean to reach India. Other Portuguese navigators pressed on, finally reaching the 'spice islands' of the

Moluccas in 1512. The Portuguese established trading ports in Goa, Macau, Timor and Japan, linked by a series of staging posts along the coasts of Africa.

But was there a quicker route to India and the Far East? The Genoese navigator Christopher Columbus was convinced that he could reach Asia by sailing west from Europe. His requests for financial support were rejected by the king of Portugal. But King Ferdinand and Queen Isabella of Spain looked upon his proposal more favourably, gave him financial backing for three caravels, and charged him with the task of taking Christianity to the Great Khan of China. On October 12, 1492, Columbus and his crew landed on an island in the Bahamas, and claimed it for Spain and Christianity. He assumed the natives were 'Indians', and that Japan and China lay within close reach. And he took this misapprehension with him to his grave. It was only in 1524 that map-makers and navigators accepted that he had found a new set of continents.

As new discoveries poured in, Spain and Portugal won approval from the Pope to divide the world between them under the Treaty of Tordesillas of 1494. This was designed to give Spain the New World of the Americas, and discoveries in Asia and Africa to the Portuguese. But in 1500

Division of the spoils: the world divided between Spain and Portugal

— Treaty of Tordesillas, 1494

-- Treaty of Zaragoza, 1529

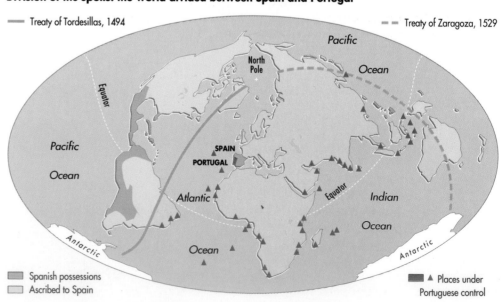

▨ Spanish possessions
☐ Ascribed to Spain

▮ ▲ Places under Portuguese control

the Portuguese navigator Pedro Álvares Cabral, heading around West Africa to continue Vasco da Gama's work, was pushed westwards by the Atlantic trade winds, and ended up in what he named Vera Cruz ('True Cross'). This was Brazil, and it fell within the Portuguese hemisphere.

The Spanish 'conquistadores' – heirs to the Reconquista – were now crossing the Atlantic to further the task of winning Christian territories from the heathens. In 1521 Hernán Cortés, at the head of a remarkably small army, seized the Aztec capital in Mexico, and had soon conquered the whole of the Aztec empire. In 1532 Francisco Pizarro, with even fewer forces, captured the vast Inca empire of the Andes, along with many tons of gold and silver. The Spanish and the Portuguese set about colonising their new domains, often with unashamed cruelty. They carved out plantations to grow sugar cane – previously another Muslim monopoly. Imported disease wiped out millions of the native Indians, so Portugal and Spain began using slave labour from Africa. Some 400 000 African slaves made the transatlantic journey from West Africa to Brazil.

After the first-ever circumnavigation of the globe by the expedition of the Portuguese navigator Ferdinand Magellan in 1522, it was clear that all the world was linked by oceans – and the new and rich markets of India, South-east Asia, China and Japan were open to all-comers. Before a century had passed, the Spanish and Portuguese had rivals in the Dutch, English and French.

Rebirth and reawakening

Back home in Europe, the royal courts of Spain, Portugal and Italy were adjusting not only to these expanded geographical horizons, but also to a new way of thinking. One of the consequences of the Reconquista of Spain was the release of Arab scholarship based on classical Greek learning. This fed into an enthusiastic review of the Classical world – its philosophy, political structures, literature, art and architecture. Later named the Renaissance, or 'Rebirth', it took place over a number of centuries, reaching maturity in the 15th and 16th centuries, and radiating outwards from its main crucible in Italy. In the great Italian cities of Florence, Milan, Bologna, Rome and Venice wealthy patrons took

pride in promoting the works of men such as Dante, Machiavelli, Leonardo da Vinci, Raphael and Michelangelo.

Economic and political power in Europe was gradually seeping northwards, as England, France and The Netherlands grew into major colonial empires. Italy remained divided into a number of states. Greece and the Balkans were under the rule of the Ottoman Empire. Under Philip II, Spain and Portugal were united in 1580, but separated again after a Portuguese revolt in the 1640s. All remained primarily rural, as the northern lands turned to industry to generate new markets and economic impetus.

Wind of change

The rise of Napoleon in France had a major impact on Southern Europe. France conquered Italy in 1800 and Spain in 1808. Although Napoleon was finally defeated

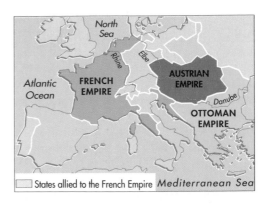

States allied to the French Empire

The Inquisition

'I would prefer to lose all my domains and die 100 times than rule over heretics', declared Philip II of Spain (reigned 1556-98). To root out Protestantism in his empire, he turned to the Inquisition, an organisation founded by the Roman Catholic Church in about 1232 to combat dissent. The Inquisitors were monks, who claimed that torture was justified in the service of God. The Spanish Inquisition – set up in 1479 to enforce the conversion of Muslim and Jews following the Reconquista -- was notoriously much harsher and freer with the death penalty.

in 1815, he helped to inspire a sense of nationalism across Europe. In Greece, this led the eight-year War of Independence against the weakening Ottoman Empire, from which it was liberated in 1830. Greece was now an independent nation again, for the first time in 2000 years. For Spain, the fervour for independence had a different consequence: by 1825 it had lost all its South American possessions. In Italy, patriots fought under the banner of the Risorgimento (Revival) for the unification of all of Italy. Led by Giuseppe Garibaldi (1807-82), they achieved this goal over the 11 years to 1870.

The Balkan powder keg

During the first Balkan war of 1912, the Serbs, allied to the Bulgarians, Greeks and Romanians, succeeded in crushing the

The Red Shirts Garibaldi's volunteer troops were key players in Italy's unification.

Turks and all but pushing them out of Europe. The Ottoman Empire was in terminal decline, igniting the hope among the Southern Slavs of a Greater Serbia, extending into Bosnia-Herzegovina – part of the neighbouring Austro-Hungarian Empire. In the game of big-power politics, Austria-Hungary suspected Russia of meddling in the Balkans and supporting their fellow Slavs for territorial gain.

In 1914 Archduke Franz Ferdinand, the heir to the Austro-Hungarian throne, was assassinated in the Bosnian capital Sarajevo by a young Serb nationalist, who cannot possibly have imagined the consequences of his action. As Germany

Death in Sarajevo The assassination of Archduke Franz Ferdinand of Austria in 1914 unleashed the First World War.

encouraged its ally Austria-Hungary to crush the Serbs in response, Russia felt obliged to intervene, causing Germany to declare war on Russia and its ally France, which brought their ally Great Britain into play. The crisis ballooned into the First World War, which claimed the lives of 20 million people.

At the end of the First World War, the Habsburg monarchy collapsed and the Austro-Hungarian Empire was dismantled and broken up. In the Balkans, the Serbs, Croats and Slovenes formed a single kingdom in 1918, which in 1929 was renamed the Kingdom of Yugoslavia.

The rule of dictators

Italy came out of the war in economic disarray, having suffered some 600 000 casualties. Unemployment and economic crisis exacerbated all the underlying social problems, creating political turmoil between Communists and right-wing conservatives. Supported by big industry, Mussolini founded the Fascist Party to impose social order, using the coercive tactics of the Black Shirts to forge his power base. Rising rapidly to the position of prime minister in 1922, he triggered the collapse of Italy's parliamentary monarchy to assume absolute power.

Spain remained neutral during the First World War. But the country was sorely divided by this position, with the Left in favour of the Allies, and the Right in favour of Germany and Austria-Hungary. Military rule was imposed in 1923, and Spain began a belated transition to a modern industrial economy.

By popular vote, a republican administration came to power in 1931, and King Alfonso XIII abdicated. The activities of Marxists, anarchists and regional separatist movements in Catalonia and the Basque Region raised the spectre of national disintegration. In this fragile and impassioned climate, General Franco provoked a coup d'état in 1936, with the help of part of the army. But the military controlled only a few cities and Spain split into republicans with the left-wing on the one hand, and nationalists, monarchists and fascists on the other. They collided in the civil war of 1936-9.

In Portugal, a parallel confrontation resulted in a dictatorship supported by the army, dominated for 40 years – until 1968 – by António Salazar. Greece, meanwhile, was ruled by the military dictator Joannis Metaxas from 1936 to 1941.

El Caudillo, the Leader Franco (right) led the Nationalists to victory in the Spanish Civil War.

Fascist salute Mussolini rose to power in Italy in 1922, assisted by the intimidating antics of his militant supporters, the 'Black Shirts'.

Mussolini and Franco both gave their active support to the expansionist ambitions of Hitler in Germany, but as war enveloped Europe for a second time in 30 years, Spain remained neutral. Italy, by contrast, joined the war as one of the Axis countries, leading to bitter internal divisions, military defeat in Greece and in East and North Africa, and then in Italy itself.

The Balkans fall apart

Deep divisions between the Serbs and the Croats had already placed the new Yugoslavia under stress when the Second World War intervened. The country was quickly overrun by the Germans in 1941, and a right-wing puppet government under Ante Pavelíc was installed in Croatia; the rest was partitioned between Germany, Italy, Bulgaria and Hungary. Resistance to

Il Duce, the Chief Mussolini joins in the first harvest from the reclaimed Pontine marshes.

the occupying forces centred on two rival guerrilla movements, the Serbian royalist Chetniks and the Communist partisans led by Josip Broz, called 'Tito'. Because the Chetniks collaborated with the Germans, the Allies gave their support to Tito, whose partisans helped the Soviet Red Army to liberate Belgrade.

Assuming power as prime minister in 1945, Tito abolished the monarchy and founded the Federative People's Republic of Yugoslavia. Unwilling to be a Soviet satellite, Tito broke with the Soviet Union in 1948. When Tito died in 1980, however, he left a country mired in economic stagnation, and vulnerable to the rise of nationalist separatism. Slovenia became independent in 1992, followed by Croatia. But large minorities of Serbs feared isolation within these new states, and ethnic tensions turned to civil war, first in Croatia, then in Bosnia-Herzegovina, and then in Kosovo – conflicts that needed international intervention to bring about some kind of resolution. Albania, meanwhile, emerged impoverished from decades of repressive Communism after the death of the dictator Enver Hoxha in 1985, and groped its way towards democracy and the market economy.

Old wine in new bottles

Greece suffered acutely from postwar upheavals. In 1967, the colonels swept away the monarchy and a vicious military dictatorship ruled until overthrown by popular protest in 1974, when democracy was restored. In Spain, General Franco died in 1975, having groomed the royal heir Juan Carlos to be his successor, and to restore the monarchy. Franco appears not to have understood that Juan Carlos was a reformer, who skilfully ushered in a return to full democracy.

For most of Southern Europe, the last decades of the 20th century were a period of growing stability and prosperity. The development of the European Economic Community, later the European Union (EU), played a significant role in this. Italy was a founder-member; Greece joined in 1981; Spain and Portugal in 1986. North of the Mediterranean, the EU was beginning to shape up like the old Roman empire, buttressed by democracy of a kind more open and thorough than even the

The Marshal Tito led the partisans against German and Italian forces in Yugoslavia during the Second World War.

Yugoslavia under Tito

ancient Greeks would have countenanced. Such a strong heritage of the ancient past of Southern Europe – in institutions, culture, science, patterns of daily life – remains clear for all to see.

The carnation revolution A coup in April 1974 put an end to Portugal's right-wing dictatorship.

The Spanish Civil War

There was optimism when Spain became a republic and the king abdicated in 1931, but deep political divisions soon emerged, accompanied by unrest and violence. When the left-wing Popular Front won the election in 1936, chaos ensued, and the Spanish army tried to restore order with an unsuccessful coup d'état. The parties who opposed the Republic – Falangists, Monarchists and Nationalists – swung behind the coup leader, General Franco, and the result was three years of civil war. Franco won the support of the Fascist governments of Germany, Italy and Portugal, who supplied troops and arms. The Republicans were backed by trade unionists, anarchists, Communists and Troskyites. The Communists also organised the International Brigades, a rag-tag army of volunteers from 50 countries. Numerous foreigners were drawn to the war, including Ernest Hemingway, George Orwell, Laurie Lee, André Malraux, Willy Brandt and Tito. The conflict fired deep passions, splitting not only the nation but families, and was marked by numerous summary executions and atrocities, committed by both sides.

Standing together Republicans rally to their battle cry 'No pasaran!' (They shall not pass!)

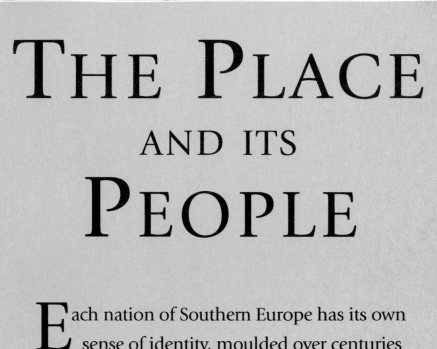

The Place
and its
People

Each nation of Southern Europe has its own sense of identity, moulded over centuries by a rich combination of language, history, climate and geography. And there are nations within these nations, fired by equally strong visions of identity. This passion can be held responsible for the ugly aspects of nationalism which came to a head in the early 20th century. But it also has more constructive and endearing qualities, such as a deep pride in cultural heritage and traditions, and the love of regional foods – olives, pasta and tapas – and wines.

CHAPTER 1

A TALENT FOR NATURAL COLOURS

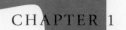

The beauty and variety of the southern European landscape masks a tormented geological past – characterised by the volcanic paroxysms that still rumble on in Stromboli, Etna and Vesuvius, and by surreal landscapes caused by millennia of erosion. To see this landscape in the raw, you need only look at the high sierras of Spain, the Dolomites of Italy, or the bone-dry islands of the Dalmatian coast. But if it is the climate that has shaped the harsh landscape, it is the region's natural vegetation that softens it with a profusion of rich colours. Humans have also lent a hand, sometimes achieving a felicitous balance between what they contribute and what is there already – as in the hills of Tuscany, or the orchards of the Algarve.

Spring flowers in a field near Fermo, in the Marche region of central Italy.

The Cyclades: balcony on the Aegean

A scattering of small, rocky islands in the southern Aegean, the Cyclades reverberate with their long history. Since ancient times, their people have evolved a way of life that balances the benefits and handicaps of the sea, of the fierce sun, and of a rocky but fertile soil. The pristine, whitewashed houses of the villages are the perfect expression of the finely tuned equilibrium they have found.

On the edge *At Thira, on Santorini, houses cling to the rim of a huge drowned crater.*

According to legend, the sea-god Poseidon struck the mountains of Greece with his trident and sent divots of earth and rock flying into the Aegean Sea, creating the Cyclades – an archipelago of 23 large islands and about 100 smaller ones, so named because of its roughly circular formation. These islands once enjoyed a pivotal position on the trade routes between Greece,

Crete and Asia Minor. Delos, birthplace of the Greek gods Apollo and Artemis, was a wealthy pilgrimage and commercial centre, and is now a treasured archaeological site. Síros had the busiest port of the Aegean, and its capital Ermoúpolis is still the capital city of the Cyclades. Coveted for their strategic and commercial importance, the islands were occupied by the Venetians after 1204, and by the Turks in the 16th century, completing the long chain of conquerors that ended with independence under Greece in 1832.

Fire and sun

Ancient authors praised the great beauty of the Cyclades. This inflated the expectations of later travellers, who were struck by the grim austerity of the landscape: in the intervening period, most of the cedars and cypress trees that were once an essential feature of the islands' charm had been cut down and turned into charcoal. Today, the heat of the sun and occasional brush fires have conspired to preserve that lean look. Some islands are uncompromisingly bald, while others have a covering of spiny shrubs, gnarled trees, and tough grasses that turn the landscape yellow from July on. But each island has its own character, with different assortments of the 200 or so plants that grow in this arid landscape – oleander, wild almond, pistachio and lemon trees, prickly holly oak, and aromatic juniper, thyme and marjoram.

Bare rigging *Windmills on the island of Mikonos once ground wheat into flour, but now the sails have gone.*

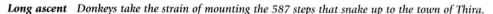

Long ascent *Donkeys take the strain of mounting the 587 steps that snake up to the town of Thira.*

The savage past

Throughout history, the islands were plagued by the warships of competing empires, and, in lawless times, by pirates in search of food, church treasures, women and slaves. For this reason, villages were built on high clifftops, or hidden from view in inland valleys. Christian monks built robust towers, from which they could scan the horizon – and with an interior accessible only by ladder, which could be drawn up in times of attack. On some islands, mothers would resort to scarring the faces of their daughters in an effort to protect them from the attentions of marauders.

The heart of the Sardinian maquis

Nature dominates in Sardinia, the second largest island of the Mediterranean. The interior is rocky, arid, turned crisp under the summer sun – in contrast to its blue rim of coastline, pockmarked with marine caves and rocky outcrops, interspersed with superb beaches.

Resisting the waves *A granite outcrop on the Arbatax peninsula shows the resilience of the island geology.*

There is an old Sardinian saying: 'Whoever comes from the sea is a robber.' Like the Cyclades, Sardinia suffered a long history of aggression from the sea: the Carthaginians, Romans, Vandals, Byzantines and Spanish all staked a claim to the island. In response, its people regularly took to the hills, retreating to the high plateaus and deep valleys of the interior. The tradition dates back over 4000 years, when shepherd communities protected themselves in squat stone towers called *nuraghi*, so robust that 6000 survive to this day. If Sardinian culture is the product of isolation, this is on account more of the interior than of the sea.

More mountain folk than seafarers

The mountains of Sardinia were thrust up 450 million years ago in a jumble of tough basalt and granite, now rising to 6017 ft (1834 m) at Monti del Gennargentu. Still jagged with the first rough-cut of erosion, the ruggedness of this landscape had a profound impact on its inhabitants, who lived in villages isolated from each other by their steep valleys. Sardinia was always a poor island, surviving primarily on goats and sheep, and constantly faced with the dual threat posed by a lack of water and scrub fires. The hard sheep's cheese, pecorino Sardo, remains one of its most famous products.

Once forested

The small railway line that crosses the country from north to south offers one of the best windows on the Sardinian maquis – a scrubland of thorn thickets, prickly pears and stunted oaks strewn around arid pastures. Today, Sardinia jealously protects its natural beauty with a number of reserves and parks. These are home to mouflon (wild mountain sheep), wild boar and the Sardinian deer – protected from hunters since the 1970s, with a stiff fine for shooting one.

Cactus fruit *The fruits of the prickly pear are eaten as a delicacy.*

Blue shallows *Translucent waters in the Gulf of Orosei glitter under the summer sun.*

Loneliness that inspired a book

Today, Sardinian shepherds drive around in cars and take their cheeses to the cooperatives for marketing. But 50 years ago they led a very different kind of life, governed by the seasonal movement of flocks, sleeping rough in cabins in the remote hills. Among them was Gavino Ledda, an illiterate shepherd, who lived in the mountains of the central Barbagia region until the age of 20. He then learned to write, became a teacher, and revisited his past in a book called *Padre Padrone* (1975), made into a highly successful film by the Taviani brothers in 1977.

Rocky heartlands *Much of the interior is covered in dry pasture scented with herbs – good grazing for the herds of sheep and goats.*

The fabled hills of Tuscany

Vine view   The Villa Poggio alle Mura dominates a hilltop.

To many people the landscape of Tuscany is the image of perfection, a harmony of ancient, worked land coupled with a deep respect for its gifts. So intimate is this bond between humans and nature that the old farmhouses seem almost a part of the geology.

Tuscany stretches from the coast of the Tyrrhenian Sea to the Apennines, the mountainous backbone of Italy. The landscape varies from coastal islands to the chestnut-forested hills around Monte San Savino; from the hectic resort beaches of Viaréggio to the agricultural plains of the Val di Chiana. All the inhabitants will proudly claim to be Tuscan, the badge of dignified living. But it is the hills and vineyards of the Chianti region, south of Florence and around Siena, where classic, picture-postcard Tuscany is to be found.

Rural idyll

Here undulating hills stretch out as far as the eye can see, often softened by haze. Small roads wind among vineyards, olive groves, and the fields of ripened grain or bright-yellow sunflowers. Side-roads lined with cypress trees lead up to the hill crests crowned by solid, honey-coloured farmhouses.

A rich vein of culture runs through these valleys, fostered by the abbeys and churches once patronised by the powerful Renaissance princes and wealthy landowners. Painters such as Piero della Francesca, Simone Martini, Raphael and Pintoricchio have immortalised these landscapes by using them as a backdrop to scenes of idealised beauty. It remains essentially the same today, except where the big ploughs of agribusiness have scoured away the old field margins and woodlands in the quest for higher yields. But the canny Tuscans are aware that they cannot let this detrimental process run too far: the beauty of the landscape is as important a resource as the harvest it can produce, as the annual influx of foreign tourists bears witness. Even modern large-scale growers are sensitive to this, planting trees, and replacing unsightly concrete vineyard poles with traditional wooden ones.

Embellishing Nature

The Tuscan climate is perfect for gardening, with plenty of sun, rare winter frosts, and no shortage of water. The gardens of the grand houses are famed both for their natural beauty and for their embellishments. Wealthy owners have added staircases, grottoes, statuary, belvederes, wooded glades, topiary, formal gardens, 'green theatres' for putting on outdoor entertainments, and surprise fountains designed to soak and amuse party guests.

A Tuscan garden   Stone steps rise up the terraces of the Villa Garzoni.

Above the mist   Cypress trees surround an old farmhouse overlooking the valley of the Órcia, near Pienza.

The sierras of Aragón: a Wild West landscape

Sheer pleasure *The vertical cliffs of Los Mallos de Riglos are cherished by mountain climbers.*

Aragón spreads south from the central Pyrenees. It is arid and thinly populated, but much admired for the grandeur and uncompromising austerity of its landscape. From tip to toe, this old kingdom is peppered with geological oddities.

Wild, lunar landscapes, monumental rock outcrops, ravines and canyons, dusty plains – not for nothing has the landscape of Aragón often been compared to the Wild West of the USA.

Over millions of years, wind and water have etched out the fretted hill crests, the needles of stone, the caves and canyons. The wind here has two manifestations: the cold *cierzo*, and the warm *bochorno*, both of which are wrung dry of moisture as they cross the mountains, making the sierras bitterly cold in winter, and torrid in summer – and dry all year round. Aragón receives very little rainfall: just 14 in (350 mm) a year on average, but this might be 8 in (20 cm) one year, and 24 in (61 cm) another. The wide temperature variation is another agent of erosion, causing the rock to fissure under the stress.

Abandoned to the elements

The sparse population also contributes to the Wild West image. Almost half the entire population of Aragón lives in the capital, Zaragoza, leaving the rest of the 18 405 sq miles (47 669 km²) to a scattering of towns and villages. A process of chronic desertification

Seeing red *Poppies turn the fields scarlet in spring.*

– land degradation through growing aridity – led to a major exodus during the 19th century. So, both to the north and south of the River Ebro, which bisects the region, abandoned villages now line the old roadways that were once busy with people and trade – the Roman roads, Muslim trade routes, and old paths that led Christian pilgrims to Santiago de Compostela.

Some of the land is turned over to the dry-farming of wheat, olives and grapes. And some, where irrigation is possible, produces a rich abundance of crops of all kinds. But Aragón for the most part remains quite untamed. It is famed for its remote corners – the medieval towns and villages where time has stood still, set against a magnificently stark backdrop of hills and mountains, such as the canyon-riddled Sierra de Guara, north of Huesca. Los Mallos (the 'Mallets') de Riglos, to the north-west of Huesca, rise up with extraordinary abruptness. Farther north still, in the Pyrenees proper, is the Parque Nacional de Ordesa, one of the most spectacular national parks in Spain.

The enchanted city

At the Ciudad Encantada, near Villalba, wind erosion has etched away at the limestone, producing fantastic sculptural shapes. Because the highest strata of rock is more resistant, many are like mushrooms, and some are more than 50 ft (15 m) tall. The shapes have been interpreted as seats, houses and palaces of magical giants.

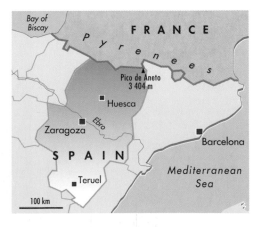

Mediterranean volcanoes: deceptive beauty

A faultline runs through the Mediterranean, from Gibraltar to Cyprus – the cause of earthquakes and volcanoes both past and present. Some volcanoes rumble benignly, releasing their energy in measured doses. Others – notably Vesuvius – pose a major threat. This precariousness may be an essential ingredient of the Mediterranean character: live for today.

Rebirth *The spherical church in Gibellina Nuova, a town in Sicily that was entirely rebuilt after an earthquake.*

Volcanic eruptions and earthquakes cast a black shadow over the history of the Mediterranean. Several key centres of civilisation have been knocked sideways by these interventions. The explosion of Thíra in the Cyclades may have contributed to the decline of the Minoan civilisation. The prosperous Roman towns of Herculaneum and Pompeii were asphyxiated by gas and buried in cinders and ash when Vesuvius erupted in AD 79.

Living with danger

The threat has not receded. Across the Mediterranean, beneath Italy and Greece, the African plate is being forced under the Eurasian plate at the rate of about 1 in (2.5 cm) a year. This causes the jolts that translate into earthquakes, and the build-up and release of magma from deep within the earth. Vesuvius has been quiet since 1944 – but this is no cause for celebration. Rather the

Volcanic islands

The seven Lipari Islands are all part of a submerged mountain, born of the same subterranean clash that forged the Tyrrhenian Sea. The most active volcano is on Stromboli: it has spat fire every two hours for the past 4000 years, but is not considered to be dangerous. Volcanic activity deep beneath the ground gives Vulcano its hot springs and mud baths. The main island, Lipari, has 12 volcanoes, but they last erupted about 4000 years ago and are believed to be extinct.

Yellow breath *On Vulcano, sulphurous gas exhales from vents or fumaroles.*

opposite: Vesuvius's cycle is well known and, in the past, long periods of dormancy have ended with catastrophic eruptions, like the one of AD 79. Periods of repeated smaller eruptions, on the other hand, have the effect of releasing the pent-up pressure within the cone at a moderate rate. In other words, the longer Vesuvius remains quiet, the greater will be the eruption. And at its foot stands the city of Naples, with a population of 3 million people. While it rests, gently smoking trails of sulphurous fumes, Vesuvius is an easily accessible tourist attraction, with a path around its blasted rim giving views over Naples and the site of Pompeii.

Etna's fury

By contrast, Etna, on Sicily, is one of the world's most active volcanoes, regularly erupting and releasing streams of molten lava down its flanks. It has four main craters and thousands of smaller outlets. During its periodic bouts of anger, these sources of lava can suddenly pool together and send a sea of molten rock chasing down the hillside at a speed of 15 ft (5 m) a second, invading the villages below and even reaching the sea 20 miles (32 km) away. By this time, the villagers will have been evacuated, returning to their homes after calm is restored to clear up the mess and rebuild their

Under the volcano San Vicenzo lies peaceably at the foot of Stromboli.

lives in time-honoured fashion. The rich volcanic soil is too bountiful to abandon: temporary inconvenience from its source is the price they are willing to pay – they have learned to live with Etna.

Rewards of risk

The inhabitants of volcanic lands would not be so persistent if volcanoes did not offer such rich rewards. In prehistoric times, they were prized for their obsidian, a glass-like stone that was used to make arrow heads and knives. Pumice – a volcanic stone riddled with air holes – is still quarried on Lipari and Thíra, for use not just as a bath-time skin cleaner, but also as a fertiliser and an abrasive in the metal industry. Volcanic action also produces the hot springs that feed numerous spas throughout Southern Europe. Vulcano is famous for its hot mud-baths, but many spas are a long way from any active volcano – at Chianciano Terme in Italy, for instance, or Baños de Sierra Alhamilla in southern Spain.

Earthquakes

Earthquakes are far more lethal and destructive than volcanoes. In 1908, in one of the worst earthquakes in European history, 200 000 people died in Sicily and southern Italy. In just 15 seconds, during the night of January 15, 1968, five towns were wiped from the map in Sicily. In 1997, part of the cathedral of Assisi in central Italy was destroyed, including paintings by Giotto considered to be pivotal in the history of Western art; 11 people died, and thousands were made homeless.

▲ Active volcanoes

Nature's fireworks Etna, the highest active volcano in Europe, has erupted at least 135 times.

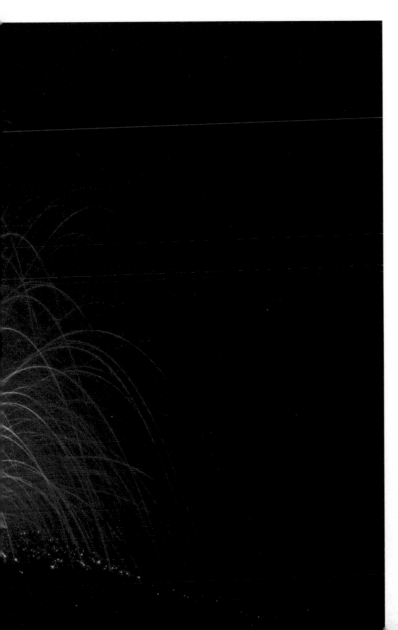

The Mediterranean: perilous, and in peril

Mariners of old learned to respect the Mediterranean's savage moods, and gave names to the regular winds that could shipwreck them. But now the boot is on the other foot: the Mediterranean itself is under assault from pollution, which threatens to alter it irreversibly.

Grey lagoon   *A photograph taken in August 1988 shows the build-up of toxic algae in Venice's lagoon, caused by agricultural fertilisers leaching into the sea.*

To the ancient Greeks and Romans, the winds were divine beings, with myths of their own. In Homer's works, the winds are ruled by Boreas, the north wind, and Zephyrus, the west wind – although they may also be in the custody of Aeolus. Special rites and sacrifices were performed before voyages to persuade the wind gods to look favourably on the travellers. The same wind patterns blow across the Mediterranean as they did in ancient times, but

now we say they are ruled by atmospheric battles, such as anticyclones, or high pressure areas, over the Azores and the Sahara. In spring and autumn, as anticyclones shift southwards, polar air is drawn into the Mediterranean. Wintery or cool spells are brought in by strong north winds such as the mistral of the Rhone Valley, the *tramontana* of the Apennines, and the *meltemi* of the Greek islands. By contrast, hot winds laden with dust may blow in from the south, such as the *khamsin* and the sirocco from the North African desert. These, and many other unnamed storms, can whip the sea into a dangerous frenzy, causing sailors to head for port at the first warning signal.

How much can it take?   *The water lapping around the limestone rocks of Capri looks crystal clear, but it already shows signs of contamination from Naples, lying across the bay.*

Man-made threats

But in a reversal of history, the Mediterranean Sea is now under threat from human activity. One of the chief problems is that it is virtually enclosed. The Strait of Gibraltar, the narrow opening to the Black Sea through the Dardanelles and Bosporus, and – since completion in 1869 – the Suez Canal, barely constitute openings of any great significance. A measure of this is the fact that the Mediterranean has virtually no tide at all. In the northern Aegean, for example, the difference between high tide and low tide is less than 2 ft (60 cm), whereas in the North Atlantic the tidal range is more like 15 ft (4.5 m). There is no low-tide exposure of rockpools and sandbars, no daily rinsing of the beaches.

As a result, the Mediterranean lacks an essential tool for self-cleaning. It is a giant pond, and anything tipped into it stays, stirred only by the wind and the waves. It is the recipient of industrial waste (some of it radioactive), run-off water carrying agricultural fertilisers and pesticides, millions of tons of oil discharged by shipping, non-biodegradable garbage such as plastic bottles and supermarket bags, and sewage that carries dangerous germs. The Mediterranean is under severe stress, a situation that is witnessed in declining fish catches, and the threat of extinction of entire species.

In addition, the population living on or close to the Mediterranean coasts is set to double by 2025. This will put even greater pressure on coastal waters, from effluent, oil spills and general waste. And it will also alter the shoreline, diminishing the areas of currently non-productive marginal land such as wetlands and salt marshes – temporary home to thousands of migratory birds, such as ducks, flamingos (found in Sardinia, for example) and pelicans.

Endangered species

Dolphins have been a symbol of the Mediterranean from ancient times, but in recent years their numbers have been greatly reduced by pollution, increased maritime traffic, and food shortages resulting from overfishing. Without conservation measures, the striped dolphin could become a threatened species. At worst, it could go the way of the monk seals. These very shy animals need undisturbed coastline to thrive and breed, but coastal development has encroached on their habitat. Plentiful about a century ago, the total population of Mediterranean monk seals has diminished to a few hundred. Many live off the Greek coast, where reserves have been set up to protect them.

Foreign invasion

Global warming is also having an impact on the range of flora and fauna in the Mediterranean. Some 85 species of tropical fish – including small barracuda – have now found their way into the sea. But a greater threat appears to have been introduced by human error. The bright-green tropical seaweed, *Caulerpa taxifolia*, was widely used in aquaria. Its remarkable resilience was noted at the tropical aquarium of Stuttgart, Germany, and in 1982 a sample was sent to the famous oceanographic museum at Monaco. Two years later – no one knows quite how – a 'green tide' began to spread out across the seabed at the base of the Monaco building.

Caulerpa taxifolia has been nicknamed the 'killer seaweed' because it contains toxins that repel other forms of sea life, can affect their reproductive systems and poison the food chain. As a result, it has few enemies to control it. Worse, it kills off the beds of the eelgrass-like *Posidonia* that form the basis of much of the Mediterranean's coastal ecology. Caulerpa can grow about 1 in (2.5 cm) a day to a depth of 325 ft (100 m). Picked up on anchors and fishing nets, it has travelled from port to port, and now covers thousands of acres of coast, in Italy, Spain and Croatia. Scientists are at a loss to know how to control it: so far, all counter-measures proposed also harm other forms of sea life.

Guardian of the past *The old lighthouse of Rethymno in northern Crete looks out upon a new vista of dense coastal development.*

Rampant seaweed *The coastal ecology of the Mediterranean is under threat from the green Caulerpa seaweed.*

Mountains, as Nature intended

In contrast to their robust and muscular image, the mountains of the Alps and the Pyrenees are fragile environments that require careful protection if they are to survive. Fortunately, national parks and nature reserves have generally succeeded in staying the hand of intrusive humans, who once threatened to hunt, fish and pick the wildlife to extinction.

The Eurasian eagle owl

Few places in the world can offer a more stunning glimpse of pristine nature than the Alps or Pyrenees. Footpaths wind upwards through the ecological strata, from woodlands and forest to high pasture dotted with wild flowers, and to the rock pinnacles of the peaks. Birds of prey soar over the valleys, mountain goats watch nervously, then scamper away across the rocks in a clatter of hoofs. Here, as in the sea, human beings are not entirely in their element: a sudden change in weather can pose a lethal threat. It is an environment that demands respect, not only because of the dangers it can pose, but because any damage caused by overuse, uncontrolled hunting and fishing, or thoughtless dumping, quickly undermines the very qualities for which it is so cherished.

National parks

Several of the most magnificent mountain regions have been placed under official protection – like the Parco Nazionale dello Stelvio in central northern Italy, founded in 1935. Together with the adjacent Swiss National Park of Engadin over the border, it forms one of the largest protected regions in Europe. It is named after the Stelvio Glacier, the biggest in Italy, which descends for 3 miles

Hanging in the balance *Ordesa canyon in northern Spain has been a national park since 1918.*

Soaring spires *The Dolomites create an awe-inspiring setting for a traditional mountain church.*

Rugged crown   Dawn illuminates a string of peaks in the Italian Dolomites.

(5 km) from almost 13 000 ft (4000 m). The park is home to marmots, chamois and deer, as well as some 130 species of birds, including the rare Eurasian eagle owl and black grouse.

To the south-east, straddling the border between Trentino-Alto Adige and the Veneto regions, are the Alpi Dolomiti, or Dolomites – a string of saw-toothed, snow-sprinkled limestone pinnacles, ridges, cliffs and gorges. They rise with heart-stopping abruptness out of gentle hills cloaked in pasture and forest. The Parco Naturale Panevéggio, to the south of the highest peaks, protects a large swathe of this forest.

The Pyrenees are a paradise for enthusiastic walkers, with paths winding up through thick forests to high ridges. They possess Spain's richest heritage in animal species. Catalonia has the Parque Nacional de Aigües Tortes ('winding water'), created in 1955, which is dominated by the great granite peaks of the Sierra dels Encantants (the 'Enchanted Mountains'). This is an important refuge for otters, eagles and grouse, as well as a breeding ground for izards, the local species of chamois that stand little more than 3 ft (1 m) high. Aigües Tortes is also one of the last remaining refuges of the lammergeier, or bearded vulture, in Europe.

Saving the ibex

The Alpine ibex, a small mountain goat with golden eyes and impressive horns averaging 26 in (67.5 cm) long, has lived in the northern Italian mountains since time immemorial. Hunted to the point of extinction, it was saved by the work of staff at the Parco Nazionale del Gran Paradiso, Italy's oldest national park. Although once down to their last 100 or so, the Alpine ibex now numbers more than 20 000 across the central Alps. Encouraged by this, Italian naturalists are now trying to reintroduce the European black vulture – the largest bird of prey in Europe.

There is a park of similar stature farther east, in Aragón: the Parque Nacional de Ordesa, famed for its towering cliffs and natural ledges called *fajas*, and shared by izards, ibexes and golden eagles.

The brown bear

Ordesa was also the natural habitat of brown bears, but their population in the entire Pyrenees is now less than half a dozen. They were once common across the mountainous regions of Southern Europe. Today there are around 80 in the Cantabrian Mountains of northern Spain, 50 in the Parco Nationale d'Abruzzo in the Apennines of central Italy, and just four in Trentino in northern Italy – but 2800 in the south-eastern Alps that descend into Slovenia. In 1996 six bears were taken from Slovenia to the Pyrenees, but they were not universally welcomed. The Slovene bears, more aggressive that their Pyrenean cousins, have been blamed for injury to sheep, and – although farmers can be reimbursed through compensation schemes – some preferred to seek redress with the gun. Only about half the bears survived.

The climbing bug

Mountaineering is called 'alpinism' in several European languages – an acknowledgment that this pursuit began in the Alps, in the 18th century. After the first ascent of Mont Blanc in 1786, climbing clubs and guide companies sprang up, and one by one the main peaks were conquered. The popularity of 'alpinism' today has its drawbacks: however careful, climbers leave their marks. But most climbers appreciate that respect for the mountains is an important component of the exhilaration they draw from them.

Onwards and upwards   A climber heads up one of the needle-like peaks of the Dolomites.

The Algarve: colours and scents of Africa

Fruit of the arbutus tree

There are echoes of North Africa not just in the history of Portugal's Algarve, but also in the colours of its landscape: saffron, ochre, baked red. The Moors created a garden-like hinterland, which, despite its tourist development, retains much of its rugged charm.

The Algarve coastline has two distinct characters. The far west, between Portimão and Cape St Vincent, is the *barlavento* – the Algarve of rocks and cliffs, of surf-beaten beaches, caves, arches and sea stacks. By contrast, the east, the *sotavento*, between Faro and the Spanish border, is a flat landscape of sand banks, dunes and salt marshes. Much of it is lined with salt lagoons, home to storks, herons and pink flamingos. The main area of tourist development lies in the central strip between Faro and Lagos, leaving the extreme east and west comparatively unscathed.

Working beach *Fishing remains an important source of income for the people of Lagos.*

Land's end *For centuries the rocky Cape St Vincent, the south-western corner of Portugal, represented the extreme limit of the known world, and was the starting point for Portuguese world exploration.*

The garden of Portugal

A ring of hills, including the Serra de Monchique and the Serra do Caldeirão, protects the coastal strip from cold north winds. These have also helped the Algarve to become the 'garden of Portugal', producing fruit, tomatoes, strawberries and avocados for export.

The ground was prepared by the Moors. This was the last part of Portugal to be wrested from the Moors, and during their five centuries of rule, until 1253, they dug wells, organised systems of irrigation, and fostered the cultivation of a range of trees that can survive with scant water: olive, fig, carob (for their sugary pulp) and, above all, almond.

According to legend, an Arab prince planted a forest of almond trees around Silves for his beautiful Scandinavian bride, who craved the winter snows of her homeland. So every year, while the cold January winds still chilled the air, the princess could see the red land of the Algarve transformed by a cloak of white and sweetly perfumed blossom.

Three climates in one

The Serra de Monchique, rising to the Foia peak at 2959 ft (902 m), demonstrates the climatic conditions of the Algarve. From base to summit, it hosts an unusual combination of plants, which benefit from protection from north winds and high rainfall blown in from the coast. Here, oaks and chestnuts more readily associated with northern Europe grow in close proximity to typical trees of the Mediterranean, such as cork oaks, mimosa, pines, eucalyptus and arbutus, or strawberry trees. And the most sheltered valleys extend the range yet further to tropical plants, such as yams and banana trees.

Dalmatia: between rock and the deep blue sea

Running down the rocky, fretted coast of Croatia is a chain of elongated islands composed of limestone. The susceptibility of the rock to erosion, and its greatly varying capacity to retain rainfall, has produced a unique landscape.

Exception proves the rule *Krk, the largest island, has plentiful streams.*

The Dalmatian coast has been shredded like a wind-torn flag. It is so riddled with indents and speckled with islands that, although measuring some 230 miles (375 km) as the crow flies, the total extent of its coastline is more than 16 times this length. It has often been compared to the fiords of Norway or Chile; but the summer heat, the scarcity of rainfall, and the brittle, desiccated nature of limestone karst have forged a landscape altogether more raw and uncompromising.

Torn shreds

Over 10 000 years ago, the Adriatic infiltrated the foothills of the Dinaric Alps. The islands that formed were aligned north-west to south-west, reflecting the orientation of the mountains, but their shape was exaggerated by winds and currents pushing from one direction. As a result, many islands, such as Otok Hvar, are exceptionally long and thin. The mountains contain large fields of limestone, such as

the plateau of Kras (Karst in German), from which the name karst is derived. One of the features of this soft and porous rock is that rainwater quickly disappears into it, leaving the surface rocky and hostile to plant growth – while beneath the ground there may be a labyrinth of caves forged by underground streams.

Hideaways

This effect can be seen on many of the islands, only 60 of which are permanently inhabited. Venice ruled the Adriatic region from 1420 to 1797, and this highly complex configuration of inlets, creeks, straits and bays provided safe anchorage for the Venetian merchants journeying between their trading ports. But they were also the notorious refuges of pirates, who preyed upon the merchant fleets. Today, they are a popular haunt of yachting enthusiasts, divers and sun-worshippers.

Bleak shores *The Zadar channel passes between arid rock walls.*

The garden of Korcula

The Dalmatian islands are not all rocky semi-deserts. The presence of water on some has permitted a covering of maquis-type vegetation. Korcula is positively green with parasol pines, pomegranate trees, aloes, oleander and olive trees. This explains its attraction to foreign powers: Korcula has been ruled by the Romans, Goths, Slavs, Byzantines, Genoese and Venetians. By some accounts, this was the birthplace of Marco Polo, in 1254. The Venetians in particular helped to preserve the island's greenery, for they needed wood to maintain their fleet. Today the people of Korcula grow olive trees and vines, producing good white wines.

Sanctuary *Some of the 125 islands of the Kornati archipelago have been earmarked as a national park.*

CHAPTER 2
PEOPLE
AND
RESOURCES

The beguiling beauty of the southern landscape cannot hide the fact that it drives a hard bargain. The sun-scorched pastures and tiny fields won from rocky soil are vivid indicators of the toil required to eke out a living. Nonetheless, the people of Southern Europe created a survival strategy characterised by three commodities: wine, olive oil and bread. Later, they added imported plants: oranges, lemons and aubergines from South Asia, peaches from Persia, tomatoes and chillies from Central America – creating the vibrant colours of the southern markets of today. Many crops are still produced by traditional methods, but intensive, industrial-style production has placed Southern Europe's agriculture among the world leaders. All too often this has created an agonising dilemma for producers: modernise or quit. This stark choice is sometimes alleviated by turning to tourism, which – despite disadvantages – can provide income that permits traditional ways of life to endure.

Workers in Albania take a rest among baskets of green olives, picked by traditional methods.

The vine: a time-honoured heritage

For the ancient Greeks and Romans, wine was a valued commodity, shipped around the Mediterranean in amphorae carefully stowed on galleys. Today Southern Europe produces many of the world's great wines. The summer sun enriches the grapes to produce dark, velvety wines such as Rioja and Barolo, and the great fortified wines of Spain and Portugal. But every region has its favourite, often produced in small quantities, and so cherished locally that it never reaches the world beyond.

Port of ports *Port shippers line the quays of Oporto, the main city of northern Portugal.*

The origins of viticulture – growing grape vines, usually for wine-making – date back at least 7000 years. The world's oldest vines have been found at Arkhanes, near Knossos in Crete. From here, perhaps, vines were taken to Greece, and then to Italy. The Etruscans passed their passion for wine on to the Romans, and they then spread the habit to France, Spain and the rest of the Roman Empire. The ancient Greeks believed that wine had medicinal properties, but they almost always drank it watered down.

They kept their wine in goatskins, casks or clay amphorae, sealed only with oil, or a greasy rag, or paper soaked in oil or wax. The presence of bacteria, and the low alcohol content of ancient wine (rarely more than 5-6° of alcohol, compared to today's 11-12°) often turned it to vinegar. It was not until the 17th century that the glass bottle and cork became widely used, largely following the pioneering work of the French monk Dom Pierre Pérignon, father of champagne.

Port: a British invention

Port is one of Portugal's most famous products. This sweet, fortified wine – mostly red – comes from the Douro area, and is named after Oporto, the city from which it is shipped. It is made by adding brandy (about 20 per cent by volume) to the grape must, which cuts the fermentation short, before all the natural sugars have been consumed. The wine is then aged in wooden barrels – the longer the better, generally. The more valuable vintage port is not blended, and only in certain years is the grape harvest considered good enough to make it.

In most European countries port is drunk as an *apéritif*, but the British have developed a taste for fine, aged vintage port, which is served as an after-meal *digestif*. In fact, port is really a British invention, developed during the late 1600s as a way of circumventing France, Britain's usual source of wine, during a trade war. This historic connection explains why many of the old port shippers have British names.

Sailsmanship *The old wine barges at Oporto were used to transport the barrels to the shippers' 'lodges' (warehouses) along the river.*

The spread of wine corresponded to the spread of Christianity: it was an essential feature of the rite of communion. Monks therefore took an active role in the development of viticulture. During the 15th century, by some estimates, four times more land was planted with vines than today. Local habits and tastes developed, such as adding honey or spices to the wine, or adding brandy to make fortified wine. In Greece, pine resin gives a distinctive flavour to the typical wine, called retsína.

Growth industry

Wine is now big business, with highly professional production methods, blending techniques tailored for the palettes of the export markets, and carefully targeted marketing and labelling. Quantity has sometimes triumphed over quality, but producers ultimately know that quality, consistency and reputation are their greatest assets in the long term.

Until the 1960s, Spain and Italy had a reputation for cheap wine of low quality, but in recent decades this has changed radically, as producers of top-quality wines began to win new markets. Italy adopted a system of 'appellations' (Denominazione di Origine Controllata, DOC), promoting the integrity of the wines from its 200 or so demarcated regions. Total production fell and the price rose, but the foreign market responded favourably, and Italy is now one of the top wine-exporting nations. Spain took a similar line by appointing 26 Denominación de Origen (DO) regions, and gained new markets for its top-quality wines such as Rioja, Valdepeñas and Rueda. The sherries of Jerez are still without rival. Outsiders' knowledge of Portuguese wine used to be limited to port and Mateus Rosé in its distinctive oval bottles, but now the regional wines such as Douro, Bairrada, Dão and Alentejo are gaining a wider popularity.

Portugal has the largest per capita wine consumption in the world, with 61 litres per head per annum. Italy comes third (53 litres) after France (60 litres), and Spain and Greece equal seventh (35 litres).

Steady hand *With theatrical skill, a bodega (wine store) worker in Jerez de la Frontera aerates a measure of barrel-fresh sherry for tasting.*

Pyramid stack *Bottles of Chianti are kept cellar-cool at the Castello di Verrazzano in Tuscany.*

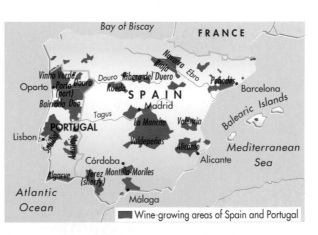

Wine-growing areas of Spain and Portugal

By the bottle or buy in bulk

There are thousands of wines in Southern Europe. Some are internationally famous, but many more are of such limited production that they have no need for an export market. Only by travelling in the region can their full range be appreciated – from the lusciously smooth Monica or Cannonau reds of Sardinia, to the sweet, rich Málaga wine of southern Spain. The big names attract big prices – such as Italy's Barolo, and some of the finest of Spain's Tempranillos. But local people tend to be rather dismissive of these, and would prefer not to buy wine by the bottle at all. Instead, they take their own demijohns and casks down to the local wine shop, or to the cooperative, where the wine is pumped out of huge stainless-steel vats and costs a fraction of the price of bottled wine. Blind tastings comparing such wines with expensive bottled ones frequently show that the locals know best.

Salute! *A Roman statue of Dionysus, Greek god of wine, raises his drinking cup.*

Produce from the hothouse of Europe

Southern Europe has a natural advantage over its huge market to the north: warmth. As buyers from international supermarkets fly in, ships and aeroplanes head out from the countries of the region loaded with tomatoes, peppers, cherries, peaches and oranges to nations less blessed with the sun.

Ready to pick *A worker tests a crop of oranges in Italy – the world's sixth largest producer.*

According to the World Health Organization, everyone should eat 165 lb (75 kg) of fresh fruit and vegetables a year, to take advantage of their natural vitamins and fibre. This is good news for Southern Europe, which is one of the main exporters of fruit and vegetables in the world.

Tent city *In Portugal, cultivation under plastic speeds growth.*

Spanish oasis *Tomato-growing land near Alicante, south-eastern Spain, shows the benefits of irrigation.*

The water tribunal

The Huerta de Valencia is Spain's most fertile region. A land of oranges and rice, it is the home of paella, the national dish. It now supports one of the highest rural population densities in Europe. Water from the surrounding hills used to be transported by canals of compacted earth. These have been largely replaced by ones made of cement, and by pipelines, while large dams and reservoirs have extended the area of land in use. Nonetheless, respect for water remains undiminished, and its distribution is organised by a community tribunal based on the ancestral model.

A meteoric expansion

It is a market that has developed exponentially over several decades. Italy is now Europe's biggest producer of fruit and vegetables, and sixth in the world – no mean feat considering that the countries ahead of it (China, Brazil, India, the USA and Turkey) are all many times larger. It is also the European market leader in pears, cherries, kiwi fruits and artichokes. Spain is top among producers of citrus fruit, strawberries and apples. Portugal and Greece may chalk up

more modest statistics, but nonetheless both have doubled their output since 1960. The Mediterranean is, effectively, Europe's market-garden. It is an efficient, modern industry, well attuned to the demands of the export market, in presentation, supermarket labelling, timing, optimum ripeness, transport and delivery.

The gift of climate

Southern Europe not only has plenty of sun, it also has a range of climates that suit all kinds of produce, from leeks, broccoli and many varieties of lettuce, to the kinds of fruit and vegetables that require more intense heat, such as tomatoes, courgettes, aubergines, and peppers – star ingredients of Mediterranean cooking. The natural warmth of the climate eliminates or reduces dependency on the greenhouses needed in less clement northern latitudes, so reducing costs. But by the same token greenhouses can be used to produce early crops, ahead of the rest of the market. So Spanish strawberries now reach the UK from early spring: the British have to wait until June for their own crop.

Southern Europe's rich harvest of fruit and vegetables has its origins in tradition – the small plots and orchards where families once grew the larger part of their own food. Fig trees, almond trees and citrus trees were widely grown because they could tolerate the summer drought. Even today, garden plots provide a large amount of produce for home consumption – salads, onions, leeks, beans, tomatoes, courgettes and melons – and any excess may be sold at the side of the road. The tradition of home produce keeps Southern Europeans loyal to seasonal food: they see little point in eating produce out of season. But the growth of supermarkets across the region is beginning to alter habits.

Vital water

Water still plays a key role in production, rigorously controlled and conserved where it is in short supply. Plastic is used to minimise evaporation, while complex modern irrigation systems extend the areas of usable land. In the Andalucian province of Almería, in southern Spain, growers are able to produce five crops a year of tomatoes, green beans, peppers and cucumbers – all the more surprising, given that in the 1950s this land was little more than hard, stony ground. In fact, the climate is so arid that Sergio Leone used the landscape to imitate the Wild West of the USA in his famous 'spaghetti Westerns'. Success is due to a remarkable degree of cooperation between workers and agricultural institutions: together they laid down an artificial soil of sand and fertiliser to provide a rich base that would resist evaporation – thus creating fertile and productive farms from land that was virtually useless.

But not everyone is pleased with such developments. The growth of plastic along the coast of southern Spain seldom adds to the beauty of the landscape, even if it has alleviated the hardships of areas such as Almería – and even if, from a distance, the vast plastic-covered strawberry fields can sometimes be mistaken for lakes.

Turning up the heat *A canopy of plastic over a melon field in Spain ensures an early crop.*

Harvest festival

The end of the harvest is cause for celebration – and wildly exuberant festivals that recall a pagan past. At Buñol, 18 miles (30 km) inland from Valencia, on the western side of La Huerta, a tomato festival takes place on the last Wednesday of August. Locals, joined by thousands of enthusiasts, take part in a tomato fight held in the town's main square.

Purée fun *The battle of the tomatoes at the Buñol festival.*

Timeless olives

With their gnarled trunks and compact, silvery leaves, olive trees cut an unmistakable profile, and command a respect not readily accorded to other trees. They are the quintessential trees of the Mediterranean coast, and a foundation stone of the region's economy.

The first olive trees in the Mediterranean were probably imported from Asia Minor and grown in Crete in the 4th millennium BC. Since then, they have been planted around all its shores – anywhere where there is just enough soil and water, a long and hot growing season, and no winter frost.

Olive trees can live for a very long time – 400 years, maybe more – and still go on producing large annual crops. They seem to pass on the gift of longevity to those who appreciate their fruits. Because olive oil contains 80 per cent oleic acid, a mono-unsaturated lipid,

it does not increase cholesterol levels, a key cause of heart disease. The ancients had an inkling of this: Hippocrates, the Greek 'father of medicine', classed olive oil as a food-medicine.

Olive picking

Mature olive trees represent a valuable family asset, usually passed down from one generation to the next. Many olive groves are still picked by hand, starting with the young green olives in September. The ground beneath the trees is carefully cleared of undergrowth, then the branches are skilfully struck by long poles, dislodging the olives, which can then be picked up off the ground. In larger, more industrial estates, the work is done by mechanical vibrators, which knock the olives into nets spread out around the base of the trees. The harvest lasts several months: the last black olives, used to make olive oil, are picked in mid-winter, when their oil content is greatest. The best and purest oil – virgin olive oil – is obtained by cold-pressing. The oil is extracted simply by crushing the olives between rollers, or in hydraulic presses. Lower-quality oil is extracted in the same way, but treated by heating and filtration.

Italy produces the most olives, but Spain is the top olive oil-exporting nation – more that 250 000 tons a year.

Field patterns *The density of olive trees depends on the water available.*

Cork

Another long-living tree of Southern Europe is the cork oak. Cork is a thick outer layer of soft, spongy bark, which is stripped off in 8 ft (2.4 m) sections every 9-12 years. Cork was first used to make shoes and floats, but in the 18th century it was adapted for wine bottles, creating a great expansion in the industry. Today it is also used for flooring tiles. Portugal accounts for 50 per cent of world production.

Net profits *Nets cover the ground beneath olive trees in Tuscany to catch the fallen fruit.*

Marble: the white gold of the south

Marble has been exploited since ancient times as the most desirable medium for sculpture. It is comparatively easy to shape and polish, extremely durable, and has a unique sensual beauty. It remains a valuable economic asset for a number of Southern European countries.

Italy and Portugal are the world's biggest exporters of marble. Carrara, the focal point of the 'marble hills' of north-western Tuscany, produces more than 500 000 tons of marble a year – cut out in blocks by compressed-air drills, marble-cutting wires, abrasive slurry and diamond saws. But this is not just the centre of the Italian marble industry: it is a place of pilgrimage for sculptors and builders the world over.

The art of copying *At the marble workshops of Pietrasanta, near Carrara in Tuscany, craftsmen make copies of sculptures from plaster models – producing contemporary works as well as replicas of old classics.*

Raw material *At Borba, near Estremoz in Portugal, production methods follow the standard pattern: large rectangular blocks are extracted at the quarry, and later sawn at a factory.*

Ancient and modern

The passion for marble began in Greece. The quarries on Mount Pentelicon near Athens produced the marble used to build the Parthenon, and to create many of the masterpieces of Greek sculpture. But the most celebrated type of marble was the semi-translucent stone that came from the Greek island of Páros, which was used to create the buildings of several classic sacred sites, such as Epidauros, Delos and Delphi.

Parian marble had no rival, but its quarries were more or less exhausted by the 15th century AD. Now Carrara moved to the fore. The Romans had begun to exploit these quarries in 283 BC, but it took the Renaissance and Michelangelo in the 16th century – tramping the hills in search of the perfect white stone – to establish Carrara's supremacy. His *David* and *Pietà* were once crude blocks of Carrara marble.

All of Europe soon came to Carrara in search of the best quality marble for the grandest building projects, and during the 19th century sculptors would use little else. The quarries of Carrara still account for 75 per cent of Italy's marble production. It remains an important centre for sculpture, but today nearly 90 per cent of Carrara's marble is used for building, lining new palaces, hotels, religious buildings, embassies, and offices all over the world.

Towering asset *2100 billion cu ft (60 billion m³) of marble still remain to be quarried at Carrara.*

Purity and character

In the past, marble of pure white or cream was most prized, but mottled and coloured marble were also valued. The Romans used coloured marble to build, and during the Baroque age of the 17th century, and the Victorian period two centuries later, coloured marbles again became fashionable. Carrara produces cloudy grey *bardiglio*; elsewhere in Tuscany, Prato has a dark green serpentine marble, while Siena marble is reddish and mottled. A pinkish marble is quarried near Estremoz in the Alentejo region of Portugal.

Fishing: a noble tradition in decline

From the Greek islands to the Atlantic ports of Spain and Portugal descendants of the great seafaring nations of Southern Europe still make a living from fishing. But fleet modernisation, overfishing and pollution have plunged the industry into crisis.

Mediterranean rascasse

No escape   *Andalucian fishermen trap tuna in a circle of boats.*

Fishing is part of the image of Southern Europe. Postcards show brightly painted wooden fishing boats bobbing gently in Greek harbours, nets drying on Spanish quaysides, Italian lobster fishermen inspecting their pots in bays of turquoise blue, and glistening fish displayed on banks of ice in the coastal fishmarkets.

Collapse of fishing stocks

Pretty the fishing boats may be, but there is an alarming subtext. Today there are far fewer mullet, sea bream, mackerel, gurnard, anchovies, cod, sardines, tuna, octopus and squid to sell. Across the region, and out into the Atlantic, the fishing grounds have been depleted – in some cases virtually to the point of annihilation. Over 70 per cent of EU fishermen come from Southern Europe, so

the crisis in world fish stocks has hit particularly hard. To maintain the industry, the EU has to cut back its fleet capacity, and impose stricter quotas, and also to distribute the cuts evenly throughout Europe. Mistakes were made in the 1980s, when large investments in fishing were encouraged as a form of regional development. Fleets modernised and expanded their capacity, catches increased to breaking point. Then came the decades of painful retrenchment.

Atlantic crisis

The Spanish fishing fleet reaps one of the EU's largest catches. Vigo, in Galicia, north-western Spain, is Europe's biggest fishing port. Vigo's fleet ranges far beyond the EU territorial waters, from the Falklands to Newfoundland. But even here fishing stocks are in crisis. In the 1990s, Spanish fishermen caused considerable friction by continuing to fish fragile stocks of cod, after Canada imposed a total ban on cod-fishing within its own 200 mile (320 km) territorial fishing limits.

Tensions also run high back home. Under the Common Fisheries Policy (CFP), EU territorial fishing limits remain at 12 miles (20 km), but hard negotiations can be expected when that policy is reviewed in 2002.

Sun dried   *At Nazaré, in western Portugal, salted fish are hung out on nets to dry.*

National luxury

Portugal's national food is *bacalhau*, salt cod. Its history goes back to the 15th century, when Portuguese fishermen first began braving the Atlantic to harvest shoals of cod off Newfoundland. Expeditions took several months, so salting the catch was essential. The cod stocks of the North Atlantic collapsed in the 1990s, and now most of the *bacalhau* is imported from Norway and Iceland at great cost – making *bacalhau* dishes even more greatly prized.

Heaving to   *Oxen are still used to draw fishing boats up the beach of Areao, in Portugal.*

From nomadic grazing to battery farming

The shepherd remains a feature of the Southern European landscape to this day, but sheep farming is gradually ceding its dominant position to the industrialised production of dairy products, pigs and chickens.

On Sardinia, sheep are said to outnumber people. Their milk is used to make the famous pecorino cheeses, and they also produce wool and meat. It is a typical scenario for Southern Europe, where sheep – and goats – can tolerate the arduous climate and make best use of the open ranges of scrubland pasture and poor soils.

North-south divide

At the start of each summer, Sardinian shepherds begin moving their flocks along the ancient tracks towards the uplands in search of fresh pasture. It is a hard and lonely life, but here, as in many of the poorer regions of Southern Europe, the position of sheep farming remains unchallenged. Sheep, as well as pigs, continue to graze the fallow land in the shade of the oak trees of Extremadura in Spain, or the Alentejo region of Portugal. But it is becoming increasingly difficult to recruit young men into traditional shepherding. Farmers are no longer willing to put up with the deprivations of semi-nomadic herding. Sheep, like their owners, are becoming more sedentary.

Fleeced Sheepshearing in Sardinia (right). Below: A shepherdess tends a handful of Greece's population of 10 million sheep.

Old recipes appeal to modern tastes

Imagine an Italian delicatessen, with Parmesan and Gorgonzola cheese, olives, coffee – and the mesmerising range of salamis and ham. Although a number of countries produce preserved meats, Italy is the most celebrated source. They owe their origins to old farmhouse practices: it was a way of preserving meat and using all parts of the carcass. Today, preserved meats are a major export industry. One of the most famous is *prosciutto crudo* – literally 'uncooked ham', but preserved in salt and air-dried for eight months.

Regional flavours Ham from Andalucía in Spain has its own regional characteristics.

With EU funding, the traditional patterns of farming are evolving. Where conditions permit – and this often applies to more northerly regions – farms are switching to new, more profitable kinds of stock-raising. In Catalonia in north-eastern Spain, and Emilia-Romagna in northern Italy, intensive pig and chicken farming is developing fast, spawning at the same time a plethora of complementary food-processing industries.

Livestock producers throughout Southern Europe are gearing up and modernising. Spain and Italy now rank eighth and ninth respectively in the world meat-producers' league table. But it will be many more years before the bells of the mountain herds are finally silenced – a sound that has echoed across Southern Europe since history began.

Tides of exodus

Southern Europe has long traditions of emigration. From the 15th century on, millions have torn themselves away from their Mediterranean homelands in search of a better life in destinations near and far. They took with them cultural habits and perspectives that have had a major impact around the entire globe.

During the 15th and 16th centuries, the motivation for migration was largely profit. Spanish and Portuguese colonists headed for territories in the New World and in the Far East to make their fortunes in trade or plantations. By the 19th and 20th centuries, circumstances had changed. The migrants of Southern Europe were now in search of the better life promised elsewhere, often driven out by despair over the economic conditions at home.

There were two main waves of economic emigration: in the years leading up to the First World War, and then during the boom years of 1950-70. Politics also played their part. Those who found themselves in open disagreement with the existing regime were often forced to leave – a situation that applied particularly to the 20th century. Some 40 000 Italians fled Mussolini's Italy in the 1930s, and 250 000 Spaniards were displaced by the Civil War of 1936-9.

The workforce of Northern Europe

Many went to the USA – considered the dream goal in the early 20th century; others went to Argentina and Venezuela. After the Second World War, 650 000 Italians, Greeks and Yugoslavs went to Australia. But the destination of migrants was usually not so distant. Southern Europe has long been a source of labour for Northern Europe. The current composition of the population in many of these countries – where ethnic minorities make up around 5-6 per

New life *Italians arriving in New York in the early 20th century.*

The Italian diaspora

Emigration from Southern Europe outstrips the average for Europe as a whole. Between 1901 and 1930, 1.6 million Italians went to France, 600 000 to Germany, 2.5 million to the USA, 1.26 million to Argentina, 376 000 to Brazil, and 100 000 to Canada. In just one year – 1913 – a million Italians emigrated. In a new wave, between 1950 and 1970, 337 000 Italians went to Australia. Historically, most Italian emigrants were from southern Italy. All the while, there was the phenomenon of 'internal immigration', as 9 million southern Italians moved to northern Italy. Until the recent influx of migrants from the Balkans, the word 'immigration' generally referred to the movement of southern Italians to the north.

cent of the total – tells the tale. In France 0.44 per cent of the total population are Italian, and 0.38 per cent are Spanish. In Belgium 0.5 per cent of the population is Spanish; in Germany 1 per cent comes from the former Yugoslavia, and 0.42 per cent from Greece. In Austria a full 2.5 per cent come from the former Yugoslavia.

Urban attractions

In the past, the majority of migrants from the south were unskilled, of rural origin and poorly educated. They usually found themselves on the bottom rung of the social ladder. Seasonal fruit picking was a traditional lure – grape-harvesting in the wine-growing regions, for instance – but most migrants were drawn to industrial labour in the cities, perhaps because agricultural work symbolised the misery and seasonal uncertainties that they suffered back home. So, re-creating something of the social flavour of Mediterranean life, Southern Europeans gathered in urban clusters, using networks of friends, relatives and fellow nationals for mutual assistance. Like many emigré communities, to this day they often remain fiercely loyal to their home culture and its traditions.

Between despair and hope
Albanian men await the arrival of a Greek ship to escape the collapse of their country's economy in 1997.

Most emigrants set out with the intention of returning home one day, but the decision to stay was often made for them, as the second generation grew up and integrated with the host community. The ability to join in the social and political structures of the host country depended to a degree on government policy. Germany, for instance, treated immigrants as 'guest workers', with few rights or prospects of long-term residence, while immigrants to the USA and Australia were encouraged to stay.

Home thoughts *An Italian bakery in SoHo, New York.*

economic boom in the north of the country, are short of labour. But the arrival of countless illegal immigrants – the *clandestini* – is giving rise to anxiety, especially as this phenomenon is known to involve criminal syndicates. While the Balkans remain in a state of flux, the exodus looks set to continue. Meanwhile, large numbers of people are moving within the Balkans, in search of work, living wages and stability – the same combination of reasons that has always pushed Southern Europeans to seek a better life abroad.

New migration

For decades migration meant Italians leaving their country. Now a very different situation has arisen: migrants are pouring into Italy, at a rate of over a million a year. Most come from the Balkans – refugees from the economic crises in Albania, and the strife in Bosnia and Kosovo. The Italians, with their very low birth-rate of 1.3 children per couple and the

Group therapy *Romany women in Macedonia pool their experiences over cigarettes and coffee, and sewing.*

Crop call *Strawberry-picking in Macedonia attracts hundreds of seasonal migrants to the fruit fields.*

Snapshots from Lorraine

It took courage to be an Italian miner in the coalfields of Lorraine, north-eastern France, in the inter-war years – a courage born of despair at home. Arriving with their families, they found lodgings in wooden shacks without any comforts or sanitation, where children slept five to a bed. Unmarried men lodged in insalubrious hotels, where the beds were occupied in shifts, day and night. Few spoke any French, and the xenophobic locals nicknamed them dismissively as 'macaronis'. The miners led frugal lives in order to send their pay home. Despite the gruelling physical labour of mine work, they lived on a diet of pasta, rice and polenta – the simple staples of their homelands. For all their privations, the Italians were considered to be the aristocracy by various other immigrant communities, and were respected by their employers for their cooperation and application. Only on Sundays and public holidays did they celebrate their national identity. Wearing their best clothes, they reinforced their cultural traditions – particularly in their religious festivals, which they observed with a fervour that helped to mitigate the hardships of their daily lives.

Slovenia: defying the odds

Within a decade of breaking free of Yugoslavia and winning its independence, Slovenia achieved the highest standard of living of any ex-Communist nation. A strong candidate to join an enlarged European Union, it provides an intriguing model for economists.

It has not all been plain sailing. In 1991, the year that Slovenia declared independence and won it with comparatively little conflict, inflation was running at 247 per cent. By 1997, however, it was down to 9 per cent, and the gross domestic product compared favourably with that of Greece and Portugal. It was a remarkable feat for a country labelled by the Press as the 'dolls house of Europe', with fewer than 2 million inhabitants.

Ski Slovenia *Kranjska Gora is becoming a successful winter resort.*

Working together *The Revoz factory at Novo Mesto assembles cars for the French manufacturer Renault, a mark of confidence in Slovenia's future.*

Successful conversion

It has to be said, though, that Slovenia started with distinct advantages. It was the most prosperous republic of the Yugoslavian federation, and came to independence with a basketful of useful assets: a skilled workforce, good infrastructure, and sizable natural resources. Its modernised and competitive industries, producing steel, glass, chemicals and textiles, can draw on plentiful supplies of hydroelectric power. Forests, covering 50 per cent of its land area, yield cellulose, paper and cardboard. Agricultural producers export honey, hams, wine, muesli and a large proportion of the annual harvest of 160 000 tons of fruit. Railways link the Balkans to the rest of Europe, while a new motorway network will connect with Hungary, and hook into a cross-European network that runs from Barcelona to Kiev.

Thumbs up to investors

Foreign investment, particularly from Germany, Austria and Italy, compensated for Slovenia's modest access to capital in the early years. Joint venture projects have been set up in pharmaceuticals (Lek/Bayer), communications (Isktratel/Siemens) and the car industry (Revoz/Renault). Tourism has also flourished, despite the negative image and uncertainties of the ongoing Balkan crisis to the south.

Slovenia holds many attractions for foreign visitors, including its dramatic Alpine scenery, lakes, spas and winter sports facilities – all of which it is keen to promote as a way of putting Slovenia firmly on the map.

A reputation for science

Slovenia has produced a long line of eminent scientists, including Jozef Stefan (1835-93), one of the most distinguished physicists of the 19th century, and Fritz Pregl, a founder of microanalysis and winner of the Nobel prize for chemistry in 1923. The Jozef Stefan Institute in Ljubljana has become one of Southern Europe's leading research organisations. Founded in 1949 by Anton Peterlin, a leading specialist in macromolecules, it now has a staff of 700, working in the fields of physics, chemistry, biochemistry, electronics, nuclear technology and information science. It has also won a strong reputation for its work in environmental research.

Mountain resource *The Julian Alps rim the north of the country, providing timber, pasture and winter sports – as well as a spectacular landscape.*

Albania: anger and resignation

Albania emerged as an independent state during the Balkan Wars of 1912-13, as Serbia, Greece, Bulgaria and Montenegro fought over spoils of the crumbling Ottoman Empire. Four decades of Communist rule left the country backward and impoverished, and barely able to cope with the Balkan crisis on its doorstep.

On the death of Enver Hoxha in 1985, after 40 years of Communist tyranny, Albania seemed like a nation drained of its life forces. It slid rapidly into anarchy, which compelled thousands to flee abroad by any means they could. Mafia clans took control of business and trade, exerting their control like warlords. The people of Albania might have tolerated this as the price of an emerging market economy, but in 1997 fraudulent investment companies, known as pyramid schemes, collapsed and thousands of citizens lost their life savings. In the turmoil that followed, rioters broke into weapons depots and took up arms, the government was forced out of office, and the economy went into free fall.

Fury *The economic collapse of 1997 provoked riots.*

Picturesque poverty *Krujë, in central Albania, remains steeped in tradition.*

Forty years of isolation

Albania had a rocky career after 1913. Taken over by self-appointed King Zog I in 1924, it was invaded by Italy in 1939, then fought over by partisans. The victors were the Communists, led by Enver Hoxha, who became prime minister in 1946 and ruled like a feudal despot until his death in 1985. Private property was banned, as was foreign travel, owning a television and religion. Hoxha followed a path of extreme isolationism, falling out with a succession of would-be allies – first Communist Yugoslavia in 1948, then the Soviet Union in 1961, and lastly China in 1977. In pursuit of Albania's independence, after the age of 16 all citizens had to undergo military training and help in the construction of the 700 000 bunkers scattered throughout the country – a vivid symbol of the paranoid, hermetic isolation of Hoxha's regime.

Standing start

Albania has rich deposits of iron, oil, natural gas, chrome, nickel, copper and bauxite. Half the population lives in the fertile lowlands on the Adriatic coast, where wheat, maize, fruit and vegetables are grown, supplying an active food-processing industry. Much of the interior of rugged mountains is cloaked in forest – yet many people live by herding cattle, sheep and goats.

The war in neighbouring Kosovo in 1999 again put Albania in the spotlight, as a key supporter of Kosovo's Albanian majority. Some 320 000 Kosovar Albanians took refuge in Albania, which became a base for NATO forces, and for a number of humanitarian organisations. Albania saw some benefit from this exposure, gaining international respect and a measure of stability, but its workforce continues to leave the country in droves. Albania faces a long haul to prosperity.

Hard times *Many of Tirana's 320 000 people survive by petty trading.*

Sun, sea and tourism

Southern Europe possesses everything that many holidaymakers dream of: golden sands, azure seas, plenty of bronzing sun, cuisine and wines to relish, a plethora of world-class cultural attractions – and a tourist infrastructure to deliver satisfaction smoothly and efficiently. But tourism is always a controversial industry, with negative aspects that can easily take an ugly turn if development is uncontrolled.

Reflections *Mediterranean islands provide a dream setting for holidays.*

Holidaymakers have been coming to Southern Europe since the 19th century, but the 1960s were a watershed. Suddenly, affordable air travel and cheap package tours put the Mediterranean within reach of a much broader public. Many of the poorer parts of Europe now had something to sell to the rest of the world: their natural assets of beach, sea and sun. Mass tourism took off, generating a heated cycle of building development in places such as the Costa Brava in Spain, the Algarve in Portugal, around Rimini in Italy, in Majorca, Cyprus and along the Dalmatian coast of Yugoslavia. Many of the most popular destinations were completely transformed by the process.

The sins of 'urbanisation'

Large swathes of land were converted into tourist villages – brand new settlements of houses and apartments bought by foreigners, or rented to them. The term used in Spain, Portugal and Italy was 'urbanisation', which soon became synonymous with jerry-built developments – poorly planned and even more poorly constructed. The towns of Vilamoura and Quarteira earned the sobriquet 'the shame of the Algarve'. Once a pretty little fishing village, Quarteira was stripped of its charm by development in the 1980s, as the bulldozers and concrete mixers took over. But while tourism can unquestionably wreck a place, the income can also help to preserve traditional ways of life, encourage local enterprise, and fund the preservation of historic and cultural sites.

Míkonos developed rapidly to become the most heavily commercialised of the Greek Cyclades. In high season the streets and beaches throng with foreign visitors, and the discos throb with techno music way into the night. But here, in contrast to Quarteira, construction has been carefully moderated. The essential charm of the island is still recognisable, wisely acknowledged as its most valuable asset.

Marbella: queen of the Costa del Sol

Founded 3600 years ago by the Phoenicians, the city of Marbella in Andalucía retains vestiges of its long history: ruins from Roman occupation, which began in the 3rd century BC, and an *alcázar* (fortified palace) from the Moorish years (8th to 15th century). Now the city has taken on a new lease of life as a flagship of Spanish tourism. It is the centrepiece of the Costa del Sol, with more than 24 excellent beaches lining 17 miles (27 km) of coast. Despite new developments and villas all around the city, the old quarter maintains its authentic, Andalucían feel, with its white-washed labyrinth of alleys. In the evening, strollers thread through the narrow streets to gather at the Plaza de los Naranjos (Square of the Oranges), or head for Puerto Bañus, the new and very chic yachting marina 3 miles (5 km) to the west. Marbella is a place where authenticity and tourism have reached a *modus vivendi* – not a perfect marriage, but a mutually beneficial one.

Old ways *Marbella, in southern Spain, has preserved much of its picturesque charm.*

Imperial villa   In the 1890s Empress Elisabeth of Austria built her residence, the Achílleion, on Corfu to 'ease her soul'.

To suit all tastes

The focus of the tourist industry has changed in recent years. Southern Europe has woken up to the fact that it can offer a huge breadth of opportunities for tourism of all kinds. The choice is endless. You can go on a walking holiday in the Spanish Pyrenees; stay in a farmhouse – equipped with a swimming pool – in the Tuscan hills; rent a yacht in the Greek Islands; see Sicily in spring, the hills awash with wild flowers; or in winter head for the mountains in northern Italy or Slovenia with your skis.

Charms lost. . .
Vilamoura, on
Portugal's Algarve, has
been disfigured by huge
developments and
unsubtle architecture.

. . . and saved
The little island of
Capri, in the Bay of
Naples, receives many
thousands of visitors a
year, but protects its
charms with an air of
exclusivity.

Corfu: always a focus for admirers

Corfu is the northernmost and prettiest of the Ionian islands, off the west coast of Greece – a happy combination of a mountainous interior, a glittering collar of blue seas, and enough vegetation to earn the nickname 'the green island'. For centuries this was a Christian outpost at the gates of the Islamic Ottoman world. In Corfu town, the baroque *Dhimarkhíon*, later the town hall, recalls the island's years as part of the Venetian Republic from 1386 to 1797. The arcades of the *Spianádha* (Esplanade) are a vestige of the French occupation in the early 19th century, while the Old Palace dates from British rule (1815-64). To the south of the town is *Mon Repos*, formerly the summer residence of the British Lord High Commissioner, then of the Greek kings. This was the birthplace, in 1921, of Prince Philip, Duke of Edinburgh. Corfu has had a string of admirers since Odysseus stopped on his return to Ithaca. More recently they included the writers Goethe, Oscar Wilde and Lawrence Durrell, and the painters Alfred Sisley and Edward Lear. These days the charm of the island is not entirely unalloyed. Corfu has the most developed tourist industry of all the Greek islands, with the greatest density of package-holiday hotels and villas.

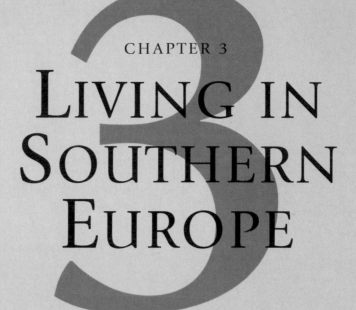

CHAPTER 3

LIVING IN SOUTHERN EUROPE

L iving together in a community, keeping in touch with
family, making friends, networking, contributing to
happy and invigorating social cohesion – these are the
forces that make Southern European society what it is. Life
revolves around them: witness the prominence of public places
in Mediterranean towns – the squares, the pedestrianised
shopping streets, the cafés, the markets – and the enthusiastic
crowds that turn out for religious festivals, spectator
sports and summer open-air concerts. Even on an
ordinary weekday, any town may take on a festive air.
The climate influences the patterns of behaviour: shade is
important in the summer heat; social activities gravitate
towards the evening and night. Essentially, it is an outdoor
life: the streets and public places are treated like extensions
of the home.

Shoppers and strollers throng the centre of Dubrovnik, on the Croatian coast.

Cones of stone *Curious little trulli houses have been a feature of Puglia, in southern Italy, for hundreds of years.*

The white villages of the south

From the Algarve in the west to the Dodecanese islands of Greece in the east, traditional villages are stamped with a common motif: the use of whitewash over plaster to deflect the heat of the sun. Many are also artful geometric configurations – cubes and rectangles, satisfyingly offset by hemispheres, cones, diagonals and spirals.

Throughout Southern Europe, traditional houses have many features in common. Thick walls keep out the summer heat and preserve the coolness within. Windows are small for the same reason: they are protected by shutters, kept closed during the daytime, but slotted so that air can circulate through the darkened interior. In arid climates, roofs may be flat, or tiled and gently sloping to collect what little rain falls.

In the past, the soil governed traditional building materials – brick, stone, terracotta tiles and lime plaster – but these days cement breeze blocks are more often used, disguised beneath a thick layer of plaster. The basic building shape is often the cube – perhaps reflecting Arab influence – as in Olhão in the Algarve, to the east of Faro. Its inhabitants maintained a close trading relationship with North Africa well after the retreat of the Moors, and its old quarter resembles a North African medina. The trulli of Puglia, in southern Italy, are the exception that proves the rule. These little houses are still being built today, with dry-stone walls crowned by roofs of stone slabs laid in concentric circles to form a cone.

Rustic charm

Traditionally, the walls of southern Mediterranean homes are painted with whitewash – and sometimes even the roof tiles and pavements outside are painted white. The whiteness makes a striking contrast against the blues of the sky and sea. The geometric shapes of the buildings throw angular shadows, while details such as windows and door frames are often picked out with a border in ochre or blue. Some villages have more daring colour schemes. The port of the island of Procida, off Naples, is all pastel shades – beige, pink and blue. In the Algarve, colour is concentrated in borders decorated with geometric or floral designs. Some houses in Greek villages have courtyards paved with mosaics in pebbles, in the form of checkerboards, zigzags or rosettes. At Pirgí, the most attractive village on the Greek island of Khíos, a fork is drawn over wet plaster to create geometric sgraffito motifs.

Portuguese *azulejos*

Imported from Moorish Andalucía in the 16th century, *azulejos* tile work is still a popular feature of architectural decoration in Portugal. The word comes from the Arabic *azraq* (azure) and *zalayja* (polished stone). The panels of painted and kiln-filed tiles may represent one-off pictorial designs – some very elaborate – or repeated motifs. Even humble houses may be decorated with an *azulejos* frieze of flowers, or interlinked stars.

Building blocks *The cuboid buildings in Valletta, Malta, are offset by arches and projecting windows.*

The shape of modern life

Looking to the future
Parque Juan Carlos I is at the heart of Madrid's financial district.

At the start of the 21st century, cities such as Bilbao and Lisbon have struck out boldly with uncompromisingly modern buildings that have drawn the eyes of the world, and shown just how well architecture can talk.

Constrained for many years by limited budgets, by the prohibitive costs of modern technology, and by a tendency towards conservative taste, Southern European cities were not widely known for architectural daring. The extraordinary Sagrada Familia church of Barcelona, by Antoní Gaudí – started in 1883 and still not completed – was the exception that proved the rule. But all this has changed since the 1990s, when a set of startling new buildings appeared, notably in Spain and Portugal, reasserting the invigorating effect of prestige architecture.

Olympic city

Barcelona was transformed by the Olympic Games of 1992, which inspired a city-wide renovation. The effect was not limited to sports stadia and the athletes' accommodation: Barcelona also radically remodelled its waterfront and a number of public spaces. International architects of renown were brought in to lead the transformation. The American 'master of whiteness' Richard Meier designed the new museum of contemporary art; the British architect Norman Foster was responsible for a landmark telecommunications tower. The Spanish architect and engineer Santiago Calatrava created the remarkable Bach de Roda bridge, while the Barcelona-based post-modernist Ricardo

New link *A road bridge has revitalised Lisbon's links with southern Portugal.*

Bilbao's facelift

Bilbao, capital of the Basque country, was a city in crisis after the collapse of the steel industry in the 1970s. In the 1990s a bold transformation began with the building of the Guggenheim Museum. It was designed by the American Frank Gehry to house a world-class collection of modern art, but the building itself is now better known than its contents. A logic-defying jumble of titanium-clad shells, it has become an icon for re-emergent Bilbao. The transformation did not stop there: it included a new airport terminal and footbridge by Santiago

Art house *The Guggenheim has given Bilbao celebrity status.*

Calatrava, and an underground railway system with stations designed by Norman Foster.

Bofill created a new airport terminal. Architecture led a sea-change in Barcelona, now celebrating its role as capital of Catalonia in the newly democratised Spain; and it helped to trumpet Barcelona's evolution into one of Europe's most dynamic and prosperous cities.

World Fair

Lisbon similarly enjoyed a renaissance during the World Exposition of 1998, Expo '98. The old Olivais docks on the banks of the River Tagus – once an eyesore of cranes, chimneys and oil tanks – were rehabilitated as a window on modern design. The star piece was the ingenious Portuguese pavilion by Álvaro Siza, Portugal's leading architect, which is due to become the seat of government.

A *passion for religion*

The exuberance of the Mediterranean countries permeates their approach to religion. Religious celebrations are frequently the focus of elaborate ceremonies, and a passionate outpouring of emotion. These are, after all, the lands where Christianity first established itself as a world religion.

Saintly protectors *In Malta each parish has its patron saint.*

Southern Europe is predominantly Christian. With the headquarters of the Roman Catholic Church in Rome, and of the Greek Orthodox Church in Athens, the two main religious blocks remain today as they were in Byzantine times, more or less. But the religious map is more complex than this. Islam plays an important role in parts of the Balkans, and there are Protestants, such as the Waldensians, in northern Italy, and Jewish communities in Spain, Italy and Greece, resulting in a mosaic that represents a long history of religious mingling – as well as confrontation and strife.

The anchor of faith

In Italy, Spain and Portugal, Catholicism still plays a central role in the life of towns and villages. Local festivals tend to be based around saints' days, to celebrate the saint who protects the community, and daily private devotion will often be directed towards the image of that saint. The year is also punctuated with the main Christian festivals. Holy Week, leading up to Easter, is celebrated with particular fervour in Seville in Spain. Huge processions bearing tableaux of the Easter story, organised by the 50 or so *hermandades* (brotherhoods), take to the streets, followed by hundreds of *nazarenos*, or penitents, in their black or white cassocks and towering conical hats.

Roman Catholicism is currently undergoing a revitalisation, bucking the trend by attracting a new generation of committed

Sources of Catholic inspiration

St Ignatius Loyola (1491-1556)
Born in his ancestral castle of Loyola in the Basque country, Ignatius was a soldier turned devout pilgrim who co-founded the Society of Jesus (the Jesuits), an Order recognised by the Pope in 1540. It undertook to spread the Christian faith through disciplined study, education and missionary work.
St Theresa of Avila (1515-82) and St John of the Cross (1542-91)
These two great Spanish mystics helped to reform the Order of Carmelites. Through their writing, and by their own example, they emphasised the necessity of frugality and poverty to achieve piety and mystic experience.
Mother Teresa (1910-1997)
At the age of 18, this nun of Albanian origin went to Calcutta to teach the children of wealthy families at a convent, but in 1948 she left the school to devote herself to working among the poor in the slums. The following year she founded the Order of the Missionaries of Charity, whose mission is to help the destitute, sick and dying. Mother Teresa was awarded the Nobel peace prize in 1979.

Light of devotion *Huge torch-lit processions accompany pilgrimages honouring Our Lady of Fátima in Portugal on May 13 and October 13.*

young people. This is reflected in the traditional pilgrimage to Santiago de Compostela in Spain. Mixing religion with camaraderie, thousands of walkers and pilgrims from all over the world now take to the age-old pilgrimage routes that thread through Spain – and indeed through most of Europe – to the shrine where St James is said to be buried. Fátima, in central Portugal, is likewise a focus of devotion, drawing thousands of pilgrims to its Basilica of Our Lady, especially from Portugal and Spain. Every year, on May 13 and October 13, they

Folklore and religion Each year in Andalucía about a million people wearing traditional dress and beating drums, celebrate the two-day romería (pilgrimage) of El Rocío, in honour of the holy image of the Virgin of El Rocío.

gather in crowds of 100 000 or more in the hope of witnessing the 'great miracle'. These are the anniversaries of the first and last monthly appearances, in 1917, of the Virgin Mary before three young children of a shepherding hamlet, and the increasing numbers of pilgrims who joined them. The Virgin of Fátima passed on three secrets to one of the girls – three prophecies about the 20th century, the last of which was revealed in 2000 (the millennial anniversary of Christ's birth) allegedly as a prophecy about the attempted assassination of Pope John Paul II in 1981.

The love of icons

The Eastern Orthodox Church separated from the Church of Rome in 1054, and remains fiercely independent to this day. It is composed of a number of churches, each practising its religion in its own language – be it Greek, Albanian or Serbo-Croat. The churches play an important role in shaping ethnic or national identity, and transcend the fragile political borders of the Balkan nations, sometimes to controversial effect.

Orthodox Churches are famous for their stately and elaborate rituals, designed to show worshippers that they are in a different realm. Icons, which represent Christ or the Virgin, angels or saints, have a central place in Orthodox traditions. They are painted on wood according to a precise tradition, and are often elaborately decorated with gold or silver. Icons are said to reveal both the human and divine nature of their subjects, and to serve as a channel of blessing from God.

Contemplation Painted icons are the focus of prayer during Easter, a period of extreme devotion in the Greek Orthodox Church.

Pleas for forgiveness Penitents parade through Seville during Holy Week.

Cranes at the ready Iron and steel were the basis of Bilbao's economy, but the industry declined in the 1970s.

The Basque region: tradition, autonomy and terrorism

In 1998, after almost 40 years of terrorist activity, which claimed the lives of some 800 people, the armed Basque separatist movement ETA announced a voluntary ceasefire. It heralded a period of optimism, calm and growing prosperity for this independent-minded corner of northern Spain. But it was a false dawn. In December 1999, after just 14 months of peace, ETA launched a new campaign of bombings and assassination.

Open country The mountainous interior of the Basque country contrasts with the industrial coast.

July 1997, it seemed, was the turning point. Following the kidnap and assassination by ETA of a young municipal councillor, Miguel Angel Blanco, thousands of Basques joined millions of Spaniards in a massive demonstration of protest. It was one death too many in a campaign that now appeared increasingly senseless and outdated in the post-Franco era. ETA (*Euzkadi Ta Azkatasuna*, 'Basque Homeland and Liberty') now realised that it could no longer count on the support – albeit mostly passive – of the Basque people for its strategy of violence to win independence for their land, or the autonomy it had briefly enjoyed in the 1930s.

provinces. Franco soon crushed this dream, but his policy of brutal repression simply hardened Basque nationalist and anti-Spanish sentiments, and pushed the radicals towards armed resistance. With the advent of democracy in 1977, the Basque country had another opportunity to move towards autonomy, but the political solutions on offer did not satisfy ETA, which intensified its campaign of violence until the unilateral suspension of hostilities in 1998. Claiming frustration over the lack of progress in talks with both France and Spain, ETA has since renewed the campaign, both in the Basque region and elsewhere in Spain.

Cultural deprivation

The Basque Nationalist Party was founded in 1894, proposing independence for the six Basque provinces straddling the Spanish and French border. In 1936 the Republicans granted autonomy to the two coastal Basque

Solidarity Red berets are worn at Irún to celebrate the festival of St Martial, and a victory over Napoleon.

68

North versus south: divided Italy

Since the 1980s, Italy has seen the rise of various secessionist movements, called 'leagues', which challenge the central government in Rome and underline the economic disparity between the north and south.

Northern protest *Members of the Lombard League demonstrate in St Mark's Square, Venice.*

The electoral success of the leagues, and their political success through affiliations in government coalitions, is a measure of the growing discontent of many northern Italians. Exasperated by the inefficiencies of central government, and fed up with paying taxes to subsidise the south, some now propose a division of Italy. After all, they say, Czechoslovakia split into the Czech Republic and Slovakia in their 'Velvet Divorce' of 1993. Why not Italy?

Two-speed Italy

There are glaring disparities between north and south. The north is the industrial heartland, a hive of activity where just about all the great Italian industrial names are based: Fiat, Ferrari, Benetton, Lavazza, Luxottica, Olivetti, Pirelli. In the south incomes are low, literacy is below the national average and unemployment is rising. There are a number of reasons why the south lags behind. The hot climate and poor soil has historically failed to support its people, causing emigration and a drain on human resources. The south has a more conservative and less flexible social structure, less well geared

Pride of place *A luxury restaurant in Milan, economic capital of Italy.*

to the modern service-industry dynamic. Then there is the Mafia, which diverts government subsidies and generally exerts a corrosive force that discourages investment.

But it remains to be seen whether the northern leagues represent more than a taxpayers' revolt. Some movements are tinged with an ugly xenophobia, not just against the southerners, but against all foreigners, who provide the labour that fuels the booming northern economy. In fact, for all their disparities, northern and southern Italy seem inseparably interdependent.

Income per head
as a percentage of the average in Italy (1997)

- more than 115
- 100–115
- 85–100
- 70–85
- less than 70

The Northern League

In 1996, 4 million voters balloted in favour of the Northern League. Its leader, Umberto Bossi, proclaimed the birth of the Republic of Padania (the Po Valley), with 25 million inhabitants, a proposed parliament to be based in Mantua and its own currency. The Northern League operates as a kind of umbrella for local leagues, such as the Lombard League, and similar organisations in the fast-developing Veneto. But they cannot agree on a long-term strategy, and in fact have mutually incompatible objectives.

The day's catch *Fishermen of the small town of Sciacca in Sicily.*

69

Living Mediterranean-style

It is eleven o'clock on a summer's evening. The streets throng with people: the carefully primped unmarrieds are on parade; young couples proudly push out their babies; grandparents on fold-up chairs keep an eye on infants playing tag. Cafés and restaurants swell with customers. This is a society at pleasure – easy-going, sociable, cohesive and backed by centuries of tradition.

To the Southern Europeans, conversation is an art. Talk flows with elegance, wit and sparkle, whether in an exchange of local gossip, or in discussing sports, politics or simply the weather forecast. Words, sociability and laughter form a key element of their culture. In a similar way, they have raised leisure into an art form. The Italians have the best expression to register this pleasure in the pursuit of leisure: *far niente*, 'doing nothing'. Better still is another Italian phrase: *dolce far niente*, 'sweet idleness'.

Outdoor life

In the heat of the day, both custom and practical necessity demand that most Southern Europeans retreat into the shade to save energy by resting or sleeping. The *siesta* is part of daily life throughout the Mediterranean, not just in Spain. Life resumes again in the evening, in the public thoroughfares, the squares and public gardens, the cafés, restaurants and ice-cream parlours, which are the centres of social life in towns and villages.

At the heart of most Spanish towns and cities is the *plaza mayor*; in Italy, it is the main *piazza*; in Portugal the *praça*; in Greece the *plateia*. The main square is the focus of public social life, and it is often surrounded by arcades that shade the cafés, restaurants and shops. Annual festivals and events usually take place here, and it is often the venue for the morning market, when it becomes radiant with vibrant colours and noisy with vendors' calls and the hubbub of customers.

Even on an ordinary weekday evening in summer people gather in the public spaces to chat and exchange news. They may have to ignore the crowds of tourists – but tradition is stronger than such modern intrusions. Indeed, customs such as the *passeggiata* – the early evening stroll that fills the streets of many Italian cities – are in themselves tourist attractions, cherished as special features of Southern European life.

Seasonal pleasures

The Italians have another expression to summarise life's pleasures: *la dolce vita*, 'sweet

Al fresco *Sardines are grilled outdoors in Lisbon.*

living'. A key element of this is the pleasure of taste: Italy is a country of gourmets. The day often begins early in the morning with a flying visit to a favourite bar or café for a shot of rich, dark coffee, prepared in a way no other country can match.

Italians do not make a great song and dance about their gastronomy. They like well-prepared food and are not much impressed by fussy, inventive cuisine. Far better to produce a good *antipasto* starter of grilled aubergines and red peppers in oil than some complex pâté with decorative trimmings – which Italians might enjoy once in a while, but are usually likely to dismiss as overrated and overpriced. Pasta and rice are eaten all over Italy, but the actual dishes remain highly regional: each locality has its treasured

Winter gathering *The Piazza Maggiore in Bologna, Italy, serves as a meeting place for local people throughout the year.*

dishes, from the *risi e bisi* (rice and peas) and *risotto alle seppie* (cuttlefish risotto) of the Veneto, to the *burrida* fish casseroles of the Ligurian coast, and the steaks *alla pizzaiola* (with enriched tomato sauce) of Naples.

Italian food is always seasonal and very fresh: not for them the year-round imports from all over the world that fill the supermarket shelves of Northern Europe. The progress from spring to autumn is marked by a succession of vegetables, salads, fruits and nuts that ripen as the growing season evolves. Lamb is rarely available outside springtime.

Second home *Old friends meet at a kafeneion in the Greek Peloponnese.*

Lunch in the sun *Outdoor tables on the Campo de' Fiori in Rome.*

On the waterfront *Diners in Venice enjoy the tranquillity of the canals.*

The art of Italian coffee

The standard Italian coffee, served in tiny cups, is rich, dark and sweetened to taste. This is espresso – simply called *un caffè* – prepared with artistic aplomb by bar tenders in control of large, shining, hissing machines. There are variations on this shot-in-the-arm coffee: *caffè lungo* has added water; *caffè latte* is coffee with a large proportion of boiled milk; *caffè macchiato* has just a dash of boiled milk in it. *Cappuccino* is an espresso mixed with frothy hot milk, sometimes sprinkled with chocolate powder for tourists. This is considered essentially a morning drink, and some establishments will not serve it after 11 am. *Caffè corretto* is an after-meal drink: it is *espresso* 'corrected' with a splash of *grappa*, a brandy made with grape skins. Most Italian coffees are 100 per cent Arabica, roasted, ground and marketed in Italy by the big houses such as Lavazza or Illy. However, their caffeine-effect is too powerful for many and decaffeinated versions – *caffè hag* – have recently become popular.

Voice of passion In a Lisbon bar, fado *music enjoys rapt attention.*

After sunset

In Spain, food is a thing of the night. Spaniards eat very late, with restaurants alive with customers from 10 pm to the early hours. If hunger calls earlier in the evening, they can always fill the gap with a tasty snack in a *tapas* bar. As in Italy, food is highly regional: the *tapas* of the green hills of Cantabria on the Atlantic coast are very different to those of Andalucía in the south, which are fired with Mediterranean heat and flamenco panache.

Spain is famed for its restless, festive spirit, witnessed not just in the country's capital, Madrid, but in virtually all the towns and cities, particularly in the south. Every summer evening in the great southern city of Seville, inhabitants of all ages – from infants in arms to aged grandparents – fill the pavement cafés and restaurants of the Barrio (quarter) de Santa Cruz, while the Triana neighbourhood, on the west bank of the River Guadalquivir, throbs to live music and dance late into the night.

Seville was one of the birthplaces of flamenco, an emotional but highly disciplined outpouring that expresses a whole culture – essentially the gypsy culture of Andalucía. A passionate mixture

Fado: Portuguese blues

The word *fado* means 'fate' – the fate of slaves, sailors or forsaken lovers. It is the sung expression of *saudade*, a special kind of Portuguese melancholy or yearning for what might have been. *Fado* probably originated in the Alfama district of Lisbon in the early 19th century and has since become part of the Portuguese soul. It is sung in cafés, bars, parks and streets to the accompaniment of a guitar. *Fado* has to be seen as well as heard. The greatest *fadistas* – such as Maria Severa in the past, or Amália Rodrigues, the star of modern times – have a charismatic stage presence, with their long, dark dresses and black shawls, and subtle movements inspired by traditional Portuguese dances. Such was the perceived power of *fado* that it was banned from the radio during the 1974 revolution, on the grounds that it induced listlessness and fatalism. But a new generation of singers has taken up the cause, ensuring that these songs of love, regret and hope will remain an inseparable part of Portuguese culture.

Starting young Boys play at bullfighting in a shaded square in Spain.

of romance, lament and spontaneity, flamenco is not just a dance, it is a way of life. This underlying passion is a feature of all Southern European countries.

Shared passions

Superficially, Portugal shares much with Spain. Portugal has its *festas*, its bullfights (on horseback), and a lively late night world of bars and cafés. But Portugal is also a world apart, perhaps a factor of being on the Atlantic rather than the Mediterranean. The Portuguese have their own brand of solemnity and dignity, and a penchant for understatement that is released in their extraordinarily mournful and emotion-packed *fado* songs. On summer evenings, the urban streets are filled with quiet strollers, the distinctive scent of grilled sardines, and the sound of cooked crab being tapped open – emanating from corner restaurants, private homes or picnic tables set up on the pavements outside.

Fiery dance Flamenco remains a genuine and living part of the folklore and culture of Andalucían gypsies.

Greek style

In Greece, families take to the streets in the cool of the evening to meet, chat and shop. Food tends to be simple and wholesome: grilled fish and meats drizzled with oil and lemon juice; salads with goat cheese; baked *moussaká* of minced meat, aubergines, tomatoes and cheese. But no one who hears contemporary Greek folk singing, accompanied by the urgent power of bouzouki playing, can be in any doubt of the intense passions that also underpin Greek society.

***Spoilt for choice** Both a gastronomic and visual feast,* tapas *can include scores of savoury dishes.*

***All welcome** A Barcelona* tapas *bar attracts a convivial crowd of all ages well into the night. The success of the* tapas *bar has resulted in it spreading beyond the borders of Spain in recent years.*

The delights of *tapas*

*T*apas are essentially little titbits, consumed with a drink before lunch or dinner – but they can also be substantial enough to make a meal in themselves. This is food to be shared among friends, placed on a bar or on the table, and consumed amid lively chatter.

The original *tapa*, so the story goes, was a slice of bread placed over a glass of sherry to keep flies out (*tapa* in Spanish means 'lid'). Ham was added to the bread, and bartenders found that the salt in this tasty titbit had the effect of increasing their customers' thirst, and so the *tapas* gradually become more elaborate. Now every region of Spain has its own specialities – and moving from one *tapas* bar to another has become something of a national pastime. The most ambitious *tapas* bars are in the cities – especially cities with a university – where people start gathering at about 8 pm. *Tapas* dishes include sliced sausage, cheese, olives, mushrooms baked with garlic, fried squid, prawns, shellfish, salt cod, omelette, fried potatoes and *albóndigas* (fish or meat balls). They can be served as a small *porción*, like an *hors d'oeuvre*, or as a *ración*, a bigger helping.

Italian television: fantasy and politics

Italian commercial television has become a byword for low-quality popular broadcasting. But many Italians admire the chief media mogul, Silvio Berlusconi, for his acumen in giving the Italian viewing public just what they wanted, and creating for himself a platform to become one of the nation's leading politicians.

Italian television is aimed at those who come into the category of 'family viewing'. Supremely self-confident presenters host sprawling events of almost music-hall diversity, sharing a stage with stars, wannabes and members of the public craving their 15 minutes of fame and exposure. This easy-on-the-eye popular entertainment is channelled into virtually every home (94 out of every 100 households), where it is often treated as animated wallpaper. The average Italian watches more than two hours of television a day.

The man behind the formula is the charismatic Silvio Berlusconi, one-time ferry-boat crooner, and now one of Italy's most powerful businessmen. Back in the 1970s, Berlusconi had a vision that the future lay in television and built up a massive portfolio of stations, including three national commercial channels – Italia Uno, Canale 5 and Retequattro – to rival the state-owned Rai 1, 2 and 3. He also controls numerous regional channels. Berlusconi's broadcasting interests are all under the umbrella company Mediaset, which is fed lucrative publicity by another of his companies, the powerful advertising agency Pubitalia. These form key elements in the overall holding company, Fininvest.

From entertainment to politics

From his position as a media tycoon, Berlusconi made a seamless transition into politics. What better way to create a political career than to be directly associated with a feel-good fantasy world filled with positive images of modern Italian life? In the early 1990s he created the right-of-centre party Forza Italia, promising to put Italy on a trajectory of success similar to his own. In 1994 his party was elected to power in coalition with other parties of the right, but within nine months he resigned amid corruption and tax-evasion scandals. But Berlusconi was never one to take defeat lying down. While his company profited from the digital revolution, he rebuilt the shattered image of Forza Italia, and his own political career.

Zapping

There are hundreds of television channels in Italy, all loaded with commercials. Much of the material is imported: soaps, especially from the USA, Australia and Brazil, have proved particularly popular. Some of the dubbed Italian versions have been recognised as an improvement on the original, and their success has spawned Italy's home-grown soap-opera industry. The restless Italian viewers, however, have a notoriously short attention span and indulge in the pastime of constant channel surfing, known as *lo zapping*. This has made Italian television even more frenetic, as schedulers and advertisers compete to catch their fickle viewers' attention.

Sales pitch *Roberto Da Crema has an unusual approach to TV shopping: he rants and raves, and smashes the goods he is promoting.*

Blessed game *Sister Paola has made a name for herself as an informed soccer commentator.*

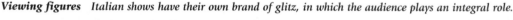

Viewing figures *Italian shows have their own brand of glitz, in which the audience plays an integral role.*

The thrill of the corrida

Few forms of entertainment cause as much controversy as bullfighting. Some sing its praises as the ultimate art form, in which bullfighters confront death with balletic discipline; others condemn it as a cruel and demeaning massacre for commercial gain. The controversy is likely to continue as long as bullfighting remains a feature of Spanish culture.

Hallowed ground *Bullrings, such as this one in Málaga, are major landmarks in many Iberian cities.*

Corridas usually take place as part of a town's annual fiesta, often in early summer. The bulls are fought by *cuadrillas* (teams) of *toreros* (bullfighters), led by the *matador* (slayer). There is a strict pattern to the ritual. After the opening parade the first bull – a specially bred *toro bravo* – will be let into the ring. The matador and his juniors (*peones*) play the bull with capes to test its character. Then the *picadores*, mounted on well-padded horses, wound the bull's neck, and *banderilleros*, on foot, plant darts in its back. This makes the bull drop its head for the final showdown. The *matador*, now alone in the ring, uses his small red cape (*muleta*) to entice the bull into charging, then performs 'passes' in a display of elegance, courage and domination. Finally, when the bull has tired, the *matador* faces it head on for the kill – which he performs swiftly and cleanly by driving his sword to the heart.

Animal courage *Horses still play a key role in bullfighting.*

The art of death

No skilled matador will allow the bull to suffer more than it must – a sentiment echoed by the crowd, which may show its satisfaction with roars of approval. The matador may then be awarded an ear, or both ears, or – in exceptional circumstances – both ears and the tail. The bull is then dragged off to be butchered – the fate, as apologists of bullfighting will argue, that would otherwise have awaited it in an ordinary abattoir.

Highlights of bullfights are presented on television, but for the Spanish bullfighting is not a sport: it is an art. While many Spaniards detest it, for others it has almost mystical, cult status. Bullfighting takes place throughout Spain, at all levels of grandeur and competence, but the world's greatest bullfighting *feria* (festival) takes place in Madrid in May and June, at the impressive Las Ventas bull ring, during the fiesta of the city's patron saint, Isidore.

On horseback

No one knows for sure the origins of bullfighting: it may be a legacy of Roman gladiatorial entertainments. In medieval times, bullfighting was performed by mounted knights and was considered a useful training for warfare. The modern form of bullfighting evolved in the 18th century. Some bullfighting is still conducted on horseback. In Spain, the *rejoneador* (rider) plays the bull skilfully before dispatching it with a steel-tipped lance, called a *rejón*. In Portugal, the *cavaleiro*, dressed in a tricorn hat, silk jacket and thigh-boots, rides on specially trained horses and performs feats of dressage-like elegance to goad and then evade the charging bull. The bull is not killed but wrestled to the ground and subdued by *forcados*; then cows are sent into the ring to lead it docilely away.

Dressed to kill *The matador, dressed in his taje de luces (suit of lights), takes aim at the climax of the fight.*

Italian flare A noisy and colourful demonstration of support by the fans of the Italian team AC Milan.

A *passion for football*

Cultural phenomenon turned industry, soccer is Southern Europe's greatest crowd-puller. Contests on the field are matched by behind-the-scenes deals and transfers worth dream-time money, while sponsorship, advertising and club ownership involve the biggest names in the industrial firmament. Despite the deep passion that football inspires, crowds are by and large well-behaved – if noisy.

Catalan pride

FC Barcelona, or Barça, is one of Europe's greatest football clubs. Over 100 years old, it has been a key focus of Catalan identity within Spain – so much so that the club was banned by the government during the 1920s for fear of inflaming separatist passions. Its strength lies in its *socios* (supporters for life), a privilege that is either inherited or awarded at birth. *Socios* are effectively the owners of the club, and elect the president. In addition, there are over 500 FC Barcelona supporters' clubs, called *penyas*, not just in Spain, but in most parts of the world.

It was an unusually quiet Sunday in Naples in June 2000. The streets were decked with blue and white banners, the colours of the Napoli football team. The city of 4 million were listening in gripped attention to their radios, or watching the TV. Suddenly the city burst into a cacophony of cheers and car horns. Out in the bay, boats sounded their horns. Naples had won a place back in Italy's top football division, Serie A, after two years in the wilderness.

Idol The Argentinian Diego Maradona helped Club Napoli to win a series of national and European championships between 1984 and 1991.

Devoted fans

Soccer incites deep passions, corresponding to the strong loyalties that citizens feel for their home town. This can be a strong galvanising force – except when there are two local teams. Turin, for example, has Juventus and Torino; Rome has Lazio and Roma; Madrid has Real Madrid and Atlético de Madrid. Derbies, when the two home teams play each other, often produce the most hotly contested games of the season, and deep-seated rivalry among the fans.

Fuelled by television rights, transfer fees for the top clubs have risen into the stratosphere. The transfer of Portuguese star Luis Figo cost £39 million, and Figo was offered an annual salary of £2.4 million for six years. More controversial still was the fact that the move took him from the top Spanish club Barcelona to its arch rival Real Madrid, and the shady shenanigans of the deal filled the papers. Such activities are all part of the great public theatre of football – guaranteed to fuel the passions of the supporters. They, too, like to put on a show. In Italy, the fans *(tifosi)* assemble behind the goals, while their leaders orchestrate proceedings with megaphones and gestures to ensure maximum noise and enthusiasm.

Mafia: organised crime

The Mafia is one export that Italy would rather not be associated with. The word has entered many languages as a synonym for organised crime – for corruption, protection rackets, and ruthless violence. The Mafia still stands at the focal point of the economy of much of southern Italy, despite the efforts of the justice system to clip its wings.

The word Mafia apparently derives from an Arabic term meaning 'refuge', and dates back to the Arab conquest of Sicily in the 9th century. From this time on, Sicilians organised themselves into secretive private armies, for protection against foreign occupiers, including the Normans and the Spaniards. Later they became powerful as the henchmen of absentee landlords, ruling by extortion and terrorism. To this day the Mafia thrives as an alternative, subversive system to government authority. The trouble is that it also thrives on criminal activity: drug smuggling, prostitution, protection rackets, blackmail, corruption. Although it looks after its own people, it is a deeply corrosive influence, creating an environment where little can be achieved outside its criminal reach.

The Mafia is based on clans or families, with pyramidal hierarchies headed by a boss or don. Similar structures exist wherever the Mafia has been exported – notably in the USA. It is underpinned by the age-old tradition of *omertà*, the conspiracy of silence: no one will assist the state authorities in the detection of crime. Any victims of crime look to the Mafia system of vendetta to see justice done. Once accepted into the Mafia, the only way to leave is to die.

Turning point   The assassination of Falcone renewed efforts to beat the Mafia.

Mass trial   In 1986-7, scores of suspects were tried in Palermo.

Taking on the Mafia

Under Benito Mussolini's Fascist government in the interwar years, thousands of *mafiosi* were arrested and imprisoned, but many were released by the Americans at the end of the war. During the 1970s, the Sicilian Mafia became involved in the drug trade to the USA. Clan warfare and a spate of murders triggered another attempt by the Italian government to control the Mafia, and the crackdown led to the 'maxi-trial' in Palermo, Sicily's capital, in 1986-7, in which 338 *mafiosi* were convicted. In 1992 they took revenge by assassinating the prosecutor, Giovanni Falcone, as well as his wife and three bodyguards. Falcone's death caused revulsion across Italy and also among Sicilians, who were tired of Mafia thuggery. Since then, the Italian judiciary has continued to pressure the *mafiosi*, but they believe the Mafia can take such knocks.

Public sympathy   The funeral of Falcone and his fellow victims drew an unprecedented crowd of 15 000 mourners.

Like an octopus

Many Italians remain pessimistic that the Mafia can ever be defeated. The term originally applied only to Sicilian criminal organisations, but on the mainland others operate in similar ways. Recently the Sacra Corona Unità has gained strength in the Puglia region, and is suspected of involvement with illegal Albanian immigration and criminal gangs. The Mafia is often compared to an octopus, with tentacles reaching deep into government, industry, the police and the justice system. Every time one tentacle is chopped off, another grows in its place.

The Balearic Islands: where all of Europe holidays

The four main islands of the Balearics – Majorca, Minorca, Ibiza and Formentera – have everything a tourist dreams of: beachside resorts with throbbing discos, and also quiet island calm, beloved of artists and poets. Many Northern Europeans have become so smitten with the islands that they have bought property there as holiday homes.

The Balearic Islands share much of the same history. Occupied since prehistoric times, they were seized by the Carthaginians, and ruled by the Moors for more than three centuries before being conquered by the Christian kings of Aragón and Catalonia in the 13th century. Then they fell into decline, suffering pirate raids, neglect and impoverishment. Their fortunes did not look bright until the 20th century, with the advent of mass tourism. Every year 8 million holidaymakers, mainly from Northern Europe, descend on the Balearic Islands to take advantage of their hot summers and mild winters.

Tourists are the first to note just how individual each of the islands is. Majorca (Mallorca)

Gothic presence Palma cathedral, built in golden limestone, dominates the old port of Majorca's capital.

Handle with care A Minorcan fisherman with his lobster catch.

White on white Despite the influx of tourism, Minorca has preserved much of its authentic charm.

Rear of approval Festivals in Minorca recall medieval times, with jousting and displays of horse-riding skills.

is the largest, about 70 miles (112 km) across, and with mountains rising to 4640 ft (1445 m). Most of its 6 million visitors go to the big resorts on the east coast, but Majorca is also famed for its idyllic beauty, found notably on the rocky north-west coast. Deià was the village made famous by the British poet and novelist Robert Graves, who lived here until his death in 1985. Even Palma, capital of Majorca, has its quiet charms, despite the discotheques and souvenir shops. The old town is still an intimate place of narrow, cobbled streets and tiny shops selling hand-crafted goods.

Smaller and different

Minorca (or Menorca) has little of Majorca's razzmatazz and is less affected by mass tourism. Its fine sandy beaches can be virtually empty, even in summer. Minorca is proud of its prehistoric heritage, and has a large number of monuments dating back to 2000 BC or earlier. Among them are the curious T-shaped megalithic monuments called *taulas*, found nowhere else in the world. As readers of Patrick O'Brian's seafaring novels will know, Minorca was occupied by the British in the 18th century, and Mahón was a strategically important naval base. The old port is now a favoured haunt of millionaires' yachts and cruisers, but around the island's picturesque coast the little fishing villages show a more typically Mediterranean face, with clusters of whitewashed houses. The north-west of the island is arid and rugged, and barely inhabited.

Two kinds of wild

Just as Majorca and Minorca form a contrasting pair, so do the smaller two islands at the western end of the archipelago. Ibiza is notorious for its wild party atmosphere. Formentera, hanging like a pendant earring to its south, is the least built-up of the islands, with a rocky coast and a flat, often bleak interior with patches of pine trees. This might be the island to get away from it all – except in the summer, when it is popular with day-trippers from Ibiza.

Far from the madding crowd Formentera is the smallest of the four main islands, and also the wildest, with rocky coastlines and deserted beaches.

Whoa! We're going to Ibiza!

As pop songs, disco music and lurid television programmes make clear, Ibiza is the party capital of the Mediterranean. It is the land of the four 'S's – sun, sea, sand and sex. The capital, Ibiza City, is the hub of the disco firmament, offering a host of state-of-the-art night spots, competing with each other for technological wizardry and big-name DJs. The second largest town, Sant Antoni de Portmany, has developed as a more rough-and-ready clubbing centre, with plenty of cheap accommodation, and a reputation for very wild nightlife. Much of the coast has been similarly developed as resorts, with high-rise hotels clustering around the pretty beaches. Ibiza now receives over a million visitors a year, outnumbering the locals by more than ten to one.

It was not always like this. In the 1960s, Ibiza was a cult destination for hippies, attracted by the climate, the unspoilt villages and the easy-going simplicity. These aspects have not been entirely swamped by the resorts and disco-mania. In fact, the tourist authorities have begun a campaign to redress the island's rather tawdry public image by promoting its quieter virtues: the old whitewashed villages; the winding ochre roads leading through a charmed landscape of dry-stone walls shaded by fig trees: vineyards, olive groves, orange and almond orchards, and fragrant pine forests. Ibiza has cultural vestiges of its history dating back to the Phoenicians and Carthaginians: the island was declared a World Heritage Site by Unesco in 1999. It also has a distinctive cuisine, with aromatic dishes such as fish stew with saffron (*le guisat de peix*), and skate with an almond sauce (*le burrida de ratjada*). To show it means business, the government has imposed a moratorium on new hotel building. And to help sustain this new public image, Ibiza will be promoted under its old Catalan name, Eivissa.

Moorish style Developments in the quiet south-western tip of Ibiza reflect the island's past,

A gulf to cross In 1994 the Bosnian civil war destroyed Mostar's ancient and symbolic bridge.

The Balkans: letting the genie of nationalism out of the bottle

For centuries the fiercely nationalist sentiments of the Balkans were sealed within the rival empires of Austria-Hungary and the Ottomans. Postwar Yugoslavia imposed unity on its six constituent republics, but when the chains were released, they were unable to contain their pent-up ambitions and resentment.

One nation for the southern Slavs. This was the dream of many Croats and Serbs in the 19th century – an ambition to gather together the Slav peoples who had migrated into the region in the 7th century, but who had been so cruelly divided by virtue of their location, on the frontier of the Ottoman Empire.

Unstable alliance

In 1912, the Serbs allied themselves to the Bulgarians, Montenegrins and Greeks, pushing the Ottomans out of Europe. But they then argued among themselves, causing an instability that alarmed the Austro-Hungarian Empire, which held sway over neighbouring Bosnia. In

Serb solidarity A demonstration in Niksic, in Montenegro, appeals to Serb nationalist sentiments.

1914, a young Serb nationalist assassinated Archduke Franz Ferdinand, heir to the Austro-Hungarian Empire, in Sarajevo, capital of Bosnia. This sparked the sudden escalation of international tension as the Big Powers faced each other down and called in their alliances, provoking the First World War. The rest of Europe has been wary of the Balkans ever since.

In 1918, the Croats, Serbs and Slovenes were united under one crown, a fragile bond that cracked during the Second World War, but was later re-established by Tito. Sponsored by the West, Yugoslavia became an unusual communist state, resisting alliance with other communist powers. This had the effect of holding back both nationalist sentiments and the economy. In 1980, at Tito's death, Yugoslavia was ready to burst. The larger groups – the Serbs, Croats and Albanians – saw this as an opportunity to redraw the map to consolidate their ethnic groupings. But the map of Yugoslavia was by this time an extremely complex patchwork quilt of peoples, often intermarried, sharing the same towns and villages but living in distinct areas or isolated pockets. There were few obvious natural borders.

New republics

Slovenia was the first republic to achieve independence from the old Yugoslavia in June 1991, after ten days of fighting. Macedonia broke free in 1992, the only nation to achieve independence without conflict. Croatia declared independence at the same time as Slovenia, but faced a rockier ride. Its driving force was the authoritarian nationalism of the Croat leader, Franjo Tudjman. Civil war erupted as the Yugoslavian government sent in the national army to protect the enclaves of the large Serb minority in Croatia. It also attempted to carve a path across Croatia to give Bosnia access to the sea – bombarding the Croatian city of Dubrovnik in the attempt.

Redrawing the map

The Croat conflict came to a close in January 1992, under a US-brokered agreement. But by this time Bosnia-Herzegovina had joined the fray by also declaring independence, which was accepted by the international community in March 1992. Here the ethnic map was extremely complex, with many disparate enclaves, and towns shared by Croats, Serbs and Muslims. Regardless of whether they had been there for generations, and lived peaceably among themselves, nationalist activists now began to exert pressure to remove all but their own people to consolidate their ethnic purity. These policies were carried out by the regular armies as well as by notorious paramilitary death squads, and a cycle of misery and revenge accelerated rapidly. Over 2 million people were now displaced as refugees across Yugoslavia; 200 000 people died in Bosnia.

Reconstruction

The savagery in Bosnia was brought under control in 1995, through United Nations and NATO intervention. In July 1999 the leaders of 30 nations gathered in Sarajevo and agreed on a plan to revive the economy of this shattered region. The European Union pledged financial aid estimated at 5-6 billion Euros a year. It also held out the prospect of future membership for the Balkan nations, provided they met certain criteria – notably the respect for human rights, for national sovereignty, and for democratic institutions.

Spoils of victory *Serb soldiers took the Croatian border town of Vukovar in August 1991 after an 86-day siege.*

Dirty war

When Croat and Serb forces clashed in the border town of Vukovar, eastern Croatia, in the late summer of 1991, more than 3000 people were killed and 4000 went missing. It was the start of the downward spiral of violence in former Yugoslavia. In the spring of 1992, the three-month siege of Sarajevo began: the Serbs sealed off the town, and its mainly Muslim population, in a long, bitter war of attrition. Deprived of electricity, heating and medicines, the inhabitants ran the constant risk of being bombed or killed by snipers. Meanwhile, Serb nationalists began clearing villages in northern Bosnia of non-Serbs. Women, children and the elderly were deported. The men were interned in camps, where they were subjected to torture and summary execution.

The outrages reached a climax in the summer of 1995, when the Serbs attacked the UN-protected town of Srebrenica in eastern Bosnia, forcing 12 000 families to flee to Tuzla, 60 miles (97 km) away, while 8000 of their menfolk disappeared – mostly, it seems, the victims of mass executions. The following month 200 000 Serbs were forced to leave their enclave in Croatia: some settled in the 'ethnically cleansed' areas of Bosnia. It was events such as these that persuaded the international community to intervene, and to enforce a political settlement.

Prisoners of war *Muslim men were held in Serb detention camps.*

Keeping the peace: putting the genie back in the bottle

In the early 1990s, Europe had a rude shock. Yugoslavia may have been economically somewhat backward, but its people were comparatively well-off. Just like any other Europeans, they watched television, shopped in supermarkets, played football. Yet their world was now collapsing into an abyss of violence and anarchy. It was an alarming illustration of the fragility of Western civilisation.

The civil war in Bosnia was widely covered by the international media. Television and newspaper reports daily told the tale of wounded children, elderly refugees, young men and women abused and tortured, pretty rural villages pillaged and burned. The world looked on in horror, but was at a loss to know what to do. This was, after all, a civil war: the integrity of international borders was not threatened. In addition, a focal point was Sarajevo – the place that had set in motion the First World War. The Balkans held a chilling lesson from history. Warned off by Russia, at first the international community stayed its hand and waited to see if the situation would resolve itself. It applied sanctions to the rump of Yugoslavia, ruled from the Serb capital of Belgrade, in an attempt to curtail its ambitions to create a Greater Serbia. But its efforts to broker peace were consistently rejected by all parties.

In 1992 the UN sent in 10 000 peace-keeping soldiers (Blue Berets) to attempt to impose peace, but they had a limited mandate. On several occasions this led to the embarrassment of impotence. At Mostar in 1993, the Croats attacked the Muslims in view of the Blue Berets, who, by their rules of engagement, were powerless to intervene. At Srebrenica in 1995, UN forces had to stand by while Serb forces 'ethnically cleansed' its Muslim population. At this point the UN, now assisted by NATO troops, decided to resort to a more aggressive aerial and land assault. This inflicted serious

military setbacks on the Serbs, and brought them to the negotiating table: at Dayton, Ohio, in November that year, a peace accord for Bosnia was hammered out. The map was redrawn, and the nation was divided in two: the Serb Republik Srpska and the Muslim-Croat Federation. A fragile stand-off was imposed by a NATO-led international peace-keeping force called IFOR (Implementation Force), superseded in 1996 by SFOR (Stabilisation Force).

Washing line *Spanish armoured cars of the UN force stationed in a Mostar block of flats in 1994.*

Armed assistance *In 1996, as tensions relax, a US soldier from IFOR in Bosnia helps with some paperwork.*

Mass grief *Muslims mourn their dead friends and relatives found in a mass grave at Ogorsko, Bosnia in 1996.*

By tractor Kosovar refugees reach the safety of Kukës, Albania, 1999.

Kosovo implodes

Yugoslavia continued to exist as a Serb-dominated federation. Besides Serbia, it now consisted of Vojvodina, with its large Hungarian-speaking population; Montenegro, with sole access to the sea; and Kosovo, where 90 per cent of the population was of Albanian origin. Under Tito, these provinces had enjoyed a fair degree of autonomy, but in 1989 President Slobodan Milosevic had rescinded this autonomy in pursuit of his dream of a Greater Serbia, and granted superior rights to the Serb minority in Kosovo.

An opposition movement in Kosovo tried to resist by peaceful means, but in 1997 a splinter group opted for armed struggle, and formed the Kosovo Liberation Army (KLA). Yugoslavia adopted a heavy-handed policy to suppress the KLA, polarising Albanian opinion. Villages sympathetic to the KLA were torched, and several massacres took place. Tens of thousands of Kosovans fled over the borders, as an orchestrated campaign of Serb intimidation suggested that a new campaign of ethnic cleansing was about to begin.

Fearing large-scale instability in the region, the international community called the Serbs and Kosovan Albanians to the negotiating table at Rambouillet, outside Paris, in February 1999. The Serbs refused the settlement on offer, which involved allowing 28 000 NATO troops access to all parts of Kosovo. As NATO prepared its forces to impose the settlement, the Serb paramilitaries escalated their campaign of intimidation, burning villages, killing over 4000 civilians, and causing nearly a million distressed Albanian Kosovans to flee into Albania, Macedonia and Montenegro.

NATO then began an unprecedented air war, bombing Serb troops and installations in Kosovo, and in Belgrade. For 79 days this war continued, while a land force was assembled in Albania, hesitant to enter. In the event, they did not have to: the Serbs suddenly capitulated and withdrew. The UN now sent in a multinational force (KFOR) of 50 000 troops to impose peace, and the refugees gradually returned to their homes and began reconstructing their lives. Despite efforts to rebuild bridges, relationships between the Albanians and the Serbs who have stayed are deeply poisoned by resentment and recriminations, and Kosovo remains politically volatile. Meanwhile, tensions have been rising in neighbouring Montenegro, where many of the population no longer wish to be associated with Milosevic's Serb-dominated Yugoslavia.

Night raid Buildings blaze in central Belgrade after another night of NATO bombing in March 1999.

The International War Crimes Tribunal

In 1993 the Security Council of the UN set up an International War Crimes Tribunal in The Hague, The Netherlands. As the immense human rights abuses in the Balkans came to light, the international community was determined to establish a body that would pursue those responsible for war crimes, as a way of delivering some justice to their victims. There are a number of Serb and Bosnian-Serb leaders on the 'wanted list', including Slobodan Milosevic. Arrests are physically and politically tricky, but the tribunal is taking a long view. Over time, it argues, circumstances will change, and the war criminals of the Balkan conflict will be brought to book.

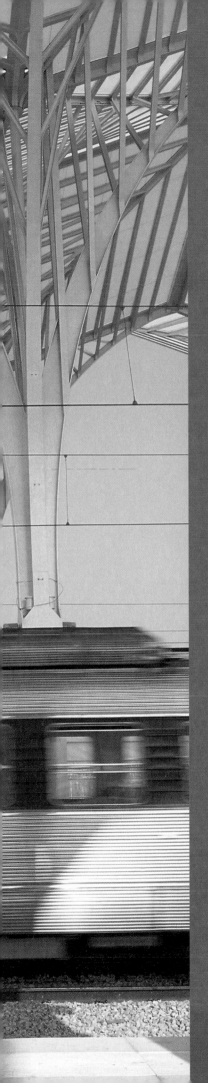

CHAPTER 4

CITIES OF SOUTHERN EUROPE

In a square like the Piazza Navona in Rome, several thousand years of continuous history can be traced. This was once the stadium of Domitian, Roman emperor from AD 81 to 96. It is now bordered by 17th-century baroque palaces and the ornate fountains of Bernini. But it is still very much a living space, with cafés and restaurants, and is often invaded by school groups, paying reverence to antiquity, and football fans who wear the history of the surroundings more lightly. This mixture of modern vibrancy and historic resonance can be found in cities all over Southern Europe. Many, such as Barcelona and Lisbon, have made a concerted effort in recent decades to represent their modernity with a new layer of contemporary architecture, underlining the fact that they are for living in now, and are not stranded in their past.

Santiago Calatrava's new railway station, the Estação do Oriente, is part of the modern face of Lisbon.

The Golden Age: Córdoba, Seville and Granada

The Moors ruled over southern Spain for seven centuries and created a glittering civilisation that has become known as the Golden Age. Its legacy is a distinctive, multicultural approach, witnessed in three great cities of Andalucía. Their rich cultural heritage has cushioned them from the unemployment and hardship that has long blighted the sun-parched south.

Exquisite suffering *Azulejos tilework depicting the Virgin, in Córdoba.*

Once a Roman city, Córdoba became the capital of Moorish Spain after the Arab invasion of AD 711, and was the capital of the Caliphate of Córdoba during the 10th and 11th centuries. Its vibrant court attracted artists, teachers and philosophers from all parts of Europe and the Arab World, and the city had a university, libraries, observatories, public gardens and public baths. Córdoba's craftworkers were famed for their leatherwork, textiles and glazed tiles. These traditions continued even after the Caliphate collapsed into aggressive anarchy in the 11th century, and they can still be sensed in the labyrinth of narrow alleys in the old centre, with its whitewashed walls and patios (courtyard gardens), decorated with *azulejos* tilework. Next to the picturesque Jewish quarter, the Judería, rises the Mezquita, the extraordinary mosque-cum-cathedral – a marriage of Muslim and Christian architecture.

Seville, modern capital of Andalucía

During its last two centuries of Moorish rule, Seville (Sevilla) rivalled Córdoba in splendour. Originally the Roman city Hispalis, under the Moorish Almohad dynasty it became capital of a realm stretching right across southern Spain, and from Morocco to Tunisia. The Alcázar fortress-palace and La Giralda tower began as

triumphant examples of Moorish architecture. Seville was conquered by the Spanish Christians under Fernando III 'El Santo' (The Saint) in 1248, but it enjoyed a second period of cosmopolitan prosperity in the 16th and 17th centuries, when it held a trading monopoly in the Spanish territories of the New World. As a

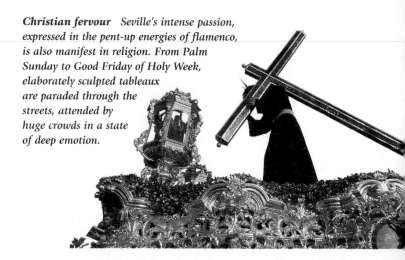

Christian fervour *Seville's intense passion, expressed in the pent-up energies of flamenco, is also manifest in religion. From Palm Sunday to Good Friday of Holy Week, elaborately sculpted tableaux are paraded through the streets, attended by huge crowds in a state of deep emotion.*

Two in one *The Mezquita of Córdoba symbolises the dual heritage of Andalucía. Surrounding the Renaissance cathedral is the extraordinary 10th-century mosque, with its labyrinth of striped horseshoe arches.*

result, it became one of the most prosperous cities in Europe. But a plague in 1649 carried off a third of the population, then the River Gualdalquivir became less navigable as ships grew in size, and Seville slid into decline. For decades it was thought of as little more than a tourist attraction, but the city has enjoyed a commercial revival since playing host to the World Expo of 1992 – on the 500th anniversary of Columbus's voyage to the Americas.

Granada: last Moorish stronghold

Against a backdrop of the snow-clad Sierra Nevada, the three hills of Granada offer an exceptional natural setting, with views out over a vast and verdant landscape. After the conquest of Córdoba and Seville in the 13th century, Granada emerged as the capital of the last of the Moorish kings, the Nasrids, and in its final 250 years ranked as one of the most prosperous in Europe. But it gradually became a Moorish outpost, hemmed in by the conquered territories of the Catholic kings, finally falling to the Christians in 1492.

Granada has preserved a rich heritage from its Moorish past, the greatest jewel of which is the Alhambra Palace. Its ornate and sumptuous architecture is matched only by the exceptional beauty of its gardens. Christian Granada can also boast the Gothic Capilla Real (Royal Chapel and mausoleum) and Gothic-Renaissance cathedral, but it is the vibrant amalgamation of cultures that distinguishes Granada, seen particularly in the winding alleys of the Albaicín quarter, and in the *gitano* (gypsy) cave-dwellings of the Sacromonte.

The gardens of Andalucía

Gardens have a special place in Islam. In a religion born of the hot, water-starved lands of the Middle East, gardens represent a vision of bounty, refreshment, order and calm – in a word, Paradise. In Spain, the Moors found a climate that could deliver this, and created superb gardens attached to the royal palaces, complete with fountains and the soothing sounds of trickling water. The most famous garden is the Generalife, attached to the summer palace of the Nasrid kings of Granada, close to the Alhambra. It has a series of terraces containing patios, fountains, trimmed hedges, cypresses, and aromatic plants, such as jasmin, roses and orange trees.

Mix and match   The Giralda of Seville was originally built as the minaret of the Great Mosque of the Almohads in the 12th century, but was integrated with the vast cathedral built three centuries later. The spire above the bells was added in the 16th century.

Swan song   The Alhambra palace in Granada was built in the 14th century and remained the centre of power of the last Moorish kingdom, until King Boabdil surrendered to the Catholic kings in 1492. Its modest exterior disguises a tiled and sculpted interior of exceptional delicacy and beauty.

Madrid, and the art of good living

According to legend, when St Isidore, patron saint of Madrid, preferred to take a siesta rather than work in his master's fields, two sympathetic angels stepped in to do the work for him. A similar divine indulgence seems to be at work today in this great Castilian city. Commercial and industrial prosperity and the bureaucracy of government cast few shadows over the Madrileños' ardour for living.

Heart of Spain *The bronze bear nibbling a* madroño *(strawberry tree) at the Puerta del Sol is Madrid's symbol. All Spain's roads are measured from here.*

From the end of the 11th century, a Moorish fortress called Magerit dominated the dry plateau at the foot of the Sierra Guadarrama, and played a strategic role at the heart of the Iberian peninsula. On this modest foundation, Philip II of Spain built his new capital in 1561, at a safe but convenient distance from his monastery-palace at El Escorial. Architecturally, it is not one of Europe's great cities, born more of the 19th and 20th centuries than any earlier era. Apart from the 16th-century Plaza Mayor, the 18th-century Palacio Real, and the Parque del Buen Retiro, Madrid's historic inheritance is seen more in its art than in its buildings. The Museo del Prado is one of Europe's greatest galleries, housing a royal collection dating back to the 16th century. It contains many of the best-known works by Velázquez, El Greco and Goya, as well as Flemish, Dutch and Italian art. Other collections include the Museo Thyssen-Bornemisza, opened in 1992, one of the world's greatest private collections of European art; and the modern art collection in the Centro de Arte Reina Sofía, which includes Picasso's *Guernica*. Above all, though, Madrid is celebrated for its unique spirit and character. The back streets of the city centre, around the Plaza Mayor and the Puerta del Sol, throb with life late into the night, engendering a festive atmosphere unmatched by any other capital city of Europe.

La Movida

At the death of Franco in 1975, a new-found sense of freedom spread rapidly through Spain. In the 1980s, Madrid became the spearhead of the revived intellectual movement and of the cultural avant-garde. This spirit also translated into social behaviour, and notably the wild late-night bar and disco scene called the *movida*, which erupted in the thousands of bars and clubs. The Spanish in general socialise well into the night, but the *Madrileños* developed such a reputation for prowling around in the early hours that they earned the nickname *los gatos*, 'the cats'.

Tropical terminus *The old hall of the Atocha railway station has been enlivened by a tropical garden.*

Commanding view *A monument to King Alfonso XII rises above the artificial lake of El Retiro park, one of the 'green lungs' of the Spanish capital.*

Festive spirit *A bar in the Plaza Mayor buzzes into the early hours.*

Barcelona: Catalan capital

Poised between sea and mountains, between the north and the south of Europe, between Catalonia and Spain, Barcelona revels in its eye-catching exhibitionism. Rated by many as Europe's most exciting city, it is driven by its own unique style of creativity and dynamism. Barcelona trumpets its boldness to be different – and different, above all, from Madrid.

This is Spain's second city, its main industrial centre, and its largest port on the Mediterranean, handling 25 million tons of cargo a year. But it wears the burden of this responsibility lightly. Barcelona sees itself as energetic, stylish and fun – the living symbol of Catalan culture, with valuable lessons to pass on to Spain.

The city was founded by the Carthaginians in about 230 BC and named after Hamilcar Barca, father of Hannibal. It has vestiges of just about all epochs of its long history: Roman walls, the vast and splendid Gothic cathedral, and a medieval quarter called the Barri Gòtic. Barcelona slumbered until the 19th century, but then began to amass riches from industry and trade. The grand boulevards of the late 19th-century district, L'Eixample (the Extension), are a model of urban planning and remain a stronghold of the well-heeled middle classes. Here, too, notably in the Passeig de Gràcia, are some of the finest examples of Barcelona's avant-garde architecture – the work of the Modernistas, led by Antoní Gaudí (1852-1926). It is no accident that Barcelona gave rise to this controversial movement. The city prides itself on its intellectual daring. The same adventurous spirit resurfaced when Barcelona hosted the 1992 Olympics. It took the opportunity to develop the waterfront, the fisherman's quarter of La Barceloneta and Port Vell. This has also enhanced the lower end of the Ramblas, the famous old promenade running through the old city, linking the city centre to the port area.

One city, two languages

Barcelona has two main languages: Spanish and Catalan. They are very different from each other, and barely related. In fact, Catalan's closest cousin appears to be Provençal of southern France, and may have come to the region with the Franks in the 8th century. Catalonia (*Catalunya* in Catalan) faced repression at various times in its history, and during such times its language became a potent symbol of Catalan identity. Because it was fiercely Republican during the civil war, Franco took his revenge by banning the use of Catalan in public, along with the Catalan flag and the national dance, the *sardana*. All have staged a remarkable comeback since Franco's death. Catalan is now spoken by 6 million people, and is an official language of Catalonia's administration. It is taught in schools, and used in literature, publishing, the press and broadcasting.

Liquid architecture Gaudí's extraordinary church, the Sagrada Familia (Holy Family), started in 1883, is still under construction. Its unique forms were inspired by dripping sand, icicles, and other shapes from nature.

Sea of people An elaborate display at the opening ceremony of the 1992 Olympics.

Stream of people The tree-lined Ramblas provide an age-old pedestrian thoroughfare linking the city centre and the port. They were built over the course of a seasonal riverbed, and named after the Arabic word for a torrent.

On display Markets serve as a colourful reminder that Barcelona is one of Spain's leading trading centres.

The hills and villages of Lisbon

A city of hills, situated along the edge of the wide estuary of the River Tagus, Lisbon is composed of a number of distinct, village-like quarters, which lend it a pleasantly low-key feel. Its striking mixture of the intimate and the grand reflect its unusual history.

Hill-climbing *Lisbon's trams run on a system laid out in the 1920s.*

Lisbon is a relaxed city, where people seem to know each other and stop to talk. With a population of under a million, or 3 million if the suburbs are included, Lisbon is small by the standards of European capitals. In keeping with the mood, its colours are soft pastel: white, blue, pink and ochre.

Lisbon's centre shows two contrasting faces. The Baixa is a low-lying grid of broad avenues and grand squares. They were laid out by the Marquês de Pombal in the late 18th century. Next to it, rising steeply up stone steps and twisting roads, is the old Alfama district, a packed jumble of tall, narrow homes, threaded with staircases. Washing hangs between balconies loaded with pot plants. Grocery shops occupy front rooms and women sit outside knitting.

The Earthquake

The contrast is the product of the tragic cataclysm of 1755. Lisbon was a Moorish port until 1147, became the capital of Christian Portugal in the 13th century, and then the focus of Portuguese world expansion in the 16th century. By 1620 it was one of the biggest and wealthiest metropolises in Europe. On All Saints' Day 1755, it was hit by an earthquake, which triggered widespread fires, then a tidal wave. Two-thirds of the city was destroyed. The Alfama was one of the few districts to remain relatively unscathed. Lisbon had to start again, and the architecture corresponds to this watershed.

Taking the lift

Most of Lisbon is laid out on a fairly orderly grid system, but the hills prevent this being very noticeable. The cool grandeur of the main promenade, the Avenida da Libertade, with its shady trees and pavement cafés, is a relief from the city's more hectic contours. An elegant public lift, the Elevador de Santa Justa, was constructed in 1902 to raise passengers vertically from the Baixa to the level of Chiado and Bairro Alto – a district once famous for its bohemian *taskas* (restaurants) and *fado* bars, now joined by chic boutiques and art galleries.

The gardens of Lisbon

Despite its coastal position, and Atlantic breezes, Lisbon can be hot and dry in summer, with average July temperatures of 28°C (82°F). Its people know the value of shade and greenery, and appreciate their gardens and public parks. The garden of the castle of São Jorge dominates the Alfama district and offers fine views of the city and the Tagus. The Saldanha district in the north of the city contains the huge Parque Eduardo VII. Part of this is given over to the Estufa Fria, meaning 'cold greenhouse'. This magical botanical garden was developed in the 1930s and is now richly cloaked in the greenery of ferns and palms.

Pride of Portugal *The Jerónimos Monastery of the Bélem district of Lisbon dates from the early 16th century, and is a masterpiece of the late Gothic style called Manueline.*

Harbour view *A statue of the Marquês de Pombal looks down the Avenida da Libertade from the base of the Parque Eduardo VII.*

Serene outlook *The gardens of the Quinta do Marquês de Fronteira date from the 17th century.*

Naples: living on the edge

Naples overlooks a bay of spectacular beauty, with Capri and the Sorrento peninsula fading into the misty distance. But much closer lie the blasted cones of Vesuvius and the ever-present threat of a volcanic eruption.

Sister city *Like Naples, Palermo has reminders of past grandeur.*

Driving in Naples is like playing an old game with new rules. Cars, most of them battle-scarred, use any available space to advance their cause, honking, swerving and revving. Red traffic lights are strictly for advice only. This is all very much in keeping with the essential character of Naples: exciting, spontaneous, showing scant respect for authority. Neapolitans know that it makes their city chaotic and dangerous, but they value their freedom and would not have it any other way.

Humble heart

Unlike most cities, the centre of Naples is occupied by poor, working-class districts. Spaccanapoli is a warren of tiny streets that still follow the grid-plan of the Greek *neapolis* (new city) founded in 600 BC. Tiny shops selling groceries and jewellery nestle among market stalls, cafés, restaurants and ancient churches. On the other side of the city's smartest shopping street, the Via Toledo, is the Quattieri Spagnuoli, a notorious slum that has become virtually a no-go area to outsiders.

Palermo

Palermo, capital of Sicily, has much in common with Naples. It, too, has a spectacular position overlooking the sea, and is sheltered by Monte Pellegrino. It also has a rich Arab, Byzantine and Norman heritage. Less well known is its legacy of buildings and villas by the architect Ernesto Basile (1857-1932), who worked in an eclectic style, mixing Art Nouveau and Moorish idioms. But while much has been done to preserve these and to modernise the city, Palermo has been disfigured by a rash of speculative building, and has been unable to shake off a reputation for violence and Mafia racketeering.

With about a quarter of the population out-of-work, people get by as best they can. This may mean petty trading, begging, selling black market cigarettes, peddling drugs, bag-snatching. The wealthy live in the outlying suburbs, such as Posillipo and Pozzuoli, in heavily guarded enclaves. This is a Mafia city, and no one can tell quite how much the local Camorro gangs control.

A threat of a different kind comes from Naples' geology. An earthquake shook the city badly in 1980. Vesuvius is overdue for a major eruption. Neapolitans grin and shake their heads when they hear of the city authority's plans for an orderly evacuation.

Nineties facelift

Naples also has its grand monuments, such as the magnificent Piazza del Plebiscito, the medieval Castel Nuovo, the 19th-century Galleria Umberto I shopping arcade, and the Teatro San Carlo, one of the world's great opera houses. After Mayor Antonio Bassolino took up his post in 1993, Naples went through a transformation. Many of its monuments have been restored, and there is a new pride and vigour in the city. But Neapolitans would not like to become overly optimistic: colourful chaos is part of their soul.

Market fresh
Vibrant with life, colour and activity, the residential quarters at the heart of Naples follow patterns that have barely changed for centuries.

Weather eye
Certosa di San Martino monastery looks out across the bay to Vesuvius.

Guardian spirit *The winged lion of St Mark looks down from the clock tower.*

Venice, a city afloat

Venice is one of the world's great dream cities. A marriage between civilisation and water, art and commerce, it has held artists and writers spellbound for a thousand years. But it faces a ceaseless battle if it is not to sink into its beautiful lagoon.

To alight from a boat at the Molo quay in the heart of Venice is like stepping onto a stage set. This is architecture at its most dramatic and theatrical. The Palazzo Ducale (Doge's Palace), the Basilica di San Marco and its splendid arcaded square, the Tore dell'Orologio (clock tower), the towering Campanile – each one of these elements startlingly different and individual – combine to form an ensemble of breathtaking magnificence. To the west, the great S-shaped Grand Canal snakes through Venice as the city's main thoroughfare, the centre of a web of canals and alleys lined with hundreds of fine mansions and dozens of beautiful churches.

Not surprisingly, Venice attracts nearly 12 million visitors a year. Tourism is its lifeblood. But 70 000 people also live in the city, and daily life goes on in the markets, the grocery shops, the bars and cafés. As if to emphasise the fact that the city does not live entirely in the past, it plays host to an influential annual film festival, and to the Venice Biennale, a leading showpiece of international contemporary art.

Saving Venice

Venice is sinking at a rate of 1-2 inches (2.5-5 cm) a century. In the postwar era, the pace of its subsidence appeared to quicken, and reached a critical stage when disastrous floods swamped the city in 1966. For a while it seemed that Venice was doomed, and this led to dire warnings from the international institutions that they might withdraw funding for restoration. But over the past two decades measures to save Venice have had considerable success. They include: the reduction of pollution from the industrial complex at Porto Marghera on the mainland, which was altering the ecology of the lagoon; a reduction in shipping in the lagoon; the prohibition of the extraction of ground water and natural gas in the lagoon area; the erection of breakwaters to preserve the islands protecting the lagoon; the restoration of natural sandbanks; and the injection of boron into the wooden piles on which Venice is founded, to prevent deterioration. Venice is still threatened by exceptionally high tides, and in order to combat these, an ambitious plan has been formulated. A series of mobile floodgates in the mouth of the lagoon would be raised to close it off whenever high water is predicted.

Jigsaw puzzle *The 118 little islands that make up Venice are divided by 177 canals, and linked by 453 bridges.*

East meets west *The Basilica di San Marco symbolises Venice's trading power.*

Fifteen centuries of maritime history

The first inhabitants of Venice were Roman families who settled on muddy islands in the lagoon to escape Barbarian invasions in the 5th century AD. They gradually stabilised the islands by driving timber piles into the mud as foundations for their buildings. In the 9th century they erected their first major church on the Rialto island to house the relics of St Mark the Evangelist, and adopted his symbol, the winged lion, as the city's emblem. The Rialto became the hub of their growing maritime trade, which extended first down the Adriatic Sea, then across the eastern Mediterranean to the Middle East, filling the vacuum left by the declining Byzantine Empire. From early days, they adopted an ingenious system of government.

Haunting memories *The domed church of Santa Maria della Salute (St Mary of Health) was built to honour a pledge for delivery from the great plague of 1630-31.*

Essentially, it was a republic– *la serinissima republicca*, 'the most serene republic' – led by the Doge, who was elected by a senate drawn from the ruling families. Ordinary people were protected from exploitation through their guilds.

Venice's trade, and its colonies, brought great wealth to the city, which was invested in art, palaces and churches. But when Venetian art reached it apogee during the Renaissance, the city was already in decline. Wars against the Turks drained its resources, while its trade in precious Eastern goods was undermined by the routes to India and the Far East, which were pioneered by navigators from other European countries.

In the 18th century Venice became better known as a city of licentious fun for North European aristocrats on the Grand Tour, who revelled in the masked balls, gambling, and the wild antics of Carnival. The city lost its independence during the Napoleonic Wars, then became part of the Austrian Empire before signing up to join Italy in 1866.

Trading on the past

The island city of Venice had little scope to develop the kind of industries that brought prosperity in the modern industrial world. During the last two centuries, it has had to make a virtue of its historic past and its great treasures to attract tourists. But it has not been sanitised; this is not a museum city. The six *sestieri* (quarters) into which Venice is divided all retain their own distinct character. The quiet backwaters, the maze of pedestrian-only *calli* (alleys) and tiny *campi* (squares), the local shops, the markets selling fresh fish and vegetables, the flowering windowboxes, the cats – all lend the city a personalised charm, giving visitors the sense that there is always something left to discover.

Daily delivery *Fresh produce comes up the Grand Canal to the market beside the Rialto Bridge.*

Romantic connections *The 15th-century Palazzo Contarini-Fasan is the supposed home of Desdemona, Shakespeare's tragic heroine in Othello.*

Florence: Renaissance perfection

Leonardo da Vinci walked these streets; so too did Dante, Giotto, Botticelli, Michelangelo, Machiavelli and Galileo. Florence was at the heart of the Renaissance. Heir to an extraordinarily rich tradition in arts and crafts, the city's natural dynamism has also allowed it to flourish in the modern world.

Time span   *The Ponte Vecchio (old bridge) was built in 1345 to replace a Roman bridge spanning the River Arno at its narrowest point. The buildings lining its sides have housed jewellers' shops since the 15th century.*

From surrounding hills such as Fiesole, Florence (Firenze) looks serene beneath its sea of terracotta tiles. But scooters, cars and trucks roar through the medieval streets, and crowds throng the pavements. This is not just a city with one of the richest artistic and architectural heritages in the world: it is also a modern, working metropolis, capital of Tuscany.

From the 12th century Florence grew in wealth on banking and wool, until in the 15th it eclipsed the surrounding city-states of Lucca, Siena and Pisa. Its influence spread far and wide: Florence is the fount of much of Italy's culture – its language, art and philosophy. The Medicis, rulers in the 15th century, were lavish patrons, creating a political environment in which art and learning flourished.

The city resounds with the greatest names of art: Giotto and Fra Angelico, Michelangelo, Donatello. Today, the 3.5 million tourists who visit Florence each year have a choice of 68 museums and 6000 palaces and historic monuments. Outstanding are the Uffizi Gallery, the Pitti Palace, the Museo Nazionale in the Bargello, and the Accademia, which contain much of the most celebrated Renaissance art.

Bronze masterpiece   *The relief sculptures on the doors of the Baptistry are by Lorenzo Ghiberti.*

Engineering marvel   *Brunelleschi's landmark dome for the cathedral was built in 1446-67.*

94

Pompeii: snapshots of daily Roman life

On August 24, AD 79, life in the prosperous town of Pompeii came to a sudden halt, buried by the eruption of Mount Vesuvius. As citizens fled, bread was still baking in the oven and guard-dogs chained to their posts. Deep layers of ash preserved the town virtually intact for the next 1700 years.

Cult figures A Villa of the Mysteries fresco.

We have a dramatic first-hand account of the eruption of Vesuvius by the 17-year-old Pliny the Younger, who witnessed it from just beyond the volcano's deadly reach. His uncle, Pliny the Elder, was one of its victims.

The events he described took on a new relevance after 1748, when excavations at Pompeii began. Beneath 20 ft (6 m) of hardened ash and lava lay a whole Roman town, almost perfectly preserved. Excavations still continue – about a quarter of the town has yet to be unearthed. Even so, the 2 million visitors to Pompeii each year need a full day to do justice to the vast site.

Tragedy preserved

Pompeii had received a warning in AD 62, when an earthquake caused widespread damage. But the volcano had not erupted in living memory. It was not thought a threat until it began spewing smoke and debris in August AD 79. When it erupted, most of the 20 000 citizens had fled: some 2000 died. Their final terror is graphically recorded by casts of their bodies in the ash.

Life in Pompeii, a trading and manufacturing town of moderate size, was ordered and stylish. Villas of wealthy merchants, like the

The Villa of the Mysteries

For the early archaeologists, Pompeii revealed a disturbing secret. The Romans were upheld as a model society: refined, courageous, moral. But Pompeii contained countless depictions of earthy carnality. In the 19th century, many of these were confined to a 'secret cabinet' in the Museo Archeologico, but the collection is now one of the most famous features of the museum. In their context, such artefacts are neither surprising nor shocking: the Romans were deeply interested in fertility, and they were frank about the processes involved. Pompeii perhaps had a heightened interest, as the city was said to be under the protection of Venus, goddess of love. The Villa of the Mysteries, just outside Pompeii, also points to the presence of the outlawed cult of Dionysus, or Bacchus, who was worshipped in orgiastic rites. Mural paintings seem to show an initiation ceremony into the cult.

Living in style The House of the Faun, named after a statue found there, had mosaic floors and its own baths.

House of the Vettii, were lavishly decorated with wall-paintings and floor mosaics. Public baths were adorned with stuccowork and sculpture. There were two theatres in town, along with a large amphitheatre outside.

But it is the insights into daily life that leave the deepest impression: paved streets worn by carts, shop counters where hot snacks were sold, laundries, latrines, graffiti in Latin scratched onto the walls. Most of the objects found are preserved in the nearby Museo Archeologico Nazionale in Naples. The sculptures, mirrors, dishes, oil lamps and spoons help to complete the vivid picture of what it was like to be a Roman in AD 79.

The Vatican: a tiny world capital

The Vatican City-state is a country like no other. It is the world's smallest nation, contained in the heart of Rome. It has a population of about 1000, mainly men, but as the headquarters of the Roman Catholic Church, and seat of the Pope, it is considered the spiritual capital of nearly a billion adherents worldwide.

Public blessing *Pope John Paul II addresses the crowds.*

The Vatican has been a sacred site since about AD 65. It marks the place where St Peter is believed to have been martyred and buried. A church was built over the saint's tomb by Emperor Constantine in AD 324, and the Vatican has been the residence of the Popes – successors to St Peter – since 1378, after their 70-year sojourn in Avignon, southern France.

In the early 16th century, the Vatican City began to take on the shape it has today, when a series of Popes, keen to make their headquarters a visual symbol of their immense power and wealth, transformed St Peter's Basilica into the world's largest church. The artist Donato Bramante drew up the plans, and the ageing Michelangelo designed the dome from 1546. An enlarged version based on his plan was consecrated in 1626, after over a century of work. The sculptor Gian Lorenzo Bernini added the massive colonnaded Piazza San Pietro (St Peter's Square) in the 1650s, topped by the statues of 140 saints. The result was an extraordinary piece of architectural theatre, a majestic and dramatic setting for the great public rites of the Catholic Church.

Reduced circumstances

In the 16th century, the Vatican was also the capital of the Papal States, which covered a large part of central and northern Italy. During the Unification of Italy in 1861-70, the Papal States were reduced to the Vatican, and the popes began a voluntary imprisonment behind the city walls. Relations were normalised only in 1929, when Mussolini granted the Vatican independence in return for the Pope's recognition of the Italian state.

Today the Vatican City-state, covering just 109 acres (44 hectares), has a population of about 1000, mainly priests, monks, nuns, students, altar boys, and the Swiss Guard. It is a curious mixture of sacred site, bureaucracy, and tourist attraction. The Pope is assisted by the Curia Romana, a civil service that runs the Church, under the direction of cardinals and senior clerics. The Pope also has a diplomatic corps, with an influential role in international politics.

Gathering of the faithful *Crowds assemble in St Peter's Square to hear papal pronouncements. The square is said to hold 300 000 people comfortably.*

Age of information *The richly decorated Vatican Library contains over 700 000 books, including 6000 manuscripts, plus 100 000 prints and maps.*

These days, the media plays a large part in the Vatican's work. Vatican Radio broadcasts around the globe in 32 languages. A dedicated television station uses satellite to relay Masses celebrated by the Pope, while a daily paper and a weekly, translated into several languages, is issued by the Vatican's own printers.

Packed with treasures

From the days of the Renaissance onwards, the Vatican has also accumulated an extraordinary wealth in art, housed in the palace adjacent to the Basilica. The Museo Pio Clementino has many of the best known Roman and Greek sculptures. The Pinacoteca holds Renaissance and Italian art, with work by Giotto, Raphael and Leonardo. There is also a museum of ancient Egypt, and an ethnological museum. Best known of all is the Sistine Chapel. In 1508 Pope Julius II commissioned Michelangelo to repaint the chapel ceiling with a series of powerful Biblical scenes, from the Creation to the Flood. Twenty years later, he also painted the *Last Judgement*, a wall-sized image of the ultimate meaning of Christianity.

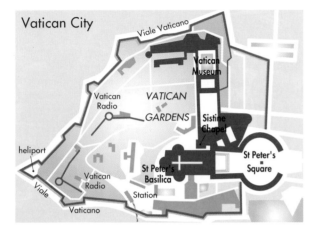

Masterpieces The Vatican holds many of Raphael's works, including the Expulsion of Heliodorus from the Temple *(detail).*

The Sistine Chapel: controversial restoration

Soon after Michelangelo had completed the *Last Judgement* in 1541, the ceilings and walls of the Sistine Chapel began to darken with the grime of candles and charcoal braziers; protective varnish also turned dark with time. From 1980 to 1994, a team of experts undertook a major restoration, ending with the *Last Judgement* itself. The restorers made delicate decisions about the removal of clothing added later to the figures. But more controversial was the colour. Clearly, Michelangelo used a much more vivid palette than anyone had expected – many art-lovers were shocked by the result.

The Swiss Guard

Since the early 16th century, the Pope has been protected by the élite Swiss Guard. Today there are about 100 soldiers in the Guard: all must be Swiss nationals, Roman Catholics, born to legitimate marriages, and younger than 25. Many serve just for the minimum two years, but some make a career of the Guard. Only the officers may marry: their children are among the very few living in the Vatican. The Swiss Guard's dress uniform was supposedly designed by Michelangelo in the 16th century, but looks are deceptive: in fact, guardsmen are highly trained in modern commando warfare.

Rome

1. The Fountain of the Four Rivers, among the greatest works of the 17th-century sculptor Gian Lorenzo Bernini, is the centrepiece of the Piazza Navona. The square itself occupies the site of the stadium of Emperor Domitian.

2. Mussolini erected many bombastic monuments in Rome, but the Palazzo della Civiltà del Lavoro (Palace of the Civilisation of Work), of 1938, is unusually restrained. It was part of a planned 1942 Esposizione Universale di Roma, cancelled because of the war.

3. The Piazza del Populo (People's Square) was laid out in the early 19th century, but retained a gate by Bernini through the 3rd-century wall. The obelisk of Ramses II was brought to Rome by Augustus, and has stood here since the 1580s.

4. The Palatine Hill, one of the Seven Hills of Rome, overlooks the Forum. This was where the founders of Rome, Romulus and Remus, were brought up by a she-wolf. It became the chief residence of the emperors – and origin of our word 'palace'.

5. The River Tiber curves through the city from north to south. Near the Vatican, it passes the massive medieval Castel Sant' Angelo. The bridge, the Ponte Sant' Angelo, is decorated by ten statues of angels by Bernini.

6. The Capitoline Hill is now topped by the city hall, the Campidoglio. The smallest of the Seven Hills, the Capitoline was the site of the Temple of Jupiter, spiritual heart of the Roman world.

The rich small cities of northern Italy

Padua, Mantua, Ferrara, Urbino, Pisa … their names conjure up images of Renaissance art, pioneer universities, architectural refinement and pageant. Today, these cities are all intensely proud of the spirit that forged their individuality.

In perspective Wood inlay designed by Bramante for the ducal palace of Urbino.

Picture Italy in the 15th century, a mosaic of duchies and principalities. These are troubled times, as rival factions jostle for power and territory. But the wealthy aristocratic families, in their fortified cities, have also developed a taste for the trappings of fine living, and the rewards of art and learning. Their courts vie with each other to attract and nurture the greatest talents in architecture, painting, sculpture and scholarship. The result is a series of charmed cities with a cultural heritage of extraordinary richness, and – compared to most cities in the rest of Europe – quite out of proportion to their economic importance today.

Making a scene The Teatro Olympico, of 1588, was the first covered theatre in Europe. It was part of a utopian city at Sabbioneta, Lombardy.

The shadow of history *The Piazza del Campo, in Siena, is one of the great historic squares of Italy. Shell-shaped and paved with bricks, it is overlooked by the Palazzo Publicco (seen here in shadow). Twice a year the piazza is packed with people for the Palio horse-race which hurtles around it.*

Learned Padua

Padua (Padova), just 22 miles (35 km) west of Venice, was rich and successful enough to declare itself an independent republic in 1164. The medieval heart of the city still bears witness to its precocious enlightenment. The university, founded in 1222, and the old law courts, the Palazzo della Ragione (Palace of Reason) helped Padua to earn its nickname, La Dotta, 'The Learned'. But art was celebrated as well as ideas. The jewel in Padua's crown is the Capella degli Scrovegni, a chapel decorated with frescoes by Giotto (1266–1337). These represent as significant a leap forward in Western art as Michelangelo's Sistine Chapel in Rome, painted two centuries later. A continuing artistic heritage can be seen in the Museo Civico Eremitani, with work by other medieval artists and by Bellini, Tintoretto, Titian, Veronese and Tiepolo.

The glories of Mantua

Mantua (Mantova), in the fertile plains of Lombardy, was ruled for nearly four hundred years by the Gonzaga family, who brought to it their taste for art and luxury. They attracted some of the most prodigious talents of the Renaissance, such as Mantegna (1431-1506), who painted the beautiful frescoes of the Camera degli Sposi (Chamber of the Spouses), in the old Castello. Giulio Romano (1492-1546), a pupil of Raphael, designed the interior of the cathedral and the Palazzo del Tè, the duke's summer palace. Monteverdi composed the first modern opera, *Orfeo* for Vincenzo I in 1607. Another extraordinary product of the Gonzaga family

is Sabbioneta, a village south-west of Mantua which was converted in the 16th century into an ideal humanist town – a 'Little Athens', complete with palaces, gardens and the ornate Teatro Olympico.

Refined Ferrara

With its massive walls, drawbridges and moats, the Castello Estense in Ferrara, in Emilia-Romagna, serves as a reminder of the military imperatives of the age. But far from being the feudal tyrants this architecture suggests, the 15 Este dukes who ruled from 1264 to 1597 created an enlightened Renaissance city. Its broad streets are bordered by gardens and a number of superb residences, such as the Palazzo Schifanoia (meaning 'the palace where boredom is spurned'), the Palazzo di Ludovico il Moro, and the Palazzo dei Diamanti – so named because of 8500 sculpted stones on the façade shaped like diamonds, emblem of the Este family. Ferrara was also the home of the poet Ludovico Ariosto, author of one of the great classics of Italian literature, *Orlando Furioso* (1532).

Humanist Urbino

Ochre-hued Urbino, set on a hill in the Marche, also benefited from an enlightened and wise ruling family, the dukes of Montefeltro. The late 15th-century Palazzo Ducale, built for Federico da Montefeltro, is decorated with fine tapestries and furniture. It includes Federico's remarkable study, with walls inlaid with ornate *trompe l'oeil* marquetry, to designs by Botticelli and Bramante. The palace paintings, assembled as the Galleria Nazionale delle Marche, include Piero della Francesca's *Flagellation*, and paintings by Raphael, who was born in Urbino.

The mighty fallen The Fall of the Giants *is one of the remarkable set of Mannerist frescoes in the Palazzo del Tè at Mantua, by Giulio Romano. It illustrates the doomed attempt of the Giants to climb Mount Olympus.*

The Leaning Tower of Pisa

Close to the centre of Pisa is the Campo dei Miracoli (The Field of Miracles), occupied by the cathedral, baptistry and campanile (bell tower). All are magnificent examples of ornate Romanesque architecture, built in the 12th and 13th centuries. The campanile, known as the Leaning Tower, began to lean before construction was completed in 1271, and the crowning drum has been set at a compensating angle. The top now leans out some 14ft (4.2m). Recent work on the foundations has halted the subsidence that threatened the tower's eventual collapse. But visitors may no longer enter the tower, nor experience the odd sensation of seeming to descend when actually climbing the spiral staircase.

Upstaged Pisa's cathedral walls lend emphasis to the Leaning Tower.

Quiet power Ferrara's Castello Estense.

Malta: sentinel of the southern Mediterranean

Maltese cross
The Knights of St John were known as the 'monks of war', and in Malta they adopted the symbol of a cross composed of four arrowheads.

To the west of Malta, the Mediterranean narrows into the Strait of Sicily. Everything about the Maltese islands reflects their key strategic position. Traffic drives on the left, along roads named in English, past French-named buildings, while the Maltese language is flavoured with Italian and Arabic. Historic crossroads of civilisations, cultures and religions, today's independent Malta is at last discovering itself.

Calypso's island Gozo, second largest of the Maltese islands, is greener and less heavily populated than Malta.

Like rocks cast into the sea, the three sunbaked islands of the Maltese archipelago lie 60 miles (96km) to the south of Sicily. They cover just 122 sq miles (315 km²), but have been occupied by Phoenicians, Greeks, Carthaginians, Romans, Vandals, Ostrogoths, Byzantines, Arabs, Normans, Aragonese, the Knights of St John, the French and – until 1964 – the British.

For over a century Malta, en route to the Suez Canal, played a vital role for British naval and merchant shipping. Malta became independent in 1964, and the British armed forces withdrew in 1979, so the islands have had to find new sources of income. These include shipbuilding and repairs, textile manufacture, computer assembly, and tourism. Malta has luxury hotels, where visitors can sunbathe by the pool, enjoy watersports and scuba-diving, and visit the island's many historic sites. But many Maltese still live by fishing, or growing grain, potatoes, citrus fruit, olives and tomatoes in the dry, stony soil.

Knights of St John

Malta, Rhodes and Cyprus have all have been ruled by the Knights of St John. The Order owes its origin to Italian merchants who founded a hospital in Jerusalem for Christian pilgrims in the 11th century. After the First Crusade, in 1099, the 'Hospitallers of St John of Jerusalem' developed into a powerful military force, becoming known as The Knights. Driven from the Holy Land in 1291, they moved first to Cyprus, then Rhodes, which they ruled until 1522, when both islands fell to the Ottoman Turks. In 1530 the Holy Roman Emperor Charles V gave the islands of Malta to the Order. The Knights withstood a long Ottoman siege in 1565, and fought at Lepanto in 1571. Malta was seized by Napoleon in 1798, and then by Britain in 1814. Since 1834 the Knights have been based in Rome, and they undertake humanitarian work in various places around the world.

Holy days A whole series of Christian festivals fill the Maltese calendar. Legend says the islanders were converted by St Paul when he was shipwrecked there.

Map: Gozo, Victoria, Comino, 14°30', 36°, MALTA, Valletta, Rabat, Mediterranean Sea, Malta, 50 km

First defence Valletta, capital of Malta, was founded by the Knights of St John in the 16th century and named after their grand master Jean de la Vallette. In the Second World War the city was heavily bombed by the Italians and Germans, and the island was awarded a George Cross for collective bravery.

Dubrovnik: pearl of the Adriatic

Over a period of eight months in 1991-2, Serb shells rained down on the Croatian city of Dubrovnik, causing horror around the world. This long-independent trading city, built on a medieval grid, had remained almost intact since the 17th century. Now, it seemed, one of the great treasures of European civilisation was about to be demolished.

Perched on a rocky headland of the Dalmatian coast, the port city of Dubrovnik (formerly Ragusa, as it is still called in Italian) was founded by Roman and Slav refugees from the Balkans. It was ideally placed to exploit trade links between Byzantium – and its successors, the Ottoman Empire – and Western Europe. Dubrovnik came under Venetian rule in the 13th century, but was effectively independent from 1358 to 1808, when it was annexed by Napoleon. After Napoleon's fall, the Congress of Vienna of 1815 assigned the city to Austria.

A tradition of tolerance

Girded by its mighty city walls, and defended by four castles, Dubrovnik grew into a tightly knit and extremely wealthy city. One of its strengths was its religious tolerance, which is still evident in the main street, the Stradun. Close to the Serb Orthodox Church is a small mosque still used regularly by the descendants of Muslims converted five centuries ago. Opposite the Church of St Blaise, patron saint of the city, is a tiny synagogue where a community of Sephardic Jews has met since the 14th century.

The fortunes of Dubrovnik were dealt a fatal blow in 1667, when a disastrous earthquake struck, followed by a fire, destroying most of the city and killing perhaps half its population. Although it was rebuilt, Dubrovnik never fully recovered. The bombardment of 1991-2 was a haunting echo of that disaster. But once again, Dubrovnik has quickly repaired the damage, and resumed its role as the most visited and admired city on the Dalmatian coast.

Protecting the faithful *The dome of the early 18th-century baroque cathedral peeks out from behind the fortress that guards the harbour.*

City limits *Dubrovnik's walls and fortresses were built and upgraded in several phases between the 13th and the 17th centuries.*

Historic pharmacy

The walls of Dubrovnik shelter a Franciscan monastery that has a famous pharmacy, founded in 1317 and still functioning. Visitors can see the huge dresser in which herbs and other preparations were kept, complete with gilded cherubs and ceramic jars from the 15th century. The pharmacy also had facilities for keeping live snakes, and a large stock of leeches.

Athens: the fount of Western civilisation

Two millennia after its construction, the Parthenon on the Acropolis of Athens still ranks as one of the world's great marvels. The city that now sprawls at its feet beneath a haze of pollution falls far short of such perfection – but it still has its own charms.

When Athens became the capital of independent Greece in 1834, it was a small town with 4000 inhabitants. It now has a population of 800 000, and a third of the total population of Greece lives in or around the city. Famed for its noisy streets, air pollution and searing summer heat, it has also acquired the unappealing nickname Tsimentoupolis: 'city of cement'.

Despite its expansion, Athens has preserved a host of ancient sites. The National Archaeological Museum contains many of the greatest sculptures and other artefacts of ancient Greece.

Visitors wanting to escape can always head for the Pláka quarter, in the heart of the old city, close to the site of the Agora, ancient Athens' public meeting place. The Pláka, all-but pedestrianised, is an oasis of calm. Its streets of restored houses date mostly from the 19th century, evoking the Athens of the immediate post-Ottoman era.

Like all Mediterranean cities, Athens sleeps during the afternoon heat in summer. But at night the city unwinds: the fashionable head for the nightclubs of Kolonaki, bars of Exarchia, or tavernas of Piraeus – and the atmosphere remains lively well into the small hours.

Hill view *The wooded slopes of Lykabettos, one of the eight hills of Athens, rise above the surrounding buildings.*

Piraeus, port of Athens

There's always something happening in Piraeus. A port since 482 BC, it remains as busy as ever. After the Second World War, entrepreneurs such as Stavros Niarchos and his brother-in-law Aristotle Onassis bought up surplus shipping, creating the largest national merchant fleet in the Mediterranean. Piraeus remains the hub of its activities.

Long and chequered histories

The Acropolis ('high town') stands atop a rocky hill 512 ft (156 m) above the ancient centre of Athens. It has been inhabited since the Stone Age, but its main buildings date from the Athenian 'Golden Age' in the 5th century BC. The Erechtheion, with its famous Caryatid Porch, was dedicated jointly to Athena and Poseidon. It has subsequently served as a church, palace and harem. The Parthenon, built between 447 and 437 BC, was a temple of Athena. A giant statue of the goddess in ivory and gold stood inside; it was the masterpiece of Phidias, architect of the building. After 700 years, the statue was lost and the building fell into decay. It became a Byzantine church, a cathedral, an Ottoman mosque, and a magazine, blown up in 1687 during a Venetian bombardment. In 1801 the sultan allowed the British ambassador, Lord Elgin, to remove the surviving sculptures. To the dismay of the Greeks, they are still in the British Museum.

Fresh today *Athenians come in large numbers to inspect and buy the produce at Athens' busy fish market.*

Greece's sacred places

Delphi is, by common consent, one of the most beautiful and evocative ancient sites in Greece. It was a religious centre in prehistoric times, and the sacred stone, the omphalos, was said to mark the centre of the world. We have other deities now, but Delphi retains a powerful spirit of place – an attribute shared by many of Greece's sacred sites, past and present.

Delphi's position is spectacular: set on the slopes of Mount Parnassus, a series of terraces forms a natural theatre, with a towering cliff as a backdrop. According to legend, an ancient shrine to the Earth Mother once stood here, guarded by the dragon Python. Apollo slew the dragon to take possession of the site for his oracle. Delphi became a hugely wealthy cult centre, at the heart of which was a lavish Temple of Apollo. Those wishing to consult Apollo addressed themselves to the priestess of the oracle, the Pythia, who sat in a trance, making incoherent utterances, which were interpreted by an attendant priest.

For about 1000 years from the 7th century BC, people came to consult the oracle of Apollo at Delphi, regarded then as the navel of the world. Today, visitors come to admire its extensive ruins in even greater numbers. Despite the passage of the centuries, many of them are still able to sense what it is about the site that resonated within the souls of the ancient Greeks.

Spiritual centre *The 4th-century tholos (rotunda) of the Temple of Athena at Delphi shares its setting with the cult centre of Apollo.*

Perfect isolation

Visitors can also experience a very different spirituality, forged in spectacular isolation. The Metéora are a set of monasteries atop precipitous rock towers rising abruptly out of the Plain of Thessaly, in central Greece. Five of the largest have survived, and have now been made more accessible by steps cut into the rocks.

Epidauros: centre for the healing arts

Among the oleanders and pine trees of the eastern Peloponnese lies one of Greece's most beguiling ancient sites. From the 6th century BC, thousands of sick pilgrims made their way to Epidauros to the cult centre of Asclepios, god of healing. In an extensive complex of temples, baths, hospitals and lodgings, the sick could consult the priest-doctors for a cure. Epidauros developed into a large health resort and spa town. A magnificent theatre was built here in the 4th century BC, the best preserved in Greece, and with acoustics that allow all 14 000 spectators to hear a whisper. Since 1950, this has been the scene of an annual festival of theatre, poetry and music, the revival of an ancient tradition.

Undisturbed *The spectacular Metéora monasteries were built from the 11th to 14th centuries. Many contain great treasures, such as the 16th-century Byzantine-style frescoes in the chapel of the monastery of Varlaam.*

Brighter future *Rebuilding in Sarajevo, after the civil war and siege of 1992-5.*

Balkan capitals: finding their role

Nationalist passions, civil strife and war have left their mark on the Balkans during every phase of modern history. Now, after a decade of tumult and conflict, a set of small cities find themselves promoted to the rank of international capitals – and some are finding it hard to cope.

Since their divorce from Yugoslavia, the citizens of Slovenia's capital Ljubljana have been enjoying all the trappings of a modern Western state. Ljubljana no longer looks to other Balkan cities for comparisons, but rather to the cities of neighbouring Italy and Austria, such as Trieste and Vienna. It is revisiting a historic orientation: the city developed as a trading centre between the Balkans and the West, and was Austrian until 1918. While the mighty

Free expression *Lively paintwork on the façade of a mansion in Ljubljana.*

medieval Grad fortress dominates the city from its hilltop site, the pastel-shaded, baroque façades in the old city below reflect later Austrian influences. But today, with a population of 300 000, Ljubljana is a vibrant commercial and industrial city, looking optimistically to the future.

Croatia's capital

It has not been such an easy ride for Zagreb. Originally it was two towns: Gradec, formerly a royal town, and Kaptol, distinguished by the spindly spires of the Cathedral of St Stephen. The two were combined during the 19th century, when the city grew rapidly as part of the Austro-Hungarian Empire. Zagreb shows few physical scars of the recent troubles, but its infrastructure has been pushed close to breaking point by the influx of refugees. The city has grown from 865 000 in 1990 to a million in 2000. But, by and large, Zagreb's population accept this as a small price to pay for independence, and the political freedoms, stability and prosperity that should flow from it.

Sarajevo

Before the civil war and siege of 1992-5, Sarajevo was a cosmopolitan, welcoming city, and host of the 1984 Winter Olympics. Set in a mountain valley, it was founded in the 15th century by the Turks as a suitable residence for the Ottoman provincial governor: its name means 'palace in the field'. It remained mainly Muslim, and had some 80 mosques – but this ethnic concentration made it an obvious target for Serb nationalists in the painful breakup of Yugoslavia. Today, with a population of under half a million, it struggles to meet its new demands as the capital of Bosnia, and remains scarred by the war. While the violence has ended, secured by the presence of UN peace-keeping forces, many of the buildings still lie in ruins. The pockmarks and bullet holes in the main thoroughfare, dubbed 'Snipers' Alley', serve as a vivid reminder of the trauma of the recent past.

Football diplomacy

When Croatia made it to the semi-final of the soccer World Cup of 1998, it put the country, emerging from civil war, on the world map. Everyone knew that Yugoslavia had some talented footballers – but no one expected the Croats to shine so brightly. Players such as Davor Suker and Robert Prosinecki made a lasting impression. Football plays a big part in the social life of the Croatians – and in the national psyche. One of the first acts of President Franjo Tudjman after independence was to alter the name of Dynamo Zagreb – which he thought smacked too much of Communism – to Croatia Zagreb. Its supporters at the World Cup in France broke a lifetime habit to join their arch rivals, Hadjuk Split, in cheering on the national team to a level of success that nobody had predicted. Croatia needed a place on the world stage – and its footballing heroes provided it admirably.

Austrian grandeur *A Zagreb arcade recalls the imperial past.*

Rising from the rubble Skopje was almost entirely rebuilt after an earthquake in 1963.

Power to the people Tirana's history museum in Skanderbeg Square is decorated with a Communist-era style mural.

People power An opposition supporter waves the Serbian flag after demonstrators entered the parliament building in Belgrade on October 5, 2000.

Emerging from isolation

Belgrade remains the capital of the Republic of Yugoslavia, as well as the capital of the constituent Republic of Serbia. It has a long history as a strategic trading centre on the Danube and Sava rivers, developed in turn by the Celts, Romans, Slavs, Byzantines, Turks and Austrians. Its name means 'white citadel', but the city was devastated by the Germans during the Second World War, and no citadel remains. It was reconstructed in Communist style as Tito's capital. War came again in 1999, when it was targeted by NATO bombers during the Kosovo conflict. Much of its infrastructure was destroyed, including communications centres and Danube bridges. But the toppling of President Milosovic in October 2000 brought immediate economic aid from the West, together with the promise that international sanctions would be removed. Belgrade looked forward to reconstruction and prosperity.

Getting by

Tirana was a small provincial town with a population of 10 000 when it was made capital of Albania in 1920. Its population has grown to about 320 000, but it has been granted few of the trappings of a capital city. Its first university opened only in 1957. At the death of Albania's ruler Enva Hoxha in 1985, Tirana's streets were flanked by characterless concrete public buildings, and furrowed with cart tracks. It remains an uneasy place, strapped by poverty, with scant law and order and a fragile administration. But with foreign aid and humanitarian assistance, Tirana has started to put a modern infrastructure in place, and its people are beginning to enjoy the enterprise – if not the criminality – that the market economy brings.

Mosques and quakes

The capital of Macedonia, Skopje, was not physically affected by the breakup of Yugoslavia. During Tito's era it was an engaging little city, where east met west in the cafés and bazaars, beneath a skyline bristling with minarets. The city suffered its worst modern disaster in 1963, when an earthquake destroyed 80 per cent of the buildings and made 120 000 people homeless. With international aid, however, Skopje was rebuilt with buildings resistant to shocks up to ten on the Richter scale. The old city centre, and its rich Ottoman heritage, escaped relatively unscathed, or has been restored, and Skopje – now a city of 550 000 – still retains much of its old easy-going, oriental mystique.

111

CHAPTER 5

CULTURE AND TRADITIONS

If climate were the sole determining factor of culture, then Southern Europe might be almost as monochrome as a blank canvas. But a wide range of other factors come into play, such as language, religion and historic heritage. They create an intensely coloured, sparkling mosaic, composed not simply of the constituent nations, but of the many regions within them, which often have their own, and quite distinctive, language, literature, dance and music. Christianity has been a powerful shaping force across the region, and this is expressed in the many Christian festivals and celebrations that punctuate the calendar throughout the year. But the Islamic traditions of North Africa and the Ottoman Turks have also subtly infiltrated the culture of the South, detected in architecture and musical cadences. One common feature that unites this diversity is the passion with which life is led and culture pursued.

Modern versions of traditional costumes are on parade at the fiestas and ferias of Spain.

Festival time

The warmth of the southern sun makes an atmosphere of festivity virtually inescapable. And the Italians, Spanish, Portuguese and Greeks rise to the occasion. Any excuse will do: a saint's day, a significant date in history, a celebration of local produce. Out comes the bunting, the folding chairs and benches, the makeshift stage and speaker systems, the costumes and fancy dress, funfair rides and fireworks. The benefits are not just the fun derived from such events: these festivities serve to reinforce the values and social ties of the community, and its historic roots.

Waiting their cue *Participants in the romaria of Viana do Castelo, Portugal.*

Across Southern Europe, communities feel a deep obligation to honour the feast day of their patron saints. Usually, the serious business of religion is coupled with fun. The fishing port of Viana do Castelo in Minho province, Portugal, for instance, holds a spectacular romaria (celebration of the patron saint) called the Festa da Senhora da Agonia, in which the sacred image of Mary is carried through the decorated streets to the port, then embarked on a boat for a trip out to sea. The event is accompanied by a procession in traditional costumes, with floats illustrating local crafts and specialities, followed by a bullfight.

Carnival – a time of traditional exuberance in the run-up to the fast of Lent – is widely celebrated in Southern Europe. In Greece, lively fairs and festivals precede a Holy Week of deep religious emotion, in which Christ's agony is poignantly relived.

Pagan echoes

Many festivals are older than recorded history, and may have been grafted onto ancient pagan rites. The fiesta of Las Fallas, in Valencia, Spain, held from March 13 to 19, takes the idea of a winter's-

In the swing *Traditional dancing is kept alive on the island of Brac, Croatia.*

end bonfire to a spectacular extreme. On the feast day of their patron saint, St Joseph, on March 18, carpenters used to burn the wooden poles of the lamps that lighted their workshops through the winter. The poles were dressed as effigies, a tradition that has ballooned into 300 or more vast papier-mâché caricatures made each year. These are celebrated with parades, food stalls, wine and music, until at midnight on March 19 they are set alight amid a colossal fireworks display.

Remembering the past

Other festivals focus on traditional dancing or folk singing, or recall a critical moment in history. The Festa das Cruzes in Monsanto, in the Beiras province of Portugal, celebrates the miraculous lifting of a siege when the last calf left to the starving

Queen of hearts *The haunting mystery of masks and extravagant costumes casts a magical spell at Venice's modern version of the traditional Lent carnival.*

The Venice Carnival

During the 18th century, Venice became notorious for its loose morals. The old Lenten carnival, which had its origins in the 11th century, had evolved into an extravaganza of masked balls, concerts and gambling, when no one knew or cared who was consorting with whom. Napoleon called a halt in 1797. But the Venice Carnival was revived in the 1980s and now attracts tens of thousands of onlookers and participants. It lacks the notoriety of the old carnival, but the masks and costumes create a vivid impression, especially in the misty early spring.

Sparkling fun *Carnival costumes at Pyrgos, in the Greek Peloponnese.*

inhabitants was thrown at the attackers, who took it for a sign of plenty. Now a 'calf' made of flowers is thrown from the city walls, amid folk dances and music.

Celebrating gastronomy

Traditional foods accompany most festivals, presented with pride and eaten with gusto. In Italy the food itself may become the focus of a sagra, a public feast celebrating a local gastronomic speciality, such as wine, porchetta (roast whole pig), trout or snails. For a moderate fee, locals and outsiders can sample the speciality, seated at trestle tables in the village square, and to the accompaniment of brass ensembles or dance bands. These local festivals are immensely memorable for their easy charm and conviviality.

Communal effort *Barcelona youngsters climb a human tower – a feature of the festival for the Virgen de la Merced, held on September 24.*

The Palio of Siena

Twice a year, in early July and mid-August, the central square of Siena, Tuscany, is packed with 50 000 spectators for a remarkable horse-race, the Palio. In a tradition dating back at least to the 12th century, ten jockeys ride bareback at breakneck speed around the square. It is the culmination of days of preparation. About two hours before the race, a parade in medieval dress circles the track, with youths tossing flags into the air and catching their poles as they fall. The flags bear the colours and emblems of the *contrade*, the 17 quarters of the city – for the horse-race is a serious contest between them. Finally the horses enter, with jockeys in *contrada* colours. The race lasts just one and a half hair-raising minutes. The first horse past the finishing line – with or without its rider – after three turns of the square is awarded the Palio (a painted banner), and will be fêted by its *contrada* in joyous street parties lasting several days.

Singing to the world

The image of the male Latin lover – with his bronzed good looks, softly persuasive voice and seductive attentiveness – may be a stereotypical myth, but it is one that fans are happy to attach to the great romantic singers of Southern Europe. In a way that singers from other nations cannot easily imitate, they inject a Mediterranean passion into their songs, and have won a huge global audience. A similar passion animates a small number of equally successful female singers from the region.

On song *Paolo Conte in concert, at the Ramatuelle festival in France.*

'It's wonderful!' sang the Italian Paolo Conte, in English, in a British television advertisement, broadcast in 2000. For many viewers, it was the first time they had heard the gruff, bar-room voice of this singer-songwriter – and they wanted to know more. In fact, since his first album in 1974, and notably *Un gelato al limon* (1979), Conte's witty, inventive lyrics and wide-ranging musical style have won him a loyal following beyond Italy, notably in France, Switzerland and Germany, and latterly in North America. But only now is he beginning to become a household name.

Southern charm

The list of Southern European singers with an international following is slim – but if they succeed, they succeed 'big time'. The Greek Nana Mouskouri, from Crete, is one of the most successful singers of recent times. She had already won major song contests in Greece when, in 1961, her famous 'White Rose of Athens' became an international hit. After learning French, she became one of France's leading recording artists. The American musician and producer Quincy Jones then invited her to the USA to record *The Girl from Greece Sings*, released in 1962 to great acclaim. Thereafter, she appeared regularly on British television, and became famous for her beautifully modulated voice and elegant choice of material. She also helped to create a vogue for Greek music in general and for Greek musicians such as the composer Mikis Theodorakis and singer Demis Roussos.

The Spanish singer Julio Iglesias has sold over 100 million albums worldwide. It has been a roller-coaster ride: his first career as a goalkeeper for the top Spanish soccer team Real Madrid was cut short by a motor accident. Recovering in hospital, he wrote poems, which he set to music – and has never looked back. A consummate professional, he appeals consistently to the market for well made, well orchestrated, romantic songs. With his bronzed good looks, sparkling smile and velvet voice, he remains, for many of his female fans, the ultimate Latin sex symbol. Now two of his sons – Enrique Iglesias and Julio Iglesias Jr – are following in his footsteps, and show every sign of inheriting his talent.

Breaking through

One of the best known of a new generation of Italian stars is Eros Ramazzotti. His international career began with a world tour in 1987. But he really made his mark when he sang with Tina Turner in 1998. It is a well-trodden path to international recognition. In the 1960s, Nana Mouskouri struck up a successful partnership with Harry Belafonte. Julio Iglesias sang with Willie Nelson and Diana Ross. But do Southern European stars always have to sing in English to make the breakthrough? It seems to be the case. But there are many hugely popular singers across Southern Europe who have not followed that route – and do not want to. They would rather the world came to them.

Glittering success *Nana Mouskouri is a top female star worldwide.*

Superstar *Julio Iglesias brings a suave, Sinatra-like approach to his cabaret appearances.*

Flamenco: dance with fire

The raw power is startling. Rattling, zinging guitars weave in and out of the impassioned voice of the singer. To handclaps of performers and cries from the audience, the dancer taps, swirls, hovers, in a dazzling mix of anguish, dignity and physical prowess. To many, this is the true expression of Spain – but in reality, it is the voice of gypsy Andalucía.

The gitanos (gypsies) have lived in Andalucía since the 15th century. This was the home of the guitar, born of the Arab lute, which proved the perfect companion for their powerful, melancholic songs. The result was the tradition of *cante jondo* ('deep song') – songs of lament, romantic yearning, oppression.

Catching the mood

The dance accompanying these songs was equally dazzling, performed with extraordinary discipline and precision. This fiery combination, developed in the back streets of Seville, Cadiz and Jerez, caught the imagination of European bohemians in the late 19th century, creating an international craze. The opera *Carmen* (1875), by the French composer Georges Bizet, helped popularise gypsy culture. Sevillana, a lighter, happier form of flamenco, also developed in Seville at this time.

Fearing that the real *cante jondo* might become extinct, the musician and playwright Federico García Lorca and composer Manuel de Falla founded a festival in 1922. This established flamenco as an art form, formalising the regional differences, styles and moods.

The late 19th and early 20th centuries were a Golden Age of flamenco, but the past two decades have also been exceptional. While young performers grip their audiences in Spain, the most celebrated flamenco artistes, such as the guitarist Paco de Lucía (Paco Peña) or the dancer Joaquín Cortés, tour the world, spreading the word. Flamenco has now become an international phenomenon.

The music Paco de Lucía (left), one of the great modern flamenco guitarists.

The song Flamenco singing (right) is a performance of the whole body.

The dance Performers at a national flamenco competition, at Córdoba.

Greek folk dance: living tradition

When Anthony Quinn danced the syrtaki in the film *Zorba the Greek* (1964), the world believed it was the quintessential Greek folk dance. But in fact the syrtaki was created for the film, to contemporary music by Mikis Theodorakis. Greek folk dancing is widely performed by ordinary people, at celebrations of all types. Its traditions are jealously guarded, but are also constantly evolving. Proof of this is the fact that the syrtaki itself has now been widely adopted by the people of Greece.

A passion for opera

An unexpected success of the 1990 soccer World Cup, held in Italy, was the music. The theme tune was 'Nessun Dorma', from Puccini's opera Turandot, *which became a popular overnight hit worldwide. The Southern Europeans, however, have always understood the popular appeal of opera.*

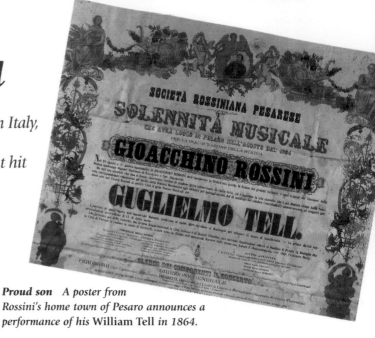

Proud son *A poster from Rossini's home town of Pesaro announces a performance of his* **William Tell** *in 1864.*

The roll call of Southern European opera stars is impressive. Maria Callas, the *prima donna assoluta* of the 1950s and 1960s was of Greek origin. The Italian Luciano Pavarotti is the natural heir to the first truly international opera star, the tenor Enrico Caruso, who became world-famous through his early gramophone recordings. Spain has produced a long line of big names, such as Montserrat Caballé, Teresa Berganza, Plácido Domingo and José Carreras.

Made in Italy

These Mediterranean lands were the birthplace of opera. Since the earliest stirrings of classical music, the Italians showed a strong preference for melody and vocal accompaniment. Claudio Monteverdi (1567-1643) combined these with the baroque love of elaborate spectacle to produce the first opera, *Orfeo*, in 1607, for the court at Mantua. He took the concept to Venice, which soon had eleven opera houses, and a passion for opera quickly spread.

The evolution of *bel canto* – operatic singing concentrating on beautiful tone and agility of voice – led to the heyday of Italian opera in the 19th century, and the careers of the 'Big Five' composers: Vincenzo Bellini (1801-35); Gaetano Donizetti (1797-1848); Gioacchino Rossini (1792-1868); Italy's all-time favourite Giuseppe Verdi (1813-1901); and Giacomo Puccini

(1858-1924). Their flair for peppering their works with memorable, singable songs made their work hugely popular, while retaining the respect of musical cognoscenti.

Italians remain passionate opera lovers: ordinary people will hum a Puccini aria as they hang out the washing or drive to work. Opera houses may retain an air of elitist exclusivity, but the music itself has always had a much broader appeal – as all football fans will now attest.

Rising from the ashes

Venice had one of the world's most beautiful opera houses, called La Fenice (the Phoenix), because it had risen from the ashes of an earlier opera house destroyed by fire in 1773. Many operas were created specially for it, including Verdi's *Rigoletto* (1851) and *La Traviata* (1853). But history repeated itself: on January 29, 1996, La Fenice was gutted by another massive blaze. Plans were immediately laid to rebuild it to identical specifications in time for the Millennium, and funds were donated from around the world. But late-Roman and medieval remains were discovered under the foundations, delaying the start of rebuilding. Nonetheless, the Teatro La Fenice will undoubtedly rise again from the ashes.

Diva *Maria Callas in 1954 at La Scala, Milan.*

Former glory *The auditorium of La Fenice, Venice, before the fire of 1996.*

Writing: in pursuit of a formidable tradition

Southern Europe can draw on a magnificent literary heritage. The modern heirs of Aeschylus, Euripides and Aristophanes, Dante, Cervantes and Portugal's Camoens demonstrate how their unique voice and perspective can still captivate a world audience.

Albanian viewpoint *Ismail Kadaré is a master of the novel and short story.*

A radical spirit surged through the literature of Southern Europe for much of the 20th century, reflecting the turmoil of the times. One outstanding writer who died in that turmoil was the Spanish playwright and poet Federico García Lorca. He created some of the most powerful tragedies of the 20th century, such as *Blood Wedding* (1933), but was killed in the Spanish Civil War.

Radical, dramatic and poetic

The century's anguish is reflected differently by Italy's Primo Levi, who wrote with great humanity on his experiences in Nazi concentration camps in books like *If this is a Man*, which won a worldwide audience. The Albanian novelist, poet, and journalist Ismail Kadaré offers another perspective. He has expressed more succinctly than most the 20th-century travails of his homeland in works like *The General of the Dead Army*.

The Italian playwright,

Screen play *Pepe Carvalho (on the left), hero of the novels of Montalbán, in a TV adaptation.*

director and performer Dario Fo has taken a more irreverent approach in his satirical revues and plays such as *Accidental Death of an Anarchist* (1974). The foundations of radical theatre were partly laid by his fellow countryman Luigi Pirandello, in plays such as *Six Characters in Search of an Author* (1921).

Many authors are not concerned with politics. The Italian Italo Calvino is famous for his allegorical novels and short stories, such as *The Baron in the Trees* (1957), about a 19th-century noblemen who conducts his life in the woods, not touching the ground. In Spain, Manuel Vázquez Montalbán has helped to turn detective stories into a major genre.

Written word *The Italian academic Umberto Eco, author of* The Name of the Rose.

Success story

Few would have predicted the runaway success of *The Name of the Rose*, by the Italian Umberto Eco, first published in 1980. A professor at the University of Bologna, Eco was known for his literary criticism and studies in communication: this was his first novel. Set in a monastery in medieval Italy, it follows the quest of an English friar to solve an unfolding multiple murder, and the mystery of the monastery's library. In 1986 it was made into a successful film by Jean-Jacques Annaud. The book and film combined have made Eco a major figure in world literature.

Film version *Sean Connery played the lead in the screen adaptation of* The Name of the Rose.

Golden Lion *Venice Festival trophy.*

European cinema: proud to be different

Ever since the Spanish director Luis Buñuel cooperated with Salvador Dalí to produce the utterly bizarre surrealist movie Un Chien Andalou *(1929), filmgoers have come to expect original and thought-provoking cinema from Southern Europe. They have not been disappointed. The reputation established by directors such as Buñuel and Italy's Federico Fellini has been admirably maintained by succeeding generations of film-makers.*

Film, some would argue, is the most complete art – a blend of images, words, mood-evoking music and narrative drama. For Italy, the birthplace of opera, it is a natural medium. Mussolini used cinema as propaganda and inaugurated the Cinecittà (Cine City), Italy's Hollywood, in Rome in 1937. After his fall from power Italian cinema blossomed. Initially it took the form of a gritty neo-realism, as seen in Roberto Rossellini's seminal film *Rome, Open City* (1945) and Vittorio di Sica's *Bicycle Thieves* (1948), which for the first time placed the lives of ordinary Italians on centre stage.

The leading Italian directors followed individual paths. Federico Fellini broke away from neo-realism to explore his penchant for the bizarre – but always held in check by a deft cinematographic touch. He made his mark with *La Strada* (1954), a road movie centring on a circus, and came to world attention with his sideways view of Rome high society in *La Dolce Vita* (1960).

By the time Fellini made *Satyricon* (1969), a haunting film of libidinous ancient Rome, and Pier Paolo Pasolini directed his earthy *Decameron* (1970), Italian cinema had won international respect. But financial constraints in Italy, and the attractions of the larger English-language market, tempted many directors to look abroad. Michelangelo Antonioni made *Blow-Up* (1966) in English, in London. Luchino Visconti made *Death in Venice* (1971) as an international production. Bernardo Bertolucci used foreign actors and a foreign city in his *Last Tango in Paris* (1972), and even for his epic of recent Italian history *1900* (1976), he used an international cast. Meanwhile, Cinecittà remained a key hub for film production in Italy. Numerous large-scale international productions were made there, from *Ben Hur* (1959) to Jean-Jacques Annaud's *The Name of the Rose* (1986), and Bertolucci's *The Last Emperor* (1987).

Buñuel and after

As in Italy, Spanish cinema mirrored politics. Luis Buñuel lived in exile, mainly in Mexico, during much of Franco's era. He continued to work until his death in 1983, and won international acclaim for his later films such as *The Discreet Charm of the Bourgeoisie* (1973), and *That Obscure Object of Desire* (1977). Pedro Almodóvar, the best-known of the post-Franco film directors, is celebrated for his hectic, sideways and often comic portrayals of contemporary Spain in films such as *Women on the Verge of a Nervous Breakdown* (1988).

Epic *Directed by Carmine Gallone,* Scipio l'Africano *(The Defeat of Hannibal, 1937), is one of the most expensive historical movies ever made.*

On the set *Marcello Mastroianni (right) with Federico Fellini (1963).*

Oscars and other prizes

Few Southern European film-makers can match the massive investment, production values and powers of promotion of Hollywood. But their work impresses art-house audiences, and occasionally the wider public – and this achievement is frequently acknowledged by film awards. *Cinema Paradiso*, written and directed by Giuseppe Tornatore, won the Oscar for best foreign-language film in 1989, a triumph repeated in 1992 with *Mediterraneo*, by Gabriele Salvatores, also of Italy. *Il Postino* (*The Postman*, 1997), an Italian-French co-production directed by Michael Radford, was nominated for the ultimate Oscar accolade of best film.

The most famous Greek name in film-making is Costa-Gavras. He is celebrated in particular for *Z* (1968), a riveting thriller of political assassination in the time of the Generals, which won an Oscar for best foreign-language film. Theo Angelopoulos has also earned considerable acclaim in recent years, winning the Golden Lion at the 1988 Venice Film Festival for *Landscape in the Mist*, and the Grand Jury Prize at the 1998 Cannes Film Festival for *Ulysses' Gaze*.

Cannes has also hailed the work of Yugoslavia's leading director Emir Kusturica, twice winner of the Palme d'Or, for *Father was Away on Business* (1985) and *Underground* (1995) – a film that explores the historical and cultural roots of the chaos in Yugoslavia.

The most recent triumph was by the Italian director Roberto Benigni. In 1998 his film of the Nazi holocaust *La Vita è Bella* (*Life is Beautiful*) was nominated for seven Oscars and won three – best foreign-language film, best actor (for Benigni) and best original music score – and also won the Grand Jury Prize at Cannes.

Film festivals

Venice held the world's first international film festival in 1932. In the postwar era it has had to contend with competition from Cannes (founded in 1946) and Berlin (1951), but it is still the biggest film festival in Southern Europe and has remained true to its aim of showing a broad spectrum of innovative international films. The highest award is the Golden Lion – the equivalent of Cannes' Palme d'Or. Italy also holds film festivals in Florence, Messina, Rimini, Salerno, Turin (new directors), Trieste (science fiction) and Verona. There are two international film festivals in Spain, at San Sebastián and Valladolid.

Daughter and mother *Victoria Abril and Marisa Paredes in Pedro Almodóvar's* Tacones Lejanos (High Heels, *1991*).

Island life *Massimo Troisi, leading actor and co-scriptwriter in* Il Postino (The Postman, *1997*).

Bathed in glory Underground, *by Emir Kusturica, was a controversial winner of the Palme d'Or at Cannes in 1995.*

121

A wealth of art

The museums and galleries of Southern Europe benefit from a rich heritage. A wealth of archaeological treasures stretches back to Mycenaean times 3000 years ago, and beyond. There are the riches of Renaissance art, works by the great Italian and Spanish masters, and Cubism, Futurism and Surrealism in the modern era. The Uffizi in Florence, the Vatican Museums, the Prado in Madrid – these are just a few of the world-class museums in the region.

Surreal *Exterior of Teatre-Museu Dalí, Figueres.*

In any illustrated book about the great civilisations of the world a large proportion of the items pictured come from the museums of Southern Europe. The reason is simple: this was where so much of Western culture was generated.

Ancient genius

The National Archaeological Museum of Athens contains an astounding collection of ancient sculpture, demonstrating the extraordinary artistic achievement of ancient Greece. The many famous pieces include the gold masks found in the shaft graves of Mycenae and the bronze statue of Zeus (or Poseidon) found in the sea off Cape Artemision. Other remarkable collections of sculpture can be seen at Delphi, the home of Apollo's oracle, and at Olympia, the sacred site where the games were first held.

The museums of archaeological finds are also treasured for what they reveal about the daily lives of ancient peoples. The Villa Giulia in Rome has a collection of Etruscan artefacts, matched by the Museo Nazionale Tarquiniense in Tarquinia, which houses many finds from the elaborate tombs nearby. Both collections contain pottery, jewellery, mirrors and cooking pots, which show the Etruscans' playful sense of design. Their humanity is powerfully represented by their sarcophagi, decorated with life-size terracotta statues of the dead. The National Archaeological Museum of Naples has everyday objects found among the debris of Pompeii and Herculaneum, as well as their finest sculptures and mosaics.

From Fra Angelico to Zurbarán

Both Italy and Spain have an immense wealth in painting. Visitors to Florence can see work by Fra Angelico, Botticelli, Leonardo da Vinci, Michelangelo, Raphael and Titian – at the Uffizi, the Pitti Palace and the Accademia. The Accademia of Venice has a collection of paintings from the 14th to the 18th centuries, with work by the Bellinis, Giorgione, Carpaccio, Titian, Veronese, Tintoretto, Guardi and Canaletto.

Face of the past *A gold mask from Mycenae, made in about 1500 BC.*

Madrid's Prado has 7000 paintings in total, only half of which are on view at any one time. It not only has work by the great Spanish painters, such as El Greco, Velázquez, Zurbarán, Murillo and Goya, but also a major collection of Italian and Flemish art, including Hieronymus Bosch and Rubens. The

The Guggenheim, Bilbao

Bilbao's Guggenheim Museum, opened in 1997, is a stroke of genius. The building, by the American architect Frank Gehry, is astonishing – a work of art in itself. Glittering with titanium tiles, it defies all architectural logic. The interior spaces, although highly unconventional, provide the setting for a remarkable collection of contemporary art. Lent by the Guggenheim Foundation of New York, it includes work by 20th-century artists such as Pablo Picasso, Egon Schiele, Marc Chagall, Alberto Giacometti, Claes Oldenburg, Robert Rauschenberg and Damien Hirst – to name but a few. The building cost $100 million, and a further $50 million has been set aside for the museum to purchase a collection of its own. It represents a huge investment for the city, but one that seems to be paying off through the thousands of visitors.

Centro de Arte Reina Sofía in Madrid is a major modern collection, with many works by Picasso, Juan Gris, Dalí and Miró. The Thyssen-Bornemisza museum in Madrid, once the private collection of a family of German-Hungarian magnates, contains a retrospective of European art from the 13th to the 20th century. Lisbon has a comparable legacy of art and artefacts, including many oriental pieces given to the nation by the wealthy Armenian oil tycoon and collector, Calouste Gulbenkian.

The Moderns

Spain has taken the lead in modern art collections. Barcelona has a museum devoted to Picasso, with a fine collection from his early years. Joan Miró was born in the medieval Barri Gòtic quarter of Barcelona. In the 1970s he set up the Fundacío Joan Miró, endowing it with 379 paintings and 500 drawings. The Teatre-Museu Dalí, created by Salvador Dalí between 1961 and 1974, is in a converted theatre in Figueres, the town of his birth. A monument to his sense of the absurd, it contains assemblages like *Rainy Taxi*, with a Cadillac, tyres, sculptures and running water, as well as several of his best paintings.

Modern eye *Picasso's* Las Meninas *(1957) is a reworking of a 17th-century painting by Velázquez.*

Eye catching *Gehry's titanium-clad Guggenheim Museum, Bilbao.*

The *Scuole* of Venice

Venice's *Scuole* (literally, 'schools') were guild-like confraternities. They were set up in the 13th century to protect the interests of various trades, such as cobblers and barbers, or groups of expatriate merchants such as the Dalmatian Slavs or Greeks. As mutual aid societies, they protected their own members in sickness, or their families in the case of death. They also performed charitable duties to the community at large. Many *Scuole* were associated with religious organisations, and were deeply pious. By the 16th century some had become wealthy and were able to commission the greatest architects to build assembly rooms and chapels, and to use the best artists to decorate the walls and ceilings, usually with works on religious subjects.

Classic
The Roman statue Apollo Belvedere in the Vatican Museum inspired Renaissance sculptors.

Light and shade *One of Giovanni Bellini's* sacre conversazioni *(Madonna and Child with Saints). In contrast to the Florentines, who championed formal composition, the Venetians took a relaxed approach and produced a more intimate effect, with the emphasis on a true-to-life rendering of people and clothing.*

The Venetian palette

As the High Renaissance evolved in the 16th century, Venetian art flourished with a blend of technical skills and self-confident panache. By comparison, much art of the rest of Italy seemed heavy-handed.

The story begins with Giovanni Bellini (*c*.1430-1516), an early master of Flemish oil-painting techniques, learned from the Sicilian Antonello da Messina. Bellini specialised in religious paintings, which possess a control of colour and light rarely seen before in Italy, and certainly not achievable by the older technique of water-based fresco painting. One of the apprentices in the Bellini studio was Giorgione (*c*.1477-1510). He invented a new kind of painting, evoking mood rather than simply illustrating a scene. His subjects – Biblical or mythological – are often set in landscapes of subtle beauty. By using portable canvases, he could appeal to private patrons as well as to religious and civil institutions.

Grand finale

Venetian painting revived in the 18th century with Canaletto (1697-1778), Francesco Guardi (1712-93) and Giovanni Battista Tiepolo (1696-1770), who resuscitated the grand Venetian tradition. He created large frescoes on Biblical or historical subjects, such as *The Banquet of Antony and Cleopatra* (left), full of *trompe-l'oeil* architecture. His light touch, sunny palette and dynamic composition radiate wit and humanity.

Stars of the Golden Age

By the time of Giorgione's early death, probably from plague, all the features of the great 16th-century flowering of Venetian High Renaissance art were in place: glittering surfaces, softly moulded contours, the impressive control of colour, detail and shading. Titian (*c*.1489-1576) was probably also a pupil of Bellini and worked with Giorgione. As he grew in confidence and became Venice's leading painter, he introduced greater dynamism into his composition. By the 1530s he was famous throughout Europe: the Holy Roman emperor Charles V and

Shimmering silk *A detail from a Biblical scene by Veronese shows his passion for sumptuous costumes.*

his son Philip II of Spain were among his patrons.

The Venetian masters were famous for the sumptuousness of their paintings, seen especially in the portrayal of cloth. Paolo Veronese (1528-88), one of the greatest decorative artists, created religious scenes on such an opulent scale that he was rebuked by the Inquisition. In a famous incident, he was forced to downgrade the title of his *Last Supper* (1573) to *The Feast in the House of Levi*.

Portraits of Spain

The history of Spanish painting is overshadowed by three towering figures: El Greco, Velázquez and Goya. Each was highly individual, and their works are instantly identifiable.

Mystic image El Greco's St Veronica *expresses the unworldly awe of humans confronting a miracle.*

With their elongated figures, emotionally charged gestures and cool colours, the works of Greek-born Dhominikos Theotocopoulos, or El Greco (The Greek, 1541-1614), represented a revolutionary departure in painting. Floating in fluid space, the figures inhabit a spiritual world, barely anchored to reality. Only the ecstatic glory of heaven appears to have any substance or poise. El Greco – born in Crete, trained in Venice, and a resident of Toledo – was making a personalised statement of faith, but it clearly chimed with the Spanish interpretation of Roman Catholicism.

Court painter

Diego Rodriguez de Silva Velázquez (1599-1660), by comparison, was a rather more conventional painter, in the Italian mould. Born in Seville, he went to Madrid aged 24 and joined the elite circle of court painters. He concentrated on portraiture, and brought to it both technical mastery and an irrepressible urge to express the humanity of his subjects – not simply to pander to their self-image. Translated to religious painting, this approach gives his work a startling realism that is easy to identify with. His great masterpiece *Las Meninas* (*The Maids of Honour*, 1656) provides an insight into the royal court of Spain. The image is seen as if from the eyes of the royal couple (reflected in the mirror at the rear of the painting), who are sitting for a portrait. In front of them they see what we see: Velázquez at his easel, and beside him some of the royal household – an informal group that includes the Infanta (princess), a dwarf and a dog. Although meticulously composed, it looks entirely spontaneous.

Painting anguish

Francisco José de Goya y Lucientes (1746-1828) was also a court painter – but of a very different kind. He took Velázquez's quest for honest portraiture to the point of insolence. His portraits are often dark, intimate and merciless: they might reveal intelligence and kindness, or self-conceit and ugliness. Much of Goya's work barely conceals his inner turmoil, exacerbated by his deafness resulting from illness in 1792. His engravings and etchings in particular could be ruthlessly scathing, satirising the vanities and follies of court life and the clergy, or, in the series made in 1810-14, using shocking images of violence to excoriate the atrocities committed during the Napoleonic Wars. After 1815 he led a reclusive life on the outskirts of Madrid, painting the walls of his house with his deeply disturbed 'black paintings', such as *Saturn Devouring one of his Children* (1820-3). Goya was the most original artist of his time in Europe, and the expressive energy of his work was a precursor of much that followed in European painting.

Infanta Margarita This detail shows Velázquez's free brushwork.

Firing squad Goya's Third of May 1808 *(painted in 1814) is a brutally realistic rendering of the execution of citizens after riots in Madrid against the French occupation.*

Neo-classical elegance The Capodimonte palace in Naples.

The grand palaces

Today, the grand palaces of Southern Europe are top tourist attractions, tramped over by a populace now privileged to glimpse a world from which the vast majority of their forebears would have been excluded. They can witness what supreme wealth and power could achieve – or how it could be squandered. Either outcome has its own fascinations.

Palaces after their own self-image: that was the aim of Philip II of Spain, of João V of Portugal, and the Bourbons in the Kingdom of Naples. They all built impressive palaces to broadcast their power and glory, and their refined taste – but not always to universal or lasting acclaim.

The austere architecture of the Escorial, the huge granite monastery-cum-palace 25 miles (40 km) north of Madrid, expresses all the fastidious rigour of Philip II, a king with absolute power driven by religious zeal. Built between 1563 and 1584, it served as an administrative centre, a religious institution and a royal mausoleum. The severity of its exterior masks a comfortable, elegant and airy interior. The modest private apartments are particularly charming, while the library is one of the finest in Europe, with frescoes, globes, maps and 40 000 books.

In 1717 the Portuguese king João V began building his vast palace-cum-monastery at Mafra, 25 miles (40 km) north-west of Lisbon, as a thanksgiving for the birth of his first child. With it, he aimed to rival both the Escorial and St Peter's in Rome. Again, the exterior is austere and imposing, while the ornate interior is cavernous and sombre. This effect is reinforced by the lack of original furniture: most of it departed with Dom João VI when he fled to Brazil in advance of the Napoleonic armies in 1807.

Bourbon showcase

The name Capodimonte is perhaps best known as the elaborate porcelain made in Naples. The factory was founded by the Bourbon kings, who ruled the Kingdom of Naples from 1738 to 1860, and it was named after their palace, built by the first king in their line, Charles III. The palace now serves primarily as an art gallery, the best in southern Italy, displaying the Bourbons' excellent collection of paintings, but the furnishings of the royal apartments are also an eloquent expression of the splendour in which they lived.

Moorish style Pedro I's throne room at the Alcázar of Seville.

Synthesis of traditions

The Alcázar of Seville is one of the most startling palaces in Europe. It looks like a gem of Moorish architecture, encrusted with ornate plasterwork and glittering tiles, pierced by arches and interspersed with soothing courtyard gardens. In fact it was built by the Christian king Pedro I of Castile, in 1364-66. Pedro struck up a close relationship with the Moorish king of Granada, Mohammed V, who sent his best craftsmen to help in the decoration of Pedro's new palace, and they worked alongside Christians and Jews. The result is a glorious synthesis of traditions.

Politics and religion Philip II dedicated the Escorial to St Lawrence in thanksgiving for a victory over the French on the saint's feast day.

The stones of faith

Two contrasting images: the simple, bare stone façades and tiled dome of a Byzantine church in Greece, and the fabulously ornate baroque altar of a Jesuit church in Spain. The churches of Southern Europe fill every gradation of a broad spectrum of Christian faith – each expresses a fundamentally different approach and each reflects different aspects of the spirituality that the entire region shares.

Simple piety   *Saint Demetrios cathedral at Mistras, Greece.*

The Christians of Europe have been building shrines and chapels since their religion began 2000 years ago. At first, they adapted Roman temples, or built to the Roman model. But a new Christian style began to emerge in the Byzantine Empire of the East. One of its distinctive features was the use of mosaics to decorate interior walls and domed ceilings. Ravenna's Byzantine churches, which date back to the 6th century, are decorated with mosaics of magical intensity, glittering like a jewel-case.

Romanesque and Gothic

The Byzantine style survived in the Balkans at least until the 18th century. The rest of Europe continued to use Roman-style round arches and domes – hence the name 'Romanesque' – until the 12th century. Then the virtues of the pointed arch were discovered, which permitted far lighter structures to be built, with bigger windows for stained glass. Later commentators, championing classical architecture, called this new style 'Gothic', because it had barbarously supplanted Roman-inspired architecture.

France was the country where these innovations took place, but the Catholic Church, based in Rome, played a unifying role across the entire region, so the new style soon reached Italy and Iberia. In 1187 the Cistercians came to Fossanova in Lazio, Italy, and built an abbey there of elegant simplicity. Likewise Alcobaça in central Portugal was given to the Cistercians by King Alfonso I in 1153. It went on to become one of the richest monasteries in Spain, but the huge church, bare of all distraction to prayer, is a model of architectural purity. However, the rediscovery of classical architecture in the Renaissance led to a rejection of the Gothic style.

Lavish praise   *The altarpiece of the Real Clerecía, Salamanca, Spain.*

Baroque exuberance

Churches now took on many classical features, such as domes and temple-like façades. In Italy during the 17th century this style was elaborated with exuberant flourishes – barley-twist columns, broken pediments, floral garlands and other sculptural details. Known as 'Baroque', this vogue soon spread throughout Western Europe. It was the visual expression of the Counter-Reformation, and appealed in particular to the Jesuits.

Meanwhile, in Spain, in the early 18th-century, a Catalan family of architects called Churriguera extrapolated the baroque into an even more elaborate style called 'churrigueresque' – seen for example in Salamanca's Catedral Nueva, or the Iglesia de Santa María del Coro in San Sebastián.

Trompe l'oeil

The French term *trompe l'oeil* means 'trick the eye' – to fool the viewer into thinking that what is painted on a two-dimensional surface is in fact three-dimensional. The first step along this path was the mastery of perspective, achieved by artists such as the Italian Andrea Mantegna (1421-1506). Renaissance artists gloried in painting grand buildings and temples that looked as though you could walk into them. Later artists took the idea one step further, decorating walls with architectural ornament and using massively foreshortened perspective on the ceilings, with columns receding into cloudy heavens filled with figures, viewed as if from below.

Trick of the eye   *A detail from Mantegna's fresco in the Chamber of the Spouses in Mantua.*

Mount Athos

Set on a long peninsula jutting out into the Aegean Sea, the monasteries of Mount Athos form an exclusively male religious colony that is unique in Western Christianity. With the accumulation of 1000 years of occupation, it is guardian of an extraordinarily rich artistic legacy.

Dwindling numbers *Today there are only 1500 monks on Mount Athos, compared to perhaps 40 000 in medieval times.*

Since the 7th century AD there have been hermits living on Ayion Oros (Holy Mountain), a rocky finger of land jutting out from Greece. Measuring 40 miles (60 km) long, the peninsula rises to the bare limestone peak of Mount Athos at 6670 ft (2033 m). This is where St Athanasios founded a monastery in AD 963, with the support and protection of the Byzantine emperor.

Heyday

The number of monasteries grew until the 14th century, when there were 40 of them housing – so it is said – 1000 monks each, who came from all over the Orthodox world. By careful diplomatic negotiation, the monks managed to maintain good relations with the sultans of the Ottoman Empire after the Fall of Constantinople in 1453.

Recent works *Most of the church frescoes date from the 17th to 19th century.*

Mount Athos was not always a haven of tranquil meditation. Many of the monasteries are well fortified by high walls and towers, perched spectacularly above the sea on the crests of rocky pinnacles, or hidden away in wooded inland valleys – a reflection of the frequent raids by wayward crusaders, Catalan pirates and Turks. But despite the pillage, theft, neglect and sale of treasures over the years, the monasteries still contain a formidable wealth of Byzantine and Orthodox religious art and artefacts – icons, frescoes, illuminated manuscripts, textiles, goldwork and furniture.

Today there are 17 Greek monasteries, plus one Russian, one Bulgarian and one Serb. The bearded monks live frugally, eating one or two meals a day of rice, cheese, fruit, fish and eggs. They attend eight hours of church services every day. In addition, there are a number of anchorites living in seclusion in cells, and hermits living in separate houses.

All-male republic

Mount Athos is an autonomous republic under the protection of Greece, and has its own rules. It allows entry to a very limited number of visitors – adult males only. In the original ruling of 1060, even female animals were forbidden on the peninsula. This stipulation has been relaxed for the sake of farm produce, but the fact that no women are allowed demonstrates Mount Athos's determination to remain true to its heritage and historic mission, regardless of how the rest of the world evolves.

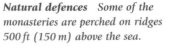

Natural defences *Some of the monasteries are perched on ridges 500 ft (150 m) above the sea.*

An archaeologist's dream

Southern Europe is peppered with archaeological sites, stretching back to prehistoric times. They inspire a deep passion and wonderment, but this heritage also has its problems: the preservation of sites is expensive, and they can be such an awkward obstacle to new building that developers are often tempted to conceal discoveries.

Archaeology began as a gentlemanly kind of pillage in the 18th century. At Pompeii and Herculaneum, locals dug into the ground and recovered artefacts to sell to European aristocrats on the Grand Tour, who were anxious for souvenirs to take back home. The ownership of the treasures unearthed amounted to little more than 'finders keepers'. As a result, the great museums in London, Berlin, Paris and other cities filled with an exceptional wealth of archaeological artefacts, ranging from precious jewellery and sculptures to whole temples. Greece, in particular, was a victim of this acquisitiveness.

They got away

Greek archaeologist Spyridon Marinatos began excavating at Akrotíri on Thíra (Santorini) in 1967, hoping to find evidence that the eruption of the huge volcano on the island caused the collapse of the Minoan civilisation on Crete. A Bronze Age town emerged, and buried in layers of volcanic ash were remains of houses, with furniture, pottery vessels, and even food. It seems that the inhabitants had fled the town before the final eruption, for no human skeletons were found, and no valuables such as jewellery or tools.

A new discipline

Unearthing the past became a more methodical and honourable science in the late 19th century, when Giuseppe Fiorelli took over excavations at Pompeii, and the German Heinrich Schliemann began work first at Troy in Asia Minor, then at Mycenae in Greece. Soon there were teams of archaeologists throughout Greece: Italians in Rhodes and Crete, Germans in Olympia, French in Delphi and Delos, and the British at Sparta. In 1900 Arthur Evans began his 25 years of excavation at Knossos on Crete.

Never-ending story

New discoveries are made every year. Eleven Roman ships were found preserved in silt during construction work at a railway station in Pisa in 1999. In Portugal a Franco-Portuguese team is working on the old Roman city of Conimbriga, near the university city of Coimbra. South of Lisbon, at Alcácer do Sal, on the estuary of the River Sado, another team has been uncovering the remains of a Phoenician trading post – the first to be found on the Atlantic seaboard. Meanwhile, excavations at Pompeii continue, and are likely to do so well into the 21st century.

Brush with the past *The villa of Herodes Atticus at Eva Kynourias in the Peloponnese has been recently excavated.*

Twice fired *Pottery of the 16th century BC has been excavated from volcanic ash and pumice on the Greek island of Thíra (Santorini).*

Massive masonry *Hagar Qim, on Malta, is one of several megalithic temples on the archipelago.*

CHAPTER 6

LANDS OF INDUSTRY AND INVENTION

6

A crossroads before history began, the Mediterranean and the countries that border it have facilitated and contributed to the thriving trade between north and south, east and west. All along, its people have absorbed and adapted ideas, products and attitudes, first from the Middle East and North Africa, later from the Americas and the Far East. While they have exported ideas to the rest of the world, their cultures and economies reflect a two-way traffic in hundreds of small details. Think of Italian coffee (originally from the Arab World), or the many dishes using tomatoes (originally from South America). In the modern process of globalisation, this cross-fertilisation happens at an even more hectic pace, and Southern Europe is far from a passive recipient. It continues to add its creative genius – and the experience of 3000 years of civilisation – in the fields of design, industry and cuisine.

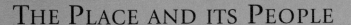

Italian couturier Giorgio Armani is a household name around the world.

Milan: the design capital with a taste for luxury

Paris, London and New York may be the fashion capitals of the world, but when it comes to design in furniture, industrial products, jewellery and clothing, Milan has made the running for more than three decades.

New look *Ettore Sottsass helped invent postmodernist furniture by taking an entirely fresh look at form and function, salted with wit and colour.*

Since the 1950s, Milan has been a fount of creativity that has made it a byword for style. Its devotion to style has generated a passion for innovation and inventiveness, with companies such as Memphis and Artemide pushing the bounds of furniture and domestic design to new and startling extremes.

Strength in luxury

Milan's innovation is well grounded in tradition, conspicuous above all in its luxury goods. To get a feel for this, one only has to take a stroll in the Quadrilatero d'Oro (Golden Quadrilateral), bounded by the Via Monte Napoleone and the Via della Spiga, where the most prestigious names in fashion and jewellery – Buccellati, Missoni, Armani, Laura Biagiotti, Fiorucci, Dolce e Gabbana, Gucci, Versace, Valentino, Mondrian – cluster.

What sets Italian design apart is a sureness of touch. Couturiers will point to the quality of Italian fabrics, and the deep traditions of tailoring – Cerruti began making fine woollen cloth in 1881. A fastidious, fashion-conscious domestic market keeps designers on their toes. The quality, diversity, speed and costs of production have placed Italy among the top manufacturers in the world – but the main consumers are still the Italians themselves.

Hothouse of design

Italian design started to make its reputation during the 1950s. Gio Ponti, creator of the classic espresso machine of 1945, was a prime mover. Cars, typewriters, furniture, electric lamps – all were championed for their technical achievement, inventiveness and aesthetic virtues. Another key figure of Milan design, especially in the 1970s and 1980s, was Ettore Sottsass. Winner of the Compasso d'Oro (The Golden Compass) for industrial design in 1970, he set up the influential Studio Alchimia with Alessandro Mendini in 1976. His inventiveness and willingness to re-think design functions, and to adopt unconventional materials and colours, had a major influence on many younger designers. He was a founder of the Memphis group of international designers, based in Milan, which became the byword for arty, innovative – and often prankish and wacky – furniture in the 1980s. Much of their work is now in design museums around the world.

Leading light *Ettore Sottsass.*

Old habits *Chic traditional style, by Borsalino, Milan.*

High fashion and the world of ready-to-wear

Top designers have the tightrope task of reflecting public taste, while also steering it and anticipating it. It is hardly surprising that their catwalk collections often look unwearable – but soon enough the more commercial world of prêt-à-porter *will follow closely in their tracks.*

Southern Europe has a natural gift for clothes – witness the host of stars in the fashion firmament. Cristobal Balenciaga of Spain became internationally celebrated as one of the promoters of the post-war New Look, and his label was relaunched in 1989. Italy's Gianfranco Ferré took over design at Dior in Paris in 1989. Valentino (Garavani) has dressed the stars with classic elegance since his debut in Florence in 1962. Gianni Versace created his own heady world of star-lit glamour and pizzazz until his murder in Miami Beach in1997. Missoni, run by a husband and wife team, make garments in exquisite textiles, decorated with designs influenced by folk art. Giorgio Armani revolutionised menswear with his smart-casual designer suits of the 1970s. The list goes on.

Despite its glamorous public image, the fashion industry is as vulnerable to commercial pressure as any other. Top fashion houses cannot survive on haute-couture clothes alone. Companies like Versace, Valentino and Gucci have had to diversify beyond their core business into perfumes, housewares and accessories, and have reinforced their brand name by emblazoning it on their products.

Colour keys

The off-the-peg world of *prêt-à-porter* has adopted parallel strategies. With its trademark low-key colours – beige, grey, black – the Spanish label Zara has enjoyed international success since its foundation in 1975. Colour was likewise the secret behind the north Italian company Benetton, which rose from its foundation in 1965 to become Europe's biggest clothing manufacturer. Its fashionable, casual clothes in a range of bright and pastel shades are marketed as the United Colors of Benetton.

Seeing stars
A landscaped dress by Missoni.

Color me   Blood-stained clothes of a Bosnian war victim, used in a Benetton publicity campaign.

Dressed in controversy

In 1992 Benetton advertised its brand name using a harrowing poster of the dying US AIDS activist David Kirby. It marked the cranking-up of Benetton's highly controversial publicity campaign that had begun in 1984 under the guidance of Oliviero Toscani. In 1986 a Jewish boy was shown holding a globe with an Arab boy. In 1989 a white baby was pictured at a black woman's breast. A series of provocative images followed – refugees, a car bomb, the electric chair, a war cemetery, starvation. The public was divided: many accused Benetton of exploitation, or just poor taste. In April 2000 the collaboration with Toscani ended, signalling a change in tack.

The beautiful people   Naomi Campbell and Elle McPherson at the launch of a Valentino boutique.

From the Medicis to the Agnellis: a tradition of patronage

The first great patron of Italian art was the Church. It set a good example to the rich and powerful, who took pride in surrounding themselves with artists and their work, then basking in the reflected glory. This tradition continues in the Italy of today, albeit in a broader variety of forms.

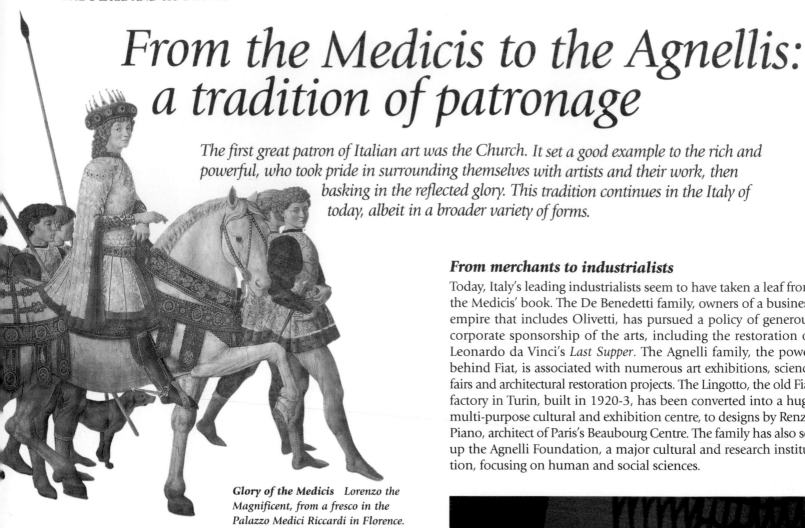

Glory of the Medicis *Lorenzo the Magnificent, from a fresco in the Palazzo Medici Riccardi in Florence.*

The tradition of private patronage in Italy goes back at least as far as Roman times, when the great sculptors received commissions from the rich and powerful. The extraordinary flourishing of art in 15th-century Florence could never have happened without the patronage of families such as the Strozzi, Rucellai, Quartesi and, above all, the Medicis.

The Medicis were a family of textile manufacturers and merchants-turned-bankers who managed to elevate themselves up the social ladder to become the equal of princes, whom they often outshone in splendour. They had a natural feeling for art, and commissioned the best practitioners of their day. Lorenzo de' Medici (1449-92), called Il Magnifico (The Magnificent) was perhaps the greatest ever patron of the arts in the Western world, nurturing the talents of Sandro Botticelli, Leonardo da Vinci and Michelangelo. Thanks to such patronage artists saw their status rise. Michelangelo was brought up in the Medici palace as one of the family, while under the patronage of the Duke of Milan, Leonardo de Vinci was able to pursue his own scientific projects and was appreciated for the universality of his interests.

The grand tradition of Medici patronage continued under Lorenzo's great-great grandson Cosimo I (1519-74), Duke of Florence and Grand Duke of Tuscany. He built the Uffizi palace as administration offices to designs by Giorgio Vasari, and refurbished the Pitti palace. The Medici family continued to rule Tuscany until the 18th century.

From merchants to industrialists

Today, Italy's leading industrialists seem to have taken a leaf from the Medicis' book. The De Benedetti family, owners of a business empire that includes Olivetti, has pursued a policy of generous corporate sponsorship of the arts, including the restoration of Leonardo da Vinci's *Last Supper*. The Agnelli family, the power behind Fiat, is associated with numerous art exhibitions, science fairs and architectural restoration projects. The Lingotto, the old Fiat factory in Turin, built in 1920-3, has been converted into a huge multi-purpose cultural and exhibition centre, to designs by Renzo Piano, architect of Paris's Beaubourg Centre. The family has also set up the Agnelli Foundation, a major cultural and research institution, focusing on human and social sciences.

Modern potentates *Giovanni Agnelli (above), president of Fiat, and Silvio Berlusconi (left), head of a huge multimedia empire and the political party Forza Italia.*

Greek shipowners: fabulous fortunes

In a country composed of islands and peninsulas, with few natural resources, Greece has always had to turn to the sea. Out of a long tradition of merchant shipping arose the phenomenon of the modern Greek shipowners.

Wife No.4 *Stavros Niarchos with Charlotte, daughter of Henry Ford II.*

Wife No.2 *Aristotle Onassis married Jackie Kennedy, widow of the American president, in 1968. The marriage had few supporters among the Kennedy family, and disappointed the American public.*

Public transport *The fleet of ferries that serves the Greek islands is largely owned by the big shipowning families.*

Aristotle Onassis and Stavros Niarchos: two names that were rarely out of the headlines of the popular Press in the postwar era, embodying the ultimate jet-setting world. They were earnest rivals, yet their families and destinies were inextricably linked.

The fortunes of billionaires

Aristotle Onassis (1906-75) was the better known of the two, through his widely publicised private life, which included his relationship with the opera diva Maria Callas, and his high-profile marriages. Onassis came from a family of tobacco merchants, ruined in 1922 by the Turkish capture of Smyrna (Izmir). The following year, aged 17, he went to Argentina and worked as a telephone operator, but meanwhile started his own tobacco business. By the age of 25 he was already a dollar millionaire, and in 1932, in the depths of the Depression, bought six Canadian freight ships at a bargain price and steadily built up one of the biggest privately owned merchant fleets in the world. He also diversified, and by the end of the 1950s his business interests included the Greek national airlines, Olympic Airways, and the Monte Carlo casino.

Crossed paths

Stavros Niarchos (1909-96) had a marginally lower profile, but shared a similar trajectory. His rise to fortune also began in the 1930s, when he persuaded his family's milling business to buy their own ships to transport the grain they imported from Argentina. Niarchos created his own shipping firm in 1939 and during the Second World War he leased his fleet to the Allies. Six of these were sunk by the Germans, but with the 2 million dollars he received in compensation he was able to build a new fleet of ships, which eventually grew to include more than 80 oil tankers.

In 1947 Niarchos married the daughter of Stavros Livanos, another powerful shipowner. The year before, her sister had married Onassis. Although related for a time by marriage, the two magnates battled constantly to outshine each other through their possessions – notably their huge private yachts, the magnificence of which regularly filled the pages of glossy magazines.

Lower profile

Greek shipping is not what it used to be. Most private fleets have been sold off, and family fortunes dissipated. The succeeding generations take a more cautious line, shy of publicity, holding court with experts in international law and commerce rather than with international politicians and stars. But the Onassis-Niarchos legacy lives on. Even though many of its ships have been 'flagged out' to Liberia or Panama, Greece still has the fourth largest fleet in the world, by gross tonnage, containing just about anything that floats: supertankers, freighters, container ships, mineral transporters, and the hundreds of ferry boats linking the islands.

Around Italy by pasta

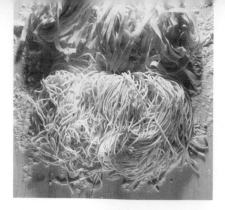

Thick or thin *Pasta takes on a different character according to its shape.*

In Italy even the cats eat pasta: it is the nation's staple food. Pasta was probably known to the Etruscans, may have been made in Pompeii, and was certainly eaten in early medieval times – so any suggestion that it was introduced to Italy from China by Marco Polo in 1295 is roundly refuted.

In 1877 Pietro Barilla opened a small pasta shop in Parma. Today his descendants control the world's biggest pasta-producing operation, employing 7900 people, and its name is celebrated for reliable quality around the world. Despite its huge exports, however, Italy remains by far Barilla's most important market. Italians are the world's biggest pasta eaters, consuming 60 lb (27 kg) per person each year.

All shapes and sizes

While everyone agrees that fresh or homemade pasta is the best, most pasta is bought in its commercially produced dried form, manufactured under government supervision, which controls the quality of the wheat used to produce the flour. The best pasta is *pasta di semola di*

Big feast *Pasta and tomato sauce can provide a hearty but economical meal for large numbers.*

grano duro, produced from the flour of high-protein durum wheat, which grows in areas with hot climates and low rainfall – like the Mediterranean. Flour and water is all that is needed to make it, but some kinds also have eggs in the mixture (*all'uovo*).

There are at least 200 pasta shapes: *maccheroni* (macaroni), *spaghetti, ravioli, fettucine, pappardelle, lasagne, tagliatelle, tortellini*, to name but a few. Many have descriptive names, such as *capelli d'angelo* (angel hair), *cappelletti* (little hats), *farfalle* (butterflies), *conchiglie* (shells), *linguine* (little tongues), *lumaconi* (snails), *orecchiette* (little ears), *penne* (pens), and *vermicelli* (little worms). The shapes are not simply for fun: the surface-to-volume ratio of the shape affects the way the pasta behaves with a particular sauce.

The sauces that go with pasta vary from region to region, and reflect the local produce and local history. In Tuscany tube-like *cannelloni* may be filled with a cream sauce with wild mushrooms and black truffles; in Sardinia, *spaghetti* might come with clams and other shellfish. Rome is said to be the home of a popular favourite, *spaghetti alla carbonara*, a cream sauce with smoked bacon pieces, egg yolks and Parmesan cheese.

Simply the best

At home, Italians eat pasta with simple dressings: for example, melted butter and a sprinkling of grated Parmesan cheese, as in *fettucine al burro*. *Spaghetti all'aglio e olio* has just a coating of hot olive oil in which crushed cloves of garlic have been fried. At the end of summer families harvest or buy large quantities of tomatoes, which they cook into their own homemade sauce, *passata di pomodoro*, to bottle and use through the coming year.

Industrial production

The word pasta means 'dough'. Commercially made dried pasta follows the same four stages of production as homemade pasta. First, the *impasto* (dough mixture) is made by combining flour with hot or cold water. Then the dough is kneaded to make it smooth and elastic. The third stage is to shape the pasta by rolling it out and cutting it, or by pressing it into moulds. Then comes the drying process, which reduces the moisture from 35 per cent to below 12 per cent. At Barilla, where production is fully automated, the drying process is carried out as part of a continual stream of manufacture. The pasta passes through jets of hot air, and then into ovens, where it dries for several hours at temperatures of between 35°C (95°F) and 55°C (131°F). After cooling, the pasta is packed into Cellophane bags or cardboard boxes.

Filling station *Agnollotti can be filled using industrial processes.*

Italian driving: second nature

Italy has the highest ratio of car ownership per head of population in Southern Europe, and fourth highest in the world: 528 per 1000 people. It reflects the Italians' love of cars – and even if they never proceed beyond ownership of a small Fiat, they will have a view about any new car on the road. An Italian driver's career often starts in adolescence with a motor scooter.

Point to a bright red racing car and most people will say 'Ferrari'. First created for Alfa-Romeo in 1929 by Enzo Ferrari, and produced independently since 1946, this great marque has produced over 5000 winners in the history of motor sport. The factory at Modena also makes high-performance luxury sports cars – but just 3300 per year in nine models, up to 90 per cent of which are exported. Their success is due not only to the technical rigour of their construction, but also to the myth created by the brand's sporting prowess. In fact, Ferrari is virtually a national religion, and for the Italians any loss on the Formula One track is taken personally. Even if they never have the chance to drive a Ferrari, most Italian men dream of doing so – and believe that they could.

Small beginnings

For years the name Fiat was associated with the diminutive Fiat 500, but this company now produces some 1.5 million cars a year – about an eighth of all European car production. Founded in Turin (Torino) in 1899 by Giovanni Agnelli, the Fabrica Italiana Automobili Torino (FIAT) is still largely owned and controlled by the family. Agnelli believed that cars were the transport of the future, and the means of liberating the masses, thus mixing socialism with industrialisation. Fiat soon became the largest corporation

The Vespa story

The name Vespa means 'wasp' – an appropriate image that combines the noise that these motor scooters make, their mobility, and the sheer number of them that buzz around Italian city streets on a summer's day. The Italians invented the motor scooter in the 1950s as a gentler alternative to the motorcycle. With its 125 cc engine, it could be ridden without helmet and goggles and suited city-dwellers, and women in skirts. The Vespa has been made by Piaggio for over 50 years, but the style has not changed substantially: it still has a front 'apron' to keep out the weather, wide handlebars, a brake pedal, small wheels with wide mudguards, and a scooter-style double seat. Even with competition from Honda and Piaggio's old rival Lambretta, made by Innocenti, the Vespa still accounts for 43 per cent of the European scooter market.

in Italy, and has since diversified into trucks, railway equipment, construction plant and aeroplanes. It also owns Lancia, Alfa-Romeo, and the agricultural machinery manufacturer New Holland. There were tough times in the 1980s, when Fiat introduced fully automated assembly lines and had to lay off 23 000 workers, but the success of models such as the Fiat Punto has established its market position, and it still employs over 280 000 people in Italy.

Drawing board *A new model begins to take shape at the design studio at Alfa-Romeo.*

Peak performance *A Ferrari driven by Michael Schumacher, at the Luxembourg Grand Prix, 1998.*

MAPS, FACTS AND FIGURES

p. 142-143
Scale 1:3 250 000
BELGRADE
YUGOSLAVIA
BLACK SEA
BULGARIA
FRANCE
ITALY
ALBANIA
TIRANA
TURKEY
SPAIN
ROME
PORTUGAL
MADRID
Barcelona
GREECE
p. 140-141
LISBON
ATHENS
Scale 1:3 500 000
p. 146-147
Palermo
ALGERIA
TUNISIA
p. 144-145
Scale 1:3 250 000
MEDITERRANEAN SEA

Map key

Place names

■ CAPITAL

● Major city

• City

· Town

Borders

—————— International borders

– – – – – Maritime national borders

———— Administrative borders

Tourist sites

★ STELVIO   Park or reserve

Topography

▲ Mulhacén
3 482 m   Peak

ALPS   Mountain range

Elevation tints

Metres

4 000
3 000
2 000
1500
1000
500
200
0
- 100

Depth tints

Metres

0
- 200
- 1 000
- 4 000
- 6 000

Spain • Portugal

ATLANTIC OCEAN

Bay of Biscay

Cabo Ortegal
Punta de Estaca de Bares
Ortigueira
Viveiro
Ribadeo
Navia
Cabo de Peñas
Corunna
Ferrol
Mondoñedo
Luarca
Avilés
Gijón
Cabo de Ajo
Carballo
Betanzos
Villalba
Tineo
Pravia
Oviedo
Llanes
Santander
Cabo Machichaco
Santiago de Compostela
Lugo
Canas
Mieres
Langreo
COVADONGA
Cuevas de Altamira
Torrelavega
Loredo
Bermeo
Guernica
Sestao

Asturias
Pico de Guadamon 1 056 m
Picos de Europa
Peña Ubiña 2 417 m
Portugalete
Barakaldo
Bilbao
Donostia-San Sebas
Eibar
Durango

Villagarcia de Arousa
A Estrada
Peña Prieta 2 933 m
Biscaye
CANTABRIAN MTS

Galicia
Pontevedra
León
Basque Country

Vigo
Ribadavia
Ourense
Monforte de Lemos
Ponferrada
Astorga
Miranda de Ebro
Vitoria-Gasteiz
Estella
Cabo Silleiro
Old
Sahagún
Logroño

Minho
2 030 m
Lago de Sanabria
Benavente
Palencia
Lerma
2262 m
Calahorra
Castile
Burgos

Minho
PENEDA-GERÊS
MONTESINHO
Chaves
Bragança
Embalse de Ricobayo
Urbion 2 228 m
SISTEM

Viana do Castelo
Braga
Minho
Trás Os Montes
Zamora
Valladolid
Tordesillas
Aranda de Duero
Soria
Póvoa de Varzim
Guimarães
ALVÃO
Duero
El Burgo de Osma
Almazán

Matosinhos
Vila Real
Embalse de Almendra
Medina del Campo
Calato
Porto
Vila Nova de Gaia
Lamego
Tua
Espinho
Ovar
Tormes
Salamanca

Beira Alta
Aveiro
Viseu
Pinhel
Semosierra
Atienza
Medinaceli

Cabo Mondego
ESTRELA
Guarda
Ciudad Rodrigo
Segovia
Sigüenza
SIERRA DE GUADARRAMA
Henares
Ojos Ge
Figueira da Foz
Coimbra
SERRA DA ESTRELA
Covilhã
Mesas 1 366 m
Ávila
Pico de Peñalara 2 430 m
Brihuega
Guadalajara

Zêzere
SIERRA DE GATA
Béjar
SIERRA DE GREDOS
Alcalá de Henares
SERR DE CU
Alagón
Pic de Almanzor 2 590 m
MADRID

Leiria
Plasencia
Cuenca
Nazaré
Fátima
Tomar
Castelo Branco
Embalse de Alcántara
Talavera de la Reina
Aranjuez
Caldas Rainha
Alcántara
Toledo
Ocaña

Cabo Carvoeiro
AIRE E CANDEEIROS
Abrantes
Nisa
Cáceres
Trujillo
Mora
SPAIN
Santarém
Tagus (Tejo)
Orgaz
New Castile
Embalse de Alarcón

Mafra
Portalegre
Extremadura
Embalse de Cijara
Sintra
Coruche
Alburquerque
SIERRA DE GUADALUPE
Alcázar de San Juan
Estoril
Cascais
PORTUGAL
Badajoz
Mérida
Guadiana
Herrera del Duque
TABLAS DE DAIMIEL
Tomelloso
Almada
LISBON
Estremoz
Elvas
Don Benito
Ciudad Real
Manzanares
Barreiro
Borba
Olivenza
Almadén
Albacete
Setúbal
SERRA DE OSSA
Évora
Cabeza del Buey
Almodóvar del Campo
Puertollano
Valdepeñas

Cabo Espichel
Baía de Setúbal
Jerez de los Caballeros
Zafra
Ju

Alentejo
Sines
Beja
Llerena
Bélmez
SIERRA MORENA
Moura
Rio Ardila
Serpa
Andújar
SIERRA DE SEGURA
Guadiana
El Pedroso
Córdoba
Linares
Úbeda
Embalse del Tranco de Beas
Caravaca de la C
SERRA DE MONCHIQUE
Tharsis
Nerva
Guadalquivir
Palma del Río
Baeza
Sagra 2 381 m
Algarve
La Palma del Condado
Carmona
Écija
Jaén
Mágina 2 167 m
Lagos
Portimão
Ayamonte
Huelva
Seville
Puente Genil
Baena
Baza
Lorca
Cabo de São Vicente
Vilamoura Quarteira
Utrera
Lucena
Iznalloz
Guadix
Cuevas
Sagres
Olhão
Palos de la Frontera
DOÑANA
Morón de la Frontera
Osuna
Santa Barbara 2 269 m
Vera
Faro
Andalucia
Loja
Granada
SIERRA NEVADA
Sorbas

Gulf of Cadiz
Lebrija
Antequera
Genil
Mulhacén 3 478 m
Almería
Sanlúcar de Barrameda
Arcos de la Frontera
Coín
Huércal-Overa
Jerez de la Frontera
Málaga
Vélez-Málaga
SIERRA NEVADA
Cadiz
San Fernando
Marbella
Torremolinos
Motril
Golfo de Almería
Cabo de Gata
Cabo Trafalgar
Fuengirola
Costa del Sol
La Línea
Estepona
Algeciras
Gibraltar (U.K.)
Europa Point
Tarifa
Strait of Gibraltar
Ceuta

0   25   50 miles
0   33   66   100 km

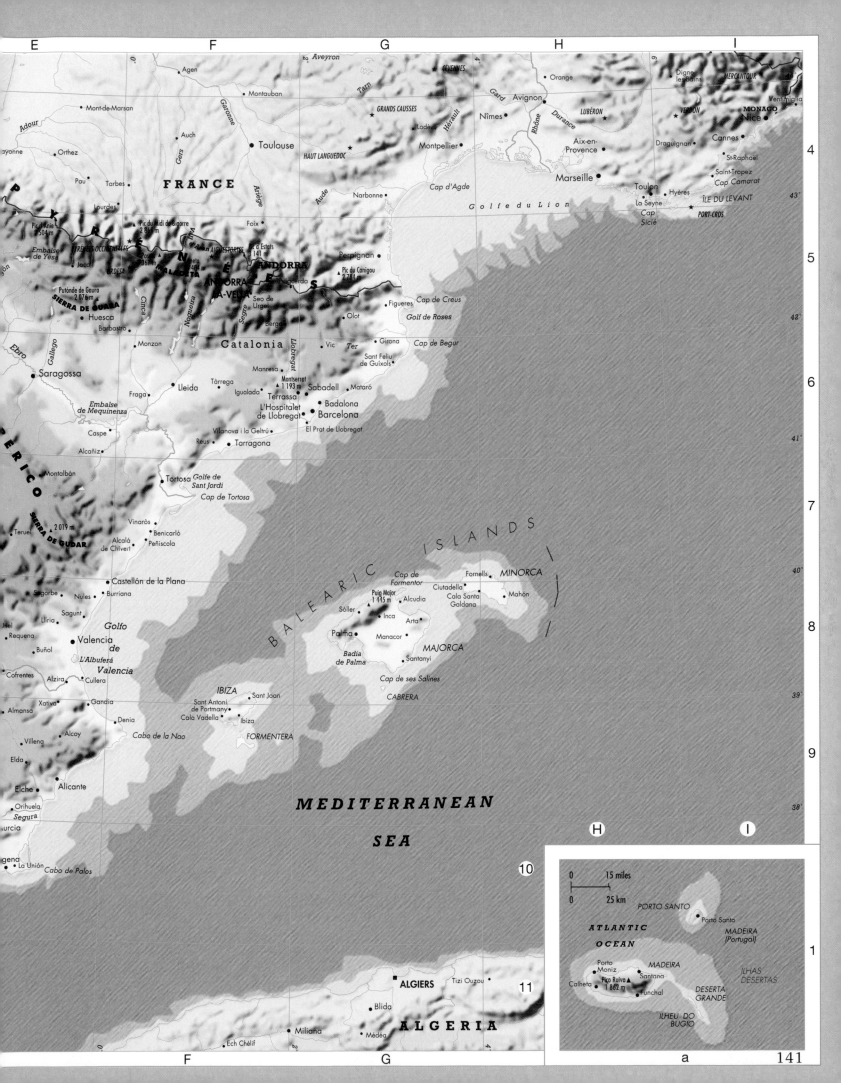

Montbéliard
Liestal
Baden
St-Gall
Innsbruck
HOHE TAUERN
Radstärtspitze 2 360
AUSTRIA
Zürich
Thalwil
Feldkirch
Spital an der Drau
NOCKBERGE
Feldkirchen in Kärnten
Völkermarkt
Ornans
Besançon
Langenthal
Wädenswil
VADUZ
Bludenz
ÖTZTAL ALPS
Lienz
GAILTALER ALPEN
Villach
Klagenfurt
Lucerne
Einsiedeln
LIECHTENSTEIN
ZILLERTALER ALPS
CARNIC ALPS
47°
Burgdorf
Lac de Neuchâtel
BERN
Thun
Lake Lucerne
Schwyz
Davos
Bressanone
Friuli
Gemona del Friuli
KARAWANKEN
Kranjska Gora
Lausanne
Fribourg
GLARUS ALPS
Rhine
Bolzano
DOLOMITES
San Daniele del Friuli
JULIAN ALPS
Sava 2 555 m
Lake Bled
Krani
SWITZERLAND
Merano
Lac de Morat
Thuner See
Interlaken
LEPONTINE ALPS
Tagliamento
1
Lake Geneva
BERNESE ALPS
Locarno
Bellinzona
DOLOMITI BELLUNESI
Feltre
Belluno
Udine
Nova Gorica
Idrija
LJUBLJANA
SLOVE
46°
Geneva
Monthey
Sion
Brenta
Trento
Rovereto
Vittorio Veneto
Conegliano
Pordenone
Palmanova
Gorizia
Postojna
Annemasse
Martigny
PENNINE ALPS
Cervin 4 478 m
Lake Maggiore
Luino
Lugano
Lake Como
Lecco
Adige
Valdagno
Bassano del Grappa
Oderzo
Latisana
Monfalcone
Trieste
Chamonix
Lac d'Annecy
Verbania
Varese
Como
Bergamo
Albino
Lake Garda
Castelfranco Veneto
Treviso
Mogliano Veneto
Ponogvaro
Koper
Opatija
Mont Blanc 4 807 m
Courmayeur
St-Vincent
Arona
Gallarate
Cantù
Monza
Brescia
Vicenza
Mestre
Burano
Venice
Gulf of Venice
Porec
Pazin
KRK
MASSIF DES BAUGES
Valle d'Aosta
GRAN PARADISO 4 061 m
Biella
Legnano
Rho
Treviglio
Verona
Padua
Rovinj
Ivrea
Novara
Magenta
Milan
Chiari
Mantova
Rovigo
Adria
CH. DE BELLEDONNE
2
Isère
VANOISE
Cirié
Vercelli
Vigevano
Pavia
Lodi
Crema
Cremona
LOMBARDY
Pô
Pula
CRES
MASSIF DE LA VAN
Chivasso
Trino
Casale Monferrato
Stradella
Piacenza
ITALY
Rt Kamenjak
UNIE
Bardonecchia
Doire Ripaire
Turin
Valenza
Voghera
Sabbioneta
Ferrara
Pô
SUSAK
45°
Chieri
Asti
Alessandria
Tortona
Fidenza
Parma
Carpi
Modena
ÉCRINS
Pinerolo
Carmagnola
Alba
Novi Ligure
Trebbia
Bologna
Ravenna
ADRIAT
Gap
CHIAN ALP
QUEYRAS
Mt Viso 3 841 m
Saluzzo
Fossano
Tanaro
APPENNINO LIGURE
Monte Cimone 2 163 m
APPENNINO TOSCO-EMILIANO
Imola
Faenza
Forlì
Cesenático
Cesena
3
Mt Pelat 3 051 m
Cuneo
Breo
GENOA
Camogli
Rapallo
Monte Falterona 1 654 m
Rimini
Cattólica
Pésaro
Digne-les-Bains
MERCANTOUR
Savona
Varazze
Finale Ligure
La Spezia
Carrara
Massa
Pistóia
Prato
FALTERONA
Florence
SAN MARINO
Fano
Urbino
Senigállia
Ancona
ALPS
Albenga
Golfo di Genova
Alassio
Viaréggio
Lucca
Arno
Livorno
Arezzo
Tiber (Tevere)
Jesi
VERDON
Imperia
Ventimiglia
San Remo
Bordighera
Pisa
Volterra
Cortona
Lago Trasimeno
Assisi
Macerata
Potenza
MONACO
Nice
Siena
Perugia
Foligno
Chienti
Fermo
4
Draguignan
Cannes
LIGURIAN SEA
Montalcino
Chiani Canal
TUSCANY
Montalcino
Monte Vettore 2 480 m
Ascoli Piceno
San del I
St-Raphaël
CAPRÁIA
Piombino
Monte Ámiata 1 734 m
Ombrone
Umbria
Spoleto
GRAN SASSO D'ITALIA
Téramo
Saint-Tropez
Cap Camarat
Cap Corse
ELBA
Portoferráio
Grosseto
Lago di Bolsena
Terni
MONTISABINI
Rieti
2 914 m
Toulon
Hyères
ÎLE DU LEVANT
PIANOSA
Orbetello
Tarquinia
Viterbo
Lago di Vico
L'Aquila
Monte Velino 2 487 m
MAIELLA
La Seyne
Cap Sicié
PORT-CROS
MONTECRISTO
GIGLIO
Lago di Bracciano
Tiber
Salto
Avezzano
5
Saint-Florent
Bastia
Calvi
Golo
Vescovato
Lago di Bolsena
Civitavécchia
ROME
Tivoli
Sora
Monte Cinto 2 710 m
Corte
VATICAN CITY
Porto
Évisa
Monte Rotondo 2 622 m
Velletri
Frosinone
ABRUZZO
Capo Rosso
CORSICA
Aléria
42°
Bastellica
Ajaccio
Anzio
Latina
Fossanova (Abbazia di)
Liri
Capo di Feno
Monte Incudine 2 136 m
Agro Pontino
Terracina
Gae
Capo di Muro
Sartène
Porto Vecchio
Sábaudia
Golfo di Gaeta
Bonifacio
CAVALLO
6
MADDALENA
CAPRERA
ISOLE PONZIANE
Gallura
Capriccioli Peninsula
Costa Smeralda
Golfo
ASINARA
Aranci
Olbia
TAVOLARA
41°
Monte Limbara 1 362 m
Porto Torrès
Sassari
MONTI DI ALA
Nuoro
Capo Caccia
Alghero
TYRRHENIAN SEA
7
Sardinia
GENNARGENTU
Golfo di Orosei
MONTI DEL
1 834 m
Arbatax Peninsula
Lago Omodeo
GENNARGENTU
Tortoli
Oristano
Golfo di Oristano
40°

0   25   50 miles
0   33   66   100 km

N   O   P   Q

1

Murska Sobota
Maribor
Ptuj
Nagykanizsa
Dombovar
Szekszard
Szeged
Kanjiza
Hunedoara
Hateg
Drava
Cakovec
Kaposvár
Komló
Baja
Subotica
Senta
Timisoara
Timis
Lugoj
2 518 m
2 103 m
Krsko
Donja Stubica
Varazdin
Pecs
Mohacs
Batina
Sombor
Kula
Becej
Novi Becej
Kikinda
Zrenjanin
Uzdin
Vrsac
Resita
1 445 m
2 290 m
Targu Jiu
45°
Bilo Gora
Bjelovar
Virovitica
Drava
Danube
Vrbas
Vojvodina
ROMANIA
Mehadia
Petrosani
ZAGREB
Slavonia
Garesnica
Kutina
Osijek
Vukovar
Backa Palanka
Novi Sad
Nera
Bazias
Orsova
Drobeta-Turnu-Severin
Filiasi
Samobor
Sisak
Petrinja
Novska
Nova Gradiska
Slavonski Brod
CROATIA
Sava
Ruma
Pancevo
Danube
Burila Mare
3
Karlovac
Krupa
Krka
Sremska Mitrovica
BELGRADE
Smederevo
Pozarevac
Majdanpek
Negotin
Cetate
Bäilesti
Vinograc
Bosanski Novi
Prijedor
Derventa
Brcko
Bijeljina
Sabac
Drina
Valjevo
Kragujevac
Zajecar
Bor
Vidin
Calafat
44°
Slunj
Bihac
Bosanska Krupa
Sana
Banja Luka
Doboj
Tuzla
Loznica
Mionica
Svilajnac
Morava
Lom
Kapela Mts
Sanski Most
Kljuc
Vrbas
Bosna
Zvornik
Krupanj
Kladanj
Srebrenica
Bajina Basta
Pozega
Zapadna Morava
Krusevac
Razanj
Knjazevac
Montana (Mikhaylovgrad)
4
Gospic
1 758 m
Drvar
Jajce
Vares
Zenica
Visoko
Cacak
Titova Uzice
BALKAN MTS
Novigrad
BOSNIA
HERZEGOVINA
SARAJEVO
Visegrad
SERBIA
Golija 1 833 m
Raska
2 017 m
KOPAONIK
Nis
Bela Palanka
Pirot
Zadar
Dinara 1 831 m
Troglav 1 913 m
Kupres
Livno
Jablanica
Prenj 2 155 m
Konjic
2 088 m
Lelija 2 032 m
Foca
Goražde
Priboj
Sjenica
Novi Pazar
YUGOSLAVIA
Leskovac
Grdelica
Pernik
43°
Sali
Knin
Listica
Mostar
Neretva
2 396 m
Tara
Zabljak
Durmitor 2 528 m
Pljevlja
Lim
Rozaje
Kosovska Mitrovica
Pristina
Medveda
Vranje
Bosilegrad
Struma
5
Sibenik
Split
Trogir
CIOVO
Omis
Markarska
Blagaj
Gacko
Bileca
Niksic
Berane
Andrijevica
Pec
Istok
Gnjilane
Kyustendil
KORNAT
KORNATI ARCHIPELAGO
ZIRJE
SOLTA
BRAC
HVAR
Ploce
Metkovic
VIDUSA
Trebinje
MONTENEGRO
Moraca
Komovi 2 488 m
2 694 m
KOSOVO
CRNA GORA
Urosevac
Dakovica
Prizren
Trgoviste
Kumanovo
MTS OSOGOV
VIS
SVETAC
BISEVO
KORCULA
Korcula
Peljesac
MLJET
Dubrovnik
Cavtat
Herceg Novi
Kotor
Orjen 1 895 m
Lovcen 1 759 m
Cetinje
Podgorica
ALBANIAN ALPS
Beli Drim
Drin
Skopje
Tetovo
Veles
Stip
Radovis
42°
LASTOVO
OTOCI PALAGRUZA (CROATIA)
Budva
Bar
Koplik
Shkodër
Lake Scutari
Puke
Kukes
Gostivar
MACEDONIA
Kavadarci
Valandovo
6
Ulcinj
Lezhe
Ulez
Crni Drim
Debar
Kicevo
Krusevo
Prilep
ISOLE TREMITI
Gjiri i Drinit
Kepi i Rodonit
Burrel
2 246 m
Zerqan
Kruje
Struga
Ohrid
Lake Ohrid
Lake Prespa
Bitola
2 517 m
NIDE
41°
Vasto
Termoli
Lago di Varano
Vieste
GARGANO
Monte Gargano 1 056 m
Monte Sant' Angelo
Manfredonia
Durrës
TIRANA
Librazhd
Elbasan
Shkumbin
Pogradec
2 600 m
Florina
Véroia
7
Biferno
Lago di Lesina
San Severo
Golfo di Manfredonia
Kavaje
Lushnjë
Devoll
Kastoriá
Kozani
2 050 m
Campobasso
Foggia
Cerignola
Ándria
Barletta
Molfetta
Bari
Ofanto
Fasano
Monopoli
Fier
Seman
Kuçovë
Tomorr 2 480 m
Korçë
Argos Orestiko
Siatista
Aliakmonas
8
Caserta
Benevento
Ariano
Melfi
Gravina in Puglia
Altamura
Matera
Mottola
Taranto
Manduria
Lecce
Selenicë
Vlorë
Vjosë
Berat
ALBANIA
Smolikas 2 673 m
Zákas
Grevená
GREECE
Naples
Pompei
Salerno
Eboli
Potenza
Basilicata
Basento
Brindisi
SAZAN
Kepi i Gjuhëzës
Palermo
Himarë
Tepelenë
Gjirokastër
Mêtsovo
Kalampaka
Meteora
Trikala
Capri
Golfo di Salerno
Agropoli
Sele
Agri
CILENTO
Monte dal Papa 2 005 m
Sapri
Pisticci
Lido di Metaponto
Gallipoli
Maglie
Casarano
Strait of Otranto
Otranto
Capo Santa Maria di Leuca
Sarande
Corfu
CORFU
EPIRUS
Ioánnina
Thiamis
Lefkimmi
Paramythian
Párga
Árta
Karditsa
Techniti Limniton Kremaston 2 315 m
39°
Golfo di Policastro
POLLINO
Monte Pollino 2 271 m
Castrovillari
Corigliano Calabro
Rossano
Punta Alice
Golfo di Taranto
PAXOI
Préveza
Lefkada
LEFKADA
Agrinio
9
Cosenza
Acri
LA SILA
1 929 m
Crati
Neto
Crotone
Capo Colonna
Calabria
1 158 m
Ithaki
ITHAKI
Astakós
Mesolongi

M   N   O   P

Southern Italy

TYRRHENIAN SEA

ISOLE PONZIANE

Sardinia

MADDALENA CAPRERA
Gallura
Capricciola
Peninsula
ASINARA
Golfo
Arancì
Costa Smeralda
Monte Limbara
1 362 m
Olbia
TAVOLARA
Porto Torrès
Sassari
MONTI DI ALA
Capo Caccia
Alghero
Nuoro
GENNARGENTU
Golfo
di Orosei
Sardinia
Lago Omodeo
MONTI DEL
GENNARGENTU
1 834 m
Arbatax
Peninsula
Tortolì
Golfo di Oristano
Oristano
Mannu
Flumendosa
Muravera
Monte Linas
1 236 m
Iglésias
Monte Caravius
1 116 m
Cágliari
SAN PIETRO
Carbonia
Golfo di
Cagliari
Capo Carbonara
SAN ANTÍOCO
Capo Teulada
Capo Spartivento

USTICA

Pale

Trápani
Alcar
ISOLE EGADI
Gibellina Co
Marsala
Belice
Mazara del Vallo

Strait
of
Sicily
PANTELLERIA
(Italy)

LA GALITE
Cap Blanc
Bizerte
Cap Serrat
Golfe
de
Tunis
Cap Bon
Mateur
Kelibia
Carthage
Tabarka
TUNIS
Hammam Lif
Skikda
Annaba
Béja
Nabeul
Jijel
Mejez el Bab
Hammamet
O. Mejerda
Zaghouan
Golfe
de Hammamet
Souk Ahras
Le Kef
Constantine
Sousse

ISOLE PELAGIE (ITAL

LINOS

LAMPIONE LAMI

Kairouan
Mahdia
TUNISIA
Batna
ALGERIA
ÎLES KERKENNAH
Sfax
Gafsa
Chott Melrhir
Chott
el-Rharsa
Gabès
DJERBA
Chott el Jerid

Naples
eum
Pompei
ammare
Salerno
Eboli
Potenza
Basento
Taranto
Manduria
Lecce
Palermo
Himarë
Gjirokastër
Metsovo
Kalampaka
Meteora ★
Trikala

8

Capri
Golfo di
Salerno
Sele
Agropoli
Basilicata
Pisticci
Lido di
Metaponto
Maglie
Otranto
Strait of
Otranto
Sarande
Ioánnina
Thíamis
Karditsa

Tanagra
Agri
CILENTO
Sapri
Monte del Papa
2 005 m
Monte Pollino
▲ 2 271 m
Golfo
di
Taranto
Gallipoli
Casarano
Corfu
Capo Santa Maria
di Leuca
Lefkimmi
Igoumenitsa
Párga
Paramythia
EPIRUS
Acheloos
Árta
Techniti
Limni
Kremaston
Timfristós
2 315 m
39°

Golfo di
Policastro
POLLINO
Castrovillari
Corigliano
Calabro
Rossano
Acri
Punta Alice
CORFU
PAXOI
Préveza

LA
SILA
▲ 1 929 m
Crati
Neto
Cosenza
Crotone
Capo Colonna
Calabria
Catanzaro
Capo Rizzuto
LEFKADA
▲ 1 158 m
Lefkada
Agrinio
Astakós
Mesolongi

9

Golfo di
Sant Eufemia
Golfo di
Squillace
Ithaki
ITHAKI
Lixouri
Argostoli
KEFALLONIA
Kyllini

38°

STROMBOLI
EOLIAN ISLANDS
PANAREA
Vibo Valentia
Punta Stilo
ZAKYNTHOS
Zakynthos
Porthmos Zakynthou
Keri

FILICUDI
ALICUDI
SALINA
LIPARI
VULCANO
Punta del Faro
Palmi

10

Milazzo
Messina
▲ 1 956 m
Réggio di Cálabria
Capo Spartivento
IONIAN
SEA
STROFADES

37°

Cefalù
MONTI NEBRODI
PELORITANI
Strait of Messina
Taormina

Términi
merese
▲ 1 847 m
Randazzo
Nicosia
Etna 3 340 m
Acireale

icily
Paterno
Catania

11

Enna
Golfo di Catania

Caltanissetta
Dittaino
Augusta

Agrigento
cle
Salso
Caltagirone
Syracuse

Licata
Gela
Golfo
di
Gela
Vittória
Ragusa
Módica
Avola
Noto
Golfo
di Noto

12

Capo Passero

GOZO
COMINO
Victoria
Valletta
MALTA

35°

MALTA
MALTA

13

MEDITERRANEAN SEA

34°

14

33°

| 0 | 25 | 50 miles |
| 0 | 33 | 66 | 100 km |

BLACK

SEA

TURKEY

ROMANIA

BUCHAREST

BULGARIA

SOFIA

YUGOSLAVIA

KOSOVO

MACEDONIA

ALBANIA

GREECE

ISTANBUL

SEA OF MARMARA

MARMARA

Dobruja

Ludogorie

Walachia

TRANSYLVANIAN ALPS

BALKAN MTS

BALKAN MTS

RILA MTS

RHODOPE MTS

PIRIN

Thrace

VARDAR

CRNA GORA

Chalcidice

YILDIZ DAGLARI

ULUDAG

SIMAVDAGLARI

Constanta
Mangalia
Durankulak
Nos Kaliakra
Balcik
Varna
Varnenski Zaliv
Nos Emine
Pomorie
Burgas
Burgaski Zaliv
Nos Emine
Ahtopol
1035 m
Iğneada
İzmit
İzmitKörfezi
Üsküdar
Bosporus
Bursa
2543 m
Büyükada
Gemlik
İMRALI
Bandirma
Edremit
Gediz
2121 m
Taysanli
Simav
Simav
Balikesir
Biga
Çan
Çanakkale
Gelibolu
Soma
Bergama
Ayvalik
Edremit
Edremit Körfezi
Foça
Manisa
Akhisar
Salihli
Alaşehir
Turgutlu

Cămpulung
Râmnicu Vâlcea
Pitesti
2518 m
Târgu Jiu
Petrosani
Hateg
Hunedoara
2291 m
145 m
Resita
Bocsa
Timisoara
Jimbolia
Deva
Lugoj
Caransebes

Câmpina
Ploiesti
Alexandria
Slatina
Craiova
Filiasi
Drobeta-Turnu-Severin
Mehadia
Majdanpek
Bor
Negotin
Zajecar
Kladovo

Giurgiu
Oltenita
Calarasi
Ialomita
Silistra
Tutrakan
Ruse
Svistov
Zimnicea
Nikopol
Turnu Magurele
Corabia
Calafat
Vidin
Lom
Kula
Vraca

Rosiorii
Turnu Magurele
Pleven
Lovec
Gabrovo
Veliko Tărnovo
Târgoviste
Sumen
Razgrad
Dobrich

Montana (Mihaylovgrad)
Pernik
Etropole
2375 m
Botev
2175 m
Kazanlăk
Stara Zagora
Sliven
Tundza
Kamcija

Pirot
Knjazevac
Nis
Bela Palanka
Dimitrovgrad
Sofia
Pazardzik
Plovdiv
Marica
Panagjuriste
Asenovgrad
Haskovo
Dimitrovgrad
Kărdzali
2191 m
Peretik
Dospat
2091 m
Musala
2925 m
Vihren
2920 m
Goce Delcev
Mesta
Blagoevgrad
Sandanski
Petrić
Sandanski

Edirne
Kırklareli
Lüleburgaz
Çorlu
Tekirdag
Ergene
Uzunköprü
Kastanigés
Didymoteicho
Svilengrad
Soufli
Feres
Enez
Evros
Alexandroupoli
Komotini
Xánthi
Feráki
Momcilgrad
Nástos
Kavála
Dráma
Sérres
Strimónas
2029 m
Falakrón
1966 m
1203 m
THÁSOS
SAMOTHRÁKI
1600 m
GÖKÇEADA
BOZCAADA
Dardanelles
İmroz
Saros Körfezi
LESVOS
Mytilini
Eresos
AGIOS
EFSTRATIOS
LIMNOS
Moudros
GIOURA
Northern

Prokuplje
Kursumlija
Leskovac
Medveda
Gnjilane
Priština
Prizren
Kosovska Mitrovica
Raska
Novi Pazar

Kriva Palanka
Kumanovo
Skopje
Tetovo
Gostivar
Kicevo
Struga
Ohrid
Debar

Kratovo
Stip
Veles
Prilep
Bitola
2600 m
2517 m
2037 m
PRESPA
OHRID

Štrumica
Valandovo
Kavadarci
Kilkis
Polýkastro
Edessa
Flórina
Kastoriá
Grevená
Kozáni
Ptolemaida
Véroia
Katerini
2918 m
Olympos
Larisa
Tírnavos
Óssa
GREECE

Thessaloníki
Gulf of Salonica
Gulf of Stymónas
Kólpos Agiou Orous
Kólpos Kassandras
Kassandra
Sithonia
Athos
2033 m
Agio Oros
Eponomi

Kyustendil
Kriva Palanka

Danube
Danube
Iskăr
Jantra
Osăm
Jiu
Olt
Motru
Arges
Morava
Južna Morava
Zapadna Morava
Iuzna Morava
Beli Drim
Axios
Vardar
Struma
Strimónas

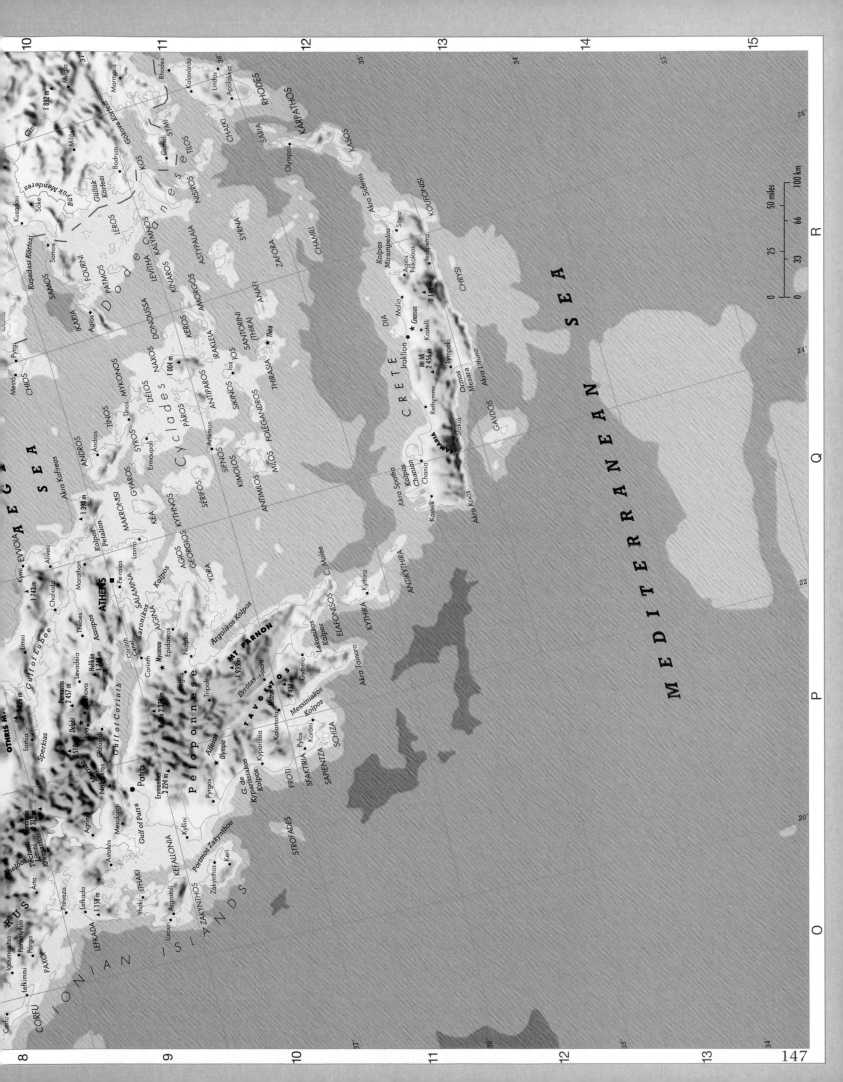

Southern Europe: the statistics

The nations of Southern Europe range in size from Spain, one of Europe's largest countries, to Andorra and San Marino, among the world's smallest.

SPAIN

Official name: Kingdom of Spain
Capital: Madrid
Area: 194 980 sq miles (505 000 km²)
Population: 39 600 000
Population density: 203 per sq mile (78.4 per km²)
Religions: Catholic 91.2%, Muslim 0.2%, other or none 7.6%
Currency: peseta/euro
GNP per head: $14 510
Languages: Spanish (Castilian), Catalan, Basque, Galician

ITALY

Official name: Republic of Italy
Capital: Rome
Area: 116 340 sq miles (301 323 km²)
Population: 57 569 000
Population density: 494.8 per sq mile (192 per km²)
Ethnic minorities: Albanian 1.1%, Austrian 0.4%, French 0.2%, Slovene 0.2%, other 0.3%
Religions: Catholic 83.2%, other or none 16.8%
Currency: lire/euro
GNP per head: $20 120
Language: Italian

GREECE

Official name: Hellenic Republic
Capital: Athens
Area: 50 965 sq miles (132 000 km²)
Population: 10 483 000
Population density: 205.7 per sq mile (79.6 per km²)
Ethnic minorities: 5% (Macedonian 2%, Albanian 0.5%, Turkish 0.5%, other 2%)
Religions: Christian 98.1% (Orthodox 97.6%, Catholic 0.4%, Protestant 0.1%), Muslim 1.5%, other or none 0.4%
Currency: drachma
GNP per head: $11 460
Language: Greek

ANDORRA

Official name: Principality of Andorra
Capital: Andorra-la-Vella
Area: 181 sq miles (468 km²)
Population: 71 000
Population density: 392.3 per sq mile (152 per km²)
Ethnic composition: Spanish 46.4%, Andorran 28.3%, Portuguese 11.1%, French 7.6%, British 1.8%, German 0.5%, other 4.3%
Religions: Catholic 92 %, other or none 1.4%
Currency: Spanish peseta and French franc/euro
GNP per head: $13 550
Languages: Catalan, Spanish, French

MALTA

Official name: Republic of Malta
Capital: Valletta
Area: 125 sq miles (324 km²)
Population : 376 000
Population density: 3008 per sq mile (1160 per km²)
Religions: Catholic 98.6%, other or none 1.4%
Currency: Maltese pound
GNP per head: $8 650
Languages: Maltese, English

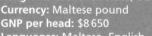

SAN MARINO

Official name: Most Serene Republic of San Marino
Capital: San Marino
Area: 23.5 sq miles (61 km²)
Population: 25 000
Population density: 1064 per sq mile (410 per km²)
Ethnic minorities: 23.2% (Italian 22%, other 1.2%)
Religions: Catholic 95.2%, other or none 4.8%
Currency: Italian lire/euro
GNP per head: $14 000
Language: Italian

MACEDONIA

Official name: Republic of Macedonia
Capital: Skopje
Area: 9927 sq miles (25 713 km²)
Population: 1 950 000
Population density: 196 per sq mile (75.8 per km²)
Ethnic composition: Macedonian 66.5%, Albanian 22.9%, Turkish 4%, Romanian 2.3%, Serb 2%, other 2.3%
Religions: Christian (mainly Orthodox), Muslim 2.5%
Currency: Macedonian dinar
GNP per head: $1 710
Language: Macedonian

BOSNIA

Official name: Republic of Bosnia and Herzegovina
Capital: Sarajevo
Area: 19 741 sq miles (51 129 km²)
Population: 3 524 000
Population density: 178.5 per sq mile (68.9 per km²)
Ethnic composition: Bosnian Muslim 44%, Serb 31.3%, Croat 17%, other 7.7%
Religions: Muslim 43.7%, Serb Orthodox 31.3%, Catholic 15%, Protestant 4%, other or none 6%
Currency: Convertible mark
GNP per head: $700
Languages: Bosnian, Serb, Croat

PORTUGAL

Official name: Portuguese Republic
Capital: Lisbon
Area: 35 552 sq miles (92 082 km²)
Population: 10 400 000
Population density: 292.5 per sq mile (113 per km²)

Ethnic minorities: 0.5% (Cape Verdean 0.2%, Spanish, British and American 0.2%, Brazilian 0.1%)
Religions: Christian 96% (Catholic 94.5%, Protestant 0.6%, other Christian 0.9%), Jewish 0.1%, Muslim 0.1%, other or none 3.8%
Currency: escudo/euro
GNP per head: $10 310
Language: Portuguese

ALBANIA

Official name: Republic of Albania
Capital: Tirana
Area: 11 100 sq miles (28 748 km²)
Population: 3 473 000
Population density: 315.9 per sq mile (120.8 per km²)

Ethnic composition: Albanian 98%, Greek 1.8%, Macedonian 0.1%, other 0.1%
Religions: Muslim 20%, Orthodox 6%, Catholic 3%, none 71%
Currency: lek
GNP per head: $914
Language: Albanian

CROATIA

Official name: Republic of Croatia
Capital: Zagreb
Area: 21 814 sq miles (56 500 km²)
Population: 4 580 000
Population density: 210 per sq mile (85.3 per km²)
Ethnic composition: Croat 78.1%, Serb 12.2%, Bosnian 0.9%, Hungarian 0.5%, Slovene 0.5%, other 7.8%
Religions: Catholic 76.5%, Orthodox 11.1%, Muslim 1.2%, other 11.2%
Currency: kuna
GNP per head: $3 800
Language: Croat

SLOVENIA

Official name: Republic of Slovenia
Capital: Ljubljana
Area: 7800 sq miles (20 200 km²)
Population: 1 948 000
Population density: 249.7 per sq mile (98.7 per km²)
Ethnic composition: Slovene 92.8%, Croat 2.8%, Serb 2.4%, Bosnian 1.4%, Hungarian 0.4%, other 0.2%
Religions: Catholic 76.5%, Orthodox 11.1%, Muslim 1.2%, other or none 11.2 %
Currency: tolar
GNP per head: $9 826
Language: Slovene

YUGOSLAVIA

Official name : Federal Republic of Yugoslavia
Capital: Belgrade
Area: 39 460 sq miles (102 200 km²)
Population: 10 872 000
Population density: 275.5 per sq mile (103,7 per km²)

Ethnic composition: Serb 62.6%, Albanian 16.5%, Montenegrin 5%, Hungarian 3.3%, Muslim 3.2%, Croat 1.1%, other 8.3%
Religions: mainly Serb Orthodox, also Muslim, Catholic and Protestant
Currency: Yugoslav dinar
GNP per head: $920
Language: Serb

Climate and landscape

Southern Europe is known for its warm, dry and sunny climate. But the picture is complicated by mountain ranges that hem in the Mediterranean basin, and the vagaries of coastal weather. The result is a mosaic of climates and landscapes – which includes arid plateaus, maquis scrub, fertile farmland, pasture and forest.

The influence of the sea

The countries of the Mediterranean and the Iberian peninsula share a feature in common: the proximity of the sea. The sea brings precipitation, especially where there are hills and mountains, which make moisture-laden coastal breezes rise and cool. The moisture then condenses and falls as rain or snow. Much of the African coast of the Mediterranean is bordered by desert, a fate that would befall Southern Europe were it not for the precipitation. In fact, areas of Spain and Sicily are semi-arid and close to desert.

Three regimes

The climate of Southern Europe can be divided into three zones. The west has Atlantic weather, with mild winters, cool summers, and high rainfall spread across the year. The Mediterranean lands have hot, dry summers and mild, wet winters, but the climate is affected by the clash of frontal systems where the tropical south and the temperate north converge. The Balkans in the east have more continental weather, with greater temperature variations between cold winters and hot summers, and considerable quantities of rain on or near the Adriatic. Tirana in Albania has almost twice as much rain as London.

HOURS OF SUNSHINE *(per year)*	
	Total
Valletta	2 995
Lisbon	2 998
Athens	2 805
Rome	2 453
Tirana	2 489
Madrid	2 848
Skopje	2 094
Sarajevo	1 850
Zagreb	1 941

Life lines Around Úbeda in Andalucía, southern Spain, highly developed irrigation systems bring life to an arid landscape.

CLIMATES ▼

Climate	
▢	Maritime (temperate)
▢	Mediterranean
▢	Semi-arid
▨	Mountains

Europe's hottest capital

Tourists travel to Greece to enjoy the Mediterranean sun. Temperatures in July and August rarely drop below 22°C (71.6°F). However, the heat in Greece can be uncomfortable, even life-threatening. Athens has an average summer temperature of 33°C (91.4°F), but anticyclones over the Balkans sometimes provoke devastating heat waves, when shade temperatures of 38°C (100.4°F) are not uncommon. The worst heat wave of recent times struck Athens in July 1987. Temperatures rose to 45°C (113°F), and a national emergency was declared as hospitals and military clinics filled with casualties, many suffering from dehydration and heart failure. Some 1200 people died. Since then, air-conditioning has become more common.

PRECIPITATION			
	Total	Wettest month	Driest month
Lisbon	26.8 in (681 mm)	Mar: 4.3 in (110 mm)	July: 0.1 in (3 mm)
Athens	15.7 in (398 mm)	Dec: 2.8 in (70 mm)	July: 0.2 in (6 mm)
Rome	29 in (740 mm)	Nov: 5.1 in (130 mm)	July: 0.6 in (15 mm)
Tirana	53 in (1345 mm)	Nov: 8.3 in (210 mm)	Aug 1.2 in (30 mm)
Madrid	18 in (456 mm)	Oct: 2.2 in (55 mm)	July: 0.4 in (11 mm)
Skopje	20 in (505 mm)	Oct: 2.4 in (60 mm)	July: 1.2 in (30 mm)
Sarajevo	40.6 in (1025 mm)	Oct: 4.1 in (105 mm)	Mar: 2.4 in (60 mm)

MEAN TEMPERATURES		
	January	July
Lisbon	+8 °C (46.4°F)	+27 °C (80.6°F)
Athens	+6 °C (42.8°F)	+33 °C (91.4°F)
Rome	+5 °C (41°F)	+28 °C (82.4°F)
Tirana	+2 °C (35.6°F)	+31 °C (87.8°F)
Madrid	+1 °C (33.8°F)	+31 °C (87.8°F)
Skopje	−3 °C (26.6°F)	+31 °C (87.8°F)
Sarajevo	−4 °C (24.8°F)	+28 °C (82.4°F)

▲ THE PHYSICAL GEOGRAPHY OF SOUTHERN EUROPE

The influence of altitude

As a rule of thumb, climate in northern temperate regions changes with altitude, just as it changes with latitude. Moving 1000 ft (300 m) up a mountain is roughly equivalent to moving 300 miles (500 km) northwards. So the higher ridges and peaks of the Pyrenees, which rise to over 10 000 ft (3050 m), have virtually Scandinavian climates. A parallel effect can be seen in the Alps of northern Italy, and across the Balkans at Mount Olympus in Greece.

The mountains rise from fertile coastal plains, or sometimes directly from the sea. With height, the landscape may progress through sun-baked maquis scrub to forest – typically oak and chestnut in the north, pines farther south – to peaks that may be snowcapped for much of the year, even in southern Spain. In Bosnia and Slovenia, forest accounts for over half the land area.

The geological past

The first great folding and mountain-building era of Europe began in the Carboniferous period of the Palaeozoic era, over 300 million years ago – but those mountains have been eroded back virtually to a plain. During the 165 million years of the Mesozoic era, the landscape was inundated repeatedly by the sea and coated with layers of sediment. During the Oligocene epoch of the Cenozoic era, a period of about 37 to 23 million years (well after the extinction of the dinosaurs) mountain-building recommenced as the African and European plates collided. This process created the Alps, which stretch in a continuous arc across northern Italy and into the Balkans. The

Pyrenees were a more distant echo of the same process. Most of the highest peaks of the region are in the Italian Alps and the Pyrenees. The Balkan mountains are generally less dramatic, but they have a greater impact on several of the nations distributed across them. The highest of Albania, for instance, is Mount Jezerce, which rises to 8835 ft (2693 m); but over three-quarters of Albania is mountainous.

The clash of the tectonic plates still continues today, witnessed in the active volcanoes of Italy (Etna, Vesuvius and Stromboli) and the frequent earthquakes that rumble through Italy and the Balkans, sometimes on a scale to cause major disasters.

HIGHEST PEAKS		
Gran Paradiso (Italy)	15 095 ft	(4061 m)
Monte Viso (Italy)	12 604 ft	(3842 m)
Mulhacén (Spain)	11 424 ft	(3482 m)
Pico de Aneto (Spain)	11 168 ft	(3404 m)
Monte Perdido (Spain)	11 007 ft	(3355 m)

LONGEST RIVERS		
Tagus	626 miles	(1007 km)
Ebro	565 miles	(910 km)
Douro	528 miles	(850 km)
Po	405 miles	(652 km)
Guadiana	359 miles	(578 km)

Major summit The Gran Paradiso, in the Alps of north-western Italy.

Mighty thoroughfare The Danube, the second longest river of Europe after the Volga, flows along the border of Croatia and through Yugoslavia.

LARGEST LAKES		
Shkodër (Albania)	143 sq miles	(370 km²)
Garda (Italy)	141 sq miles	(366 km²)
Ohrid (Macedonia)	134 sq miles	(348 km²)
Prespa (Macedonia)	106 sq miles	(274 km²)
Maggiore (Italy/Switzerland)	82 sq miles	(212 km²)

FOREST COVER (Percentage of total area)	
Slovenia	53.5%
Bosnia	53.1%
Greece	50.5%
Macedonia	38.9%
Croatia	32.6%
Portugal	31.3%
Albania	31.2%
Italy	22.1%

Population and economy

Statistics reveal a great disparity in the standards of living of Southern Europeans. After years of strife, the average income in the Balkans is less than 10 per cent that of the nations of the European Union.

POPULATION DENSITY ▼

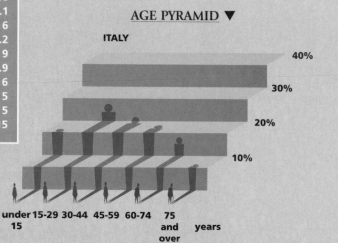

Population density
Inhabitants per sq km
- More than 200
- 100 - 50
- 50 - 100
- 10 - 50
- Fewer than 10

INFANT MORTALITY
(per thousand live births)

Albania	20.4
Andorra	4
Bosnia	19
Croatia	10
Greece	8.1
Italy	6
Macedonia	24.2
Malta	9
Portugal	6.9
San Marino	6
Slovenia	5
Spain	5
Yugoslavia	15

AGE PYRAMID ▼

ITALY

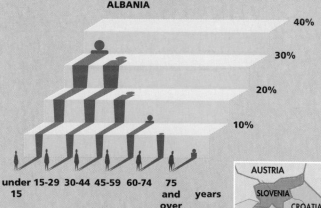

40%
30%
20%
10%

under 15   15-29   30-44   45-59   60-74   75 and over   years

ALBANIA

40%
30%
20%
10%

under 15   15-29   30-44   45-59   60-74   75 and over   years

NATIONAL POPULATIONS
(in millions of inhabitants)

Albania	3.4
Andorra	0.07
Bosnia	3.5
Croatia	4.5
Greece	10.4
Italy	57.5
Macedonia	1.9
Malta	0.3
Portugal	10.4
San Marino	0.02
Slovenia	1.9
Spain	39.6
Yugoslavia	10.8

LIFE EXPECTANCY

	Men	Women		Men	Women
Albania	70	76	Malta	73	78
Andorra	76	82	Portugal	71	78
Bosnia	72	78	San Marino	77	85
Croatia	66	75	Slovenia	69	77
Greece	75	80	Spain	73	81
Italy	74	80	Yugoslavia	69	74
Macedonia	70	74			

Former Yugoslavia: grim statistics

The Balkan wars of the early 1990s were to a large extent the result of the complex ethnic map of the former Yugoslavia. The brutal policy of 'ethnic cleansing' was an attempt to rectify this by force – 3 million people were displaced. At the beginning of the new millennium, the situation remained almost as complex.

Slovenia: Population of 1.9 million, 90 per cent of whom are Slovene.

Croatia: Population of 4.5 million, of whom between 200 000 and 300 000 are Croatian refugees. Some 4000 people died in the conflict.

Bosnia: Population of 3.5 million, 600 000 fewer than in 1992, of whom some 200 000 were killed. The Republik Srpska covers 49 per cent of the land area, and has a population of between 1-1.2 million Serbs. The 1.7 million Bosnian Muslims share a Muslim-Croat Federation with Bosnian Croats, who number 600 000.

Federal Republic of Yugoslavia: Having once been a country of 23 million, Yugoslavia is now reduced to just Serbia and Montenegro, with a population of 10.8 million. This includes some 350 000 Hungarians in Vojvodina, and 1.8 million Albanians in Kosovo. It is estimated that about 5000 Kosovars were killed by Serbs during the Kosovo crisis of 1998-9.

Ethnic groupings in former Yugoslavia (1999)
Marjority of the population:
- Croat
- Slovene
- Muslim
- Serb
- Hungarian
- Albanian
- Macedonian

The plight of Albania

Albania is the poorest country in Europe. Its plight became all the more pitiful in January 1997, when its fragile economy was shattered by the collapse of fraudulent investment companies. Anger was directed against the government, and riots turned to outright rebellion in the south of the country. A state of emergency was declared on March 2, as rebel mobs closed in on Tirana. Some 1500 people died in violent confrontations and general lawlessness. Meanwhile, thousands fled the country, 11 000 to Italy alone. Full-scale civil war was averted only by the promise of early elections, supervised by an international protection force, with a large Italian contingent. The Socialists won, but political in-fighting resulted in the fall of three governments and their premiers in as many years.

The Kosovo crisis of 1998-9 provided a brief respite from these woes: foreign aid poured in, to the benefit of Albania when the Kosovar refugees departed unexpectedly early. Although the Albanian economy is growing at a rate of 11 per cent, and inflation has been held to just 4 per cent, the country remains threadbare and fragile.

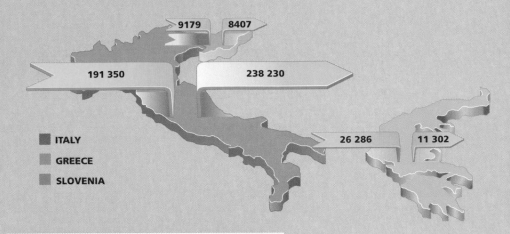

ITALY
GREECE
SLOVENIA

9179 8407
191 350 238 230
26 286 11 302

**FOREIGN TRADE OF ITALY, ▲
GREECE AND SLOVENIA**

UNEMPLOYMENT RATES

Albania	16.5%	Portugal	5.1%
Bosnia	39%	San Marino	3.6%
Croatia	18%	Slovenia	14.6%
Greece	10.3%	Spain	22.3%
Italy	12.3%	Yugoslavia	27.2%
Macedonia	35%		

▼ GROSS DOMESTIC PRODUCT PER INHABITANT (IN US DOLLARS)

Italy 18 910
Andorra 18 000
San Marino 16 900
Spain 14 256
Portugal 13 450
Greece 10 648
Slovenia 7019
Malta 6766
Croatia 2920
Yugoslavia 969
Bosnia Herzegovina 815
Macedonia 799
Albania 565

WORKING POPULATION AS A PERCENTAGE OF THE WHOLE
Italy: 40.6
Greece: 39.7
Slovenia: 39.9

SERVICE INDUSTRIES
Italy: 60.9
Greece: 48.1
Slovenia: 52.3

INDUSTRY AND MINING
Italy: 32.1
Greece: 27.4
Slovenia: 39.3

**DISTRIBUTION ▶
OF THE WORKING
POPULATION**

AGRICULTURE
Italy: 7
Greece: 24.5
Slovenia: 8.4

Andorra: the biggest duty-free shop in Europe

Landlocked in the Pyrenees, the tiny Principality of Andorra has been officially independent only since 1993. Prior to this, it was Europe's last feudal state, paying tribute to its two co-princes, the Bishop of Urgel in Spain and the President of France – an arrangement that dated back 715 years. The co-princes remain the heads of state, but Andorra now has its own elected government, an independent judiciary and a seat at the UN. It is not a member of the European Union, and has its own tax regime, with no income tax and little or no import duty. It survives mainly through a huge trade in tax-free goods. Tourism brings in more than 8 million visitors a year, and accounts for 90 per cent of the nation's income. The remaining 10 per cent comes from industries: textiles, tobacco, electrical equipment and stamps. Andorra plans to exploit its unique position – by developing its banking and financial services. Meanwhile, it remains effectively a giant duty-free shopping centre – without the airport.

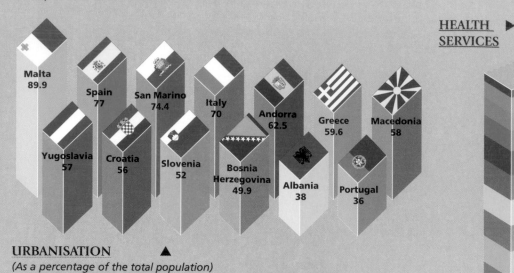

URBANISATION ▲
(As a percentage of the total population)

Malta 89.9
Spain 77
San Marino 74.4
Italy 70
Andorra 62.5
Greece 59.6
Macedonia 58
Yugoslavia 57
Croatia 56
Slovenia 52
Bosnia Herzegovina 49.9
Albania 38
Portugal 36

HEALTH SERVICES ►

DOCTORS	HOSPITAL BEDS
(Per 1000 inhabitants)	
1.60 Albania	5.47
1.54 Andorra	1.70
1.96 Bosnia-Herzegovina	5.63
2.02 Croatia	6.21
3.91 Spain	4.29
3.82 Greece	3.30
5.14 Italy	6.76
2.32 Macedonia	5.35
2.39 Malta	5.66
2.76 Portugal	3.94
2.40 San Marino	5.96
1.48 Slovenia	5.92
2.29 Yugoslavia	5.27

MAJOR URBAN AREAS
(Number of inhabitants)

Madrid	4 935 000
Barcelona	4 719 200
Milan	3 926 000
Rome	3 770 200
Athens	3 369 424
Naples	3 037 800
Turin	2 236 400
Valencia	2 126 700
Seville	1 554 500
Bari	1 540 300
Belgrade	1 440 000

TOURIST VISITORS
(Per year, in millions)

Spain	43
Italy	34.8
Greece	10.2
Portugal	10.1
Andorra	8.9
Croatia	3.8
San Marino	3.3
Malta	1.1
Slovenia	0.7
Yugoslavia	0.3
Bosnia	0.1
Albania	0.05

KEY CONSUMER GOODS ►
(Per 1000 inhabitants)

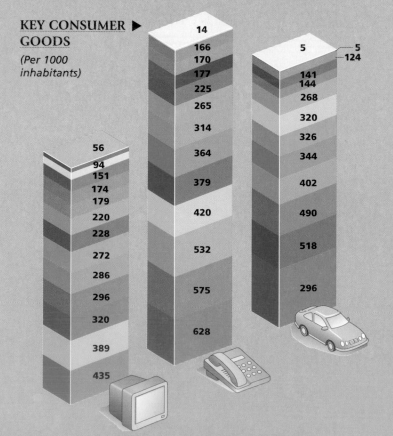

14
166
170
177
225
265
314
364
379
420
532
575
628

5
5
124
141
144
268
320
326
344
402
490
518
296

56
94
151
174
179
220
228
272
286
296
320
389
435

1.60 Albania	5.47
1.54 Andorra	1.70
1.96 Bosnia-Herzegovina	5.63
2.02 Croatia	6.21
3.91 Spain	4.29
3.82 Greece	3.30
5.14 Italy	6.76
2.32 Macedonia	5.35
2.39 Malta	5.66
2.76 Portugal	3.94
2.40 San Marino	5.96
1.48 Slovenia	5.96
2.29 Yugoslavia	5.27

Athens: doing battle with the *nefos*

Every morning, Athenians cast their eyes up to the sky and consider their prospects. If the colour is a tell-tale yellowish-brown, they can fear the worst. This is the *nefos*, meaning 'cloud' – but it is also the name for the pungent cocktail of Athens' atmospheric pollution, primarily nitrogen dioxide. The effects are aggravated by 1.7 million private cars, the bowl-like catchment area formed by the surrounding hills, and high summer temperatures. The *nefos* causes stinging eyes, pounding headaches, nausea, respiratory problems, even cardiac arrest. Various measures have been taken to reduce air pollution over the past two decades. The city authorities have campaigned to replace old vehicles, improve petrol quality and introduce catalytic converters. Public transport systems are being developed to relieve traffic pressure. According to some reports, the amount of air pollution is already 30 per cent lower than in 1990.

Index

Page numbers in *italics* denote illustrations. The letter and number references in brackets are the co-ordinates for places in the map section, p. 140-147.

Abril, Victoria *121*
Abruzzo National Park 43
Accidental Death of an Anarchist 119
Achilleion *61*
Achilles *19*
Acropolis 108, *108*
Adriatic 93, 107
Aegean Sea *13*, *17*, 34
Aeschylus 18
Agnelli, Giovanni *134*, 137
Agnelli family 134
Agnelli Foundation 134
Agora 108
Aiguës Tortes National Park *15*, 43, 141 (F5)
Akrotiri 129
Albacete 140 (E9)
Albania 59, *59*, 83, 153
    migrants from *56*, 57
    statistics 149
Alcácer do Sal 129
Alcalá de Henares 140 (D7)
Alcázar of Seville 86, 126, *126*
Alcobaça monastery 127
Alexander the Great 19
Alfa-Romeo 137, *137*
Alfonso I of Portugal 127
Alfonso XII of Spain, monument to *88*
Alfonso XIII of Spain 28
Algarve 33, 44, 60, 64
Algeciras 140 (C11)
Alhambra *24*, 87, *87*
Alicante *50*, 141 (E9)
Alicudi 145 (M9)
Almeria 51, 140 (D11)
Almodóvar, Pedro 120, *121*
Almohads, Great Mosque of *87*
alphabet 23
Alps 20, 42, 43, *58*
    Dinaric 45, 143 (N4)
    Julian *9*, *58*, 142 (L1)
Altamira, caves *11*
Ancona 142 (L4)
Andalucia, cities of 86-87
Andorra 153
    statistics 148
Andorra-la-Vella 141 (F5)
Angelico, Fra 94
Angelopoulos, Theo 121

animals 35, 41, 43
Annaud's, Jean-Jacques 120
Antonioni, Michelangelo 120
Aosta, Valle d' 142 (I2)
Apennines 40, 43, 142 (K4)
Apollo *17*, 34, 109, *109*
Apollo Belvedere 123
aqueduct, Segovia *21*
Aragón 37, *37*
Aran, Vall d' *8*, 141 (F5)
Arbatax Peninsula *35*, 142 (K8)
archaeology 129
architecture:
    church 127
    modern 65, *65*
Areao *54*
Ariosto, Ludovico 105
Aristophanes 18
Arkhanes 48, 147 (R12)
Armani, Giorgio *131*, 132, 133
Arno, River *94*
art 122-5
    portraits of Spain 125, *125*
    Venetian 124, *124*
Artemis 34
art galleries 122-3
Asclepios 109
Assisi 142 (L4)
Athanasios, Saint 128
Athena 108, *109*
Athens 18-19, 108, *108*, 122, 147 (Q10)
    pollution 154
Athos, Mount 128, *128*, 146 (R7)
Augustus, Emperor 21
Austro-Hungarian empire 28, 80
Aventine Hill *101*
Ayion Oros 128
azulejos tile work 64, *64*

bacalhau 55
Bacchus 95
Badajoz 140 (B9)
Badalona 141 (G6)
Balearic Islands 78-79, 141 (G8)
Balenciaga, Cristobal 133

Balikesir 146 (S8)
Balkans 23, 80-83
    capitals 110-11
    migrants from 57
Balkan Wars 27, 152
Bandirma 146 (S7)
Banja Luka 143 (N3)
Baños de Sierra Alhamilla 39
Banquet of Antony and Cleopatra 124
Bar 143 (O5)
Barakaldo 140 (D4)
Barbagia 35
Barcelona 65, *73*, 85, 89, *89*, *115*, 123, 141 (G6)
Barcelona, FC 76
Bari 143 (N6)
Barillo, Pietro 136
Baron in the Trees 119
Barreiro 140 (A9)
Basile, Ernesto 91
Basque region 68, *68*
bears, brown 43
Belafonte, Harry 116
Belgrade 29, 82, 83, *83*, 111, *111*, 143 (P3)
Bellini, Giovanni 124, *124*
Bellini, Vincenzo 118
Benedetti family 134
Benetton 133, *133*
Ben Hur 120
Benigni, Roberto 121
Berat 146 (O7)
Bergamo 143 (J2)
Berganza, Teresa 118
Berlusconi, Silvio 74, *134*
Bernini, Gian Lorenzo 85, 98, *99*
Bertolucci, Bernardo 120
Bicycle Thieves 120
Bihac 143 (M3)
Bilbao 65, *65*, 68, 122, *123*, 140 (D4)
birds 43
Bitola 146 (P6)
Bizet, Georges 117
Bjelovar 143 (N2)
Black Shirts 28, *28*
Blagoevgrad 146 (Q5)
Blanco, Miguel Angel 68
Bled, Lake *9*, 142 (M1)
Blood Wedding 119
Blow-Up 120
Boabdil, King 87

Bocca della Verità *102*
Boeotia, figurine *16*
Bofill, Ricardo 65
Bologna 27, *70*, 142 (K3)
Bolzano 142 (K1)
Bor 146 (Q3)
Borba *53*
Borghese, Cardinal Scipione *102*
Borghese, Villa *102*
Borghese Gardens *102*
Borsalino *132*
Bosnia 80
    statistics 149, 152
    war in 57, *80*, 81, 82, *82*
Bosnia-Herzegovina 81
Bossi, Umberto 69
Botticelli, Sandro 94, 105, 134
Brac *114*, 143 (N4)
Bramante *104*, 105
Brcko 143 (O3)
Brescia 142 (K2)
Brunelleschi, Filipo 94
Bruno, Giordano 99
Brutus 21
bullfighting 72, *73*, 75, *75*
Buñol 51, *51*, 141 (E8)
Buñuel, Luis 120
Burano 142 (L2)
Burgos 140 (D5)
Byzantine empire 22, 23, 127, 128

Caballé, Montserrat 118
Cabral, Pedro Álvares 27
Cacak 143 (P4)
Cadiz 117, 140 (B11)
Cagliari 144 (J8)
Calatayud 140 (E6)
Calatrava, Santiago 65, *85*
Caldeirão, Serra do 44
Callas, Maria 118, *118*, 135
Calvino, Italo 119
Calypso *13*, *106*
Camogli 142 (J3)
Camorro 91
Campbell, Naomi *133*
Canaletto 124, *124*
Cantabrian Mountains 43
Cape St Vincent 44, *44*
Capitoline Hill 98

Capodimonte factory 126
Capodimonte palace 126, *126*
Capri *40*, *61*, 91, 143 (M7)
Capriccioli Peninsula *15*, 142 (J6)
Carambola, El, treasures *20*
Caravaggio, Michelangelo da *102*
Carmen 117
carnation revolution *29*
Carnival 114, *115*
Carrara 53, 142 (K3)
Carreras, José 118
Cartagena 141 (E10)
Caruso, Enrico 118
Carvalho, Pepe *119*
Cassius 21
Castellón de la Plana 141 (E8)
Castille 88
catacombs, paintings in 22
Catalan language 89
Catalonia 89
Catania 145 (M10)
Catanzaro 145 (N9)
Catholicism 23, 27, 66-67
cave dwellings 87
caves:
    Altamira *11*
    Cueva de Nerja *10*
Celje 143 (M1)
ceramics:
    Greek *18*, *19*, *129*
    Moorish *24*
Cerruti 132
Charles III of Spain 126
Charles V, Holy Roman Emperor 106, 124
Chetniks 29
Chiana, Val di 36
Chianciano Terme 39
Chianti region 36
    wine 49, *49*
Chien Andalou, Un 120
Chios 147 (R9)
Christianity 22
    churches 127, *127*
    Crusades 25, 106
    Eastern Orthodox 22, 23, 67
    festivals 66, *66*, 67

Protestants 66
Roman Catholicism 23, 27, 66-67
wine and 49
churches 127, *127*
Churriguera family 127
Cinecittà 120
cinema 120-1
film festivals 121
Cinema Paradiso 121
Cirque de Sobavedo, lake 8
Cistercians 127
city-states 17
Ciudad Encantada 37, *37*
Ciutadella 141 (G8)
civilisation, Greek 16-19
Cleopatra 21
climate 150-1
cod fishing 55
coffee, Italian 71
Coimbra 129, 140 (A7)
Colosseum 101
Columbus, Christopher 26
Comino 145 (M11)
Communists 28, 29, 59, 80
Como *9*, 142 (J2)
Conimbriga 129
Connery, Sean *119*
Conquistadores 27
Constantine, Emperor 22, *22*
Constantinople 22, 25
consumer goods 154
Contarini-Fasan, Palazzo *93*
Conte, Paolo 116, *116*
Córdoba 24, 86, *86*, 87, *117*, 140 (C10)
Corfu 61, *61*, 143 (O8)
Corinth 147 (Q10)
Corinth, Gulf of 147 (Q9)
cork 52
Corleone 144 (L10)
corrida 75
on horseback 75, *75*
Cortés, Hernán 27
Cortés, Joaquin 117
Corunna 140 (A4)
Cosenza 143 (N8)
Costa Brava 60
Costa del Sol 60
Costa-Gavras 121
Costa Smeralda 142 (J6)
Crete *10*, 19, 129, 147 (R12)
Croatia 81
statistics 149, 152
Cronos 17
Crusades 25, 106
Cuenca 140 (D7)

Cueva de Nerja *10*
Cyclades *13*, 34, 60
Cyprus 60, 106
Cyril, Saint 22, *22*

Da Crema, Roberto 74
Dalí, Salvador 120, 123
Dalmatia 33, 45, 60, 143 (N4)
dance:
festivals 114
flamenco 72-73, *73*, 117, *117*
sevillana 117
syrtaki 117
Dante Alighieri 27, 94
Danube, River *151*
Dayton peace accord 82
Death in Venice 120
Decameron 120
Deià 79
Delos 34, 53, 129, 147 (R10)
Delphi 109, *109*, 129, 147 (Q9)
design, Italian 132, *132*
detention camps 81, *81*
Dias, Bartolomeu 26, 53
Dinaric Alps 45, 143 (N4)
Dionysus 95
Discreet Charm of the Bourgeoisie 120
di Sica, Vittorio 120
Doboj 143 (O3)
Dolce Vita, La 102, 120
Dolomites 33, *42*, 43, *43*, 142 (K1)
dolphins 41
Domingo, Plácido 118
Domitian, Emperor *98*
Donastia-San Sebastián 140 (E4)
Donatello 94
Donizetti, Gaetano 118
donkeys *13*, *34*
Dorians 17
Dubrovnik 81, 107, *107*, 143 (O5)
Durrës 143 (O6)

earthquakes 38, 39, 90, 111
Ebro, River 37
Eco, Umberto *119*
Ekberg, Anita *102*
Elbasan 146 (P6)
Elche 141 (E9)
Lady of *19*
Elgin, Lord 108
Elisabeth of Austria, Empress *61*

emigration 56-57
Encantants, Sierra dels *15*, 43
Eolian Islands 145 (M9)
Epidauros 53, 109
Erechtheion 108
Ermoúpolis 34
Escorial 88, 126, *126*
Estense, Castello 105, *105*
Estrela, Serra da 140 (B7)
Estremoz 53, 140 (B9)
ETA 68
ethnic cleansing 81, 83, 152
Etna 7, 33, 39, *39*, 145 (M10)
Etruscans 20
tomb painting *20*
EU (was European Economic Community) 29
Common Fisheries Policy 54
Euripedes 18
Eva Kynourias *129*
Evans, Arthur 129
exploration, voyages of 26, *26*
Expulsion of Heliodorus from the Temple 97

fado 72, *72*, 73
Falcone, Giovanni 77, *77*
Falla, Manuel de 117
Fall of the Giants 105
farming 55
Faro 140 (B10)
Fascists 28, *28*, 77
fashion:
Italian 132
ready-to-wear 133
Father was Away on Business 121
Fátima 67, 140 (A8)
Our Lady of *66*
fauna 35, 41, 43
Faun, House of the *95*
Fellini, Federico *102*, 120, *120*
Fermo *33*, 142 (L4)
Ferrara 104, 105, *105*, 142 (K3)
Ferrari, Enzo 137
Ferrari cars 137, *137*
Ferré, Gianfranco 133
festivals 114-15
cinema 121
Fiat 134, 137
Fier 143 (O7)
Fiesole 94
Figo, Luis 76
Figueres *122*, 123, 141 (G5)

Filicudi 145 (M9)
film festivals 121
Fiorelli, Giuseppe 129
First World War 28, *28*, 80, 82
fishing 54
flamenco 72-73, *73*, 117, *117*
flora 41
Florence 27, 94, *94*, 121, 122, 134, *134*, 142 (K4)
Fo, Dario 119
Foggia 143 (M6)
Foia peak 44
food 70-72, 73
at festivals 115
pasta 136, *136*
football 76
Ford, Charlotte *135*
forests 151
Forlí 142 (L3)
Formentera 78, 79, *79*, 141 (F9)
Forum, Rome *100*
Forza Italia 74, *134*
Fossanova, Abbey of 127, 142 (L6)
Foster, Norman 65
Francesca, Piero della 36
Franco, General Francisco 28, *28*, 29, 68, 88, 89
Franz Ferdinand, Archduke, assassination 28, *28*, 80
Fronteira, Quinta do Marquês de *90*
fruits 50-51
Frusades 25

Gaia 17
Galileo Galilei 94
Gallone, Carmine *120*
Garibaldi, Giuseppe 27, *27*
Garona, river, source 8
Garzoni, Villa *36*
Gaudí, Antoní 65, 89, *89*
Gehry, Frank 65, 122, *123*
Gelon 17
Generalife, gardens of 87
General of the Dead Army 119
Gennargentu, Monti del 35
Genoa 25, 142 (J3)
geology 151
Ghiberti, Lorenzo 94
Gibellina 144 (L10)
Gibellina Nuova 38
Gibraltar 24
Gibraltar, Strait of 7, 41, 140 (C12)
Gijón 140 (C4)

Giorgione 124
Giotto 39, 94, 105
Giralda of Seville 86, *87*
Giulia, Villa *102*, 122
Gjirokastër 146 (P7)
global warming 41
gods, Greek 17
Golden Age 86
gold mines *13*
Gonzago family 105
Gorazde 143 (O4)
Gospic 143 (M3)
Goya y Lucientes, Francisco José de 125, *125*
Gozo *13*, *106*, 145 (M11)
Granada 24, *24*, 87, *87*, 140 (D10)
Gran Paradiso National Park 142 (I2), *151*
Graves, Robert 79
Greco, El 125, *125*
Greece, statistics 148
Greek civilisation 16-19
gross domestic product 153
Guadalajara 140 (D7)
Guadalquivir, River 87
Guara, Sierra de 37, 141 (E5)
Guardi, Francesco 124
Gucci 132, 133
Guernica 88
Guernica y Luno 140 (D4)
Guggenheim Museum 65, *65*, 122, *123*
Gulbenkian, Calouste 123
gypsies 117

Hadrian, Emperor *100*
Hagar Qim 129
Hamilcar Barca 89
Hannibal 19, 20
health services 154
Hector *19*
Heraklion 147 (R12)
Herculaneum 122, 129, 143 (M7)
Hermes 17
Herodes Atticus, villa of *129*
Herodotus 19
Hitler, Adolf 28
Homer 16, 40
horses:
bullfighting on 75, *75*
racing, Palio 115, *115*
Hospitalet de Llobregat, L' 141 (G6)
houses, traditional 64, *64*
Hoxha, Enver 29, 59, 111

Huelva 140 (B10)
Huerta de Valencia 50, 51
Huesca 37, 141 (E5)
Hvar 45

Iberians 19, 20
ibex 43
Ibiza 78, 79, 79, 141 (F9)
Ibiza City 79
icons 67, 67
Idrija 142 (M1)
If this is a Man 119
IFOR 82, 82
Iglesias, Enrique 116
Iglesias, Julio 116, 116
Iglesias, Julio, Jr 116
Iliad 16
infant mortality 152
Innocenti 137
Inquisition 27
International Brigades 29
International War Tribes
 Tribunal 83
internment camps 81, 81
irrigation 50, 51, 150
Irún 68, 140 (E4)
Isidore, Saint 88
Islam 66, 113
 conquest by 23-24
 enforced conversion 27
 gardens 87
 prisoners of war 81
Italy:
 cars and driving 137
 migrants from 56, 56,
 57, 57
 north/south divide 69
 pasta 136, 136
 statistics 148
Ithaca 16

Jaén 140 (D10)
Jerez de la Frontera 49,
 117, 140 (B11)
jewellery, gold 20
Jews 27, 66
João V of Portugal 126
João VI of Portugal 126
John of the Cross, Saint
 66
Jones, Quincy 116
Juan Carlos of Spain 29
Julian Alps 9, 58, 142
 (L1)
Julius Caesar 21
Justinian I, Emperor 23

Kadaré, Ismail 119, 119
Karlovac 143 (M2)
Karst 45
Kastro, valley of 13

Kavajë 143 (O6)
Kavála 146 (R7)
Keats, John 99
Kennedy, Jackie 135
KFOR 83
khamsin 40
Khíos 64
Kikinda 143 (P2)
Kirby, David 133
Knights Hospitalier 25
Knights of St John 25,
 106, 106
Knossos 48, 129, 147
 (R12)
Korçë 146 (P7)
Korcula 45, 143 (N5)
Kornati Archipelago 45,
 143 (M4)
Kosovo 83
 battle of 25
 war in 57, 59, 83, 111,
 152
Kosovo Liberation Army
 (KLA) 83
Kosovska Mitrovica 146
 (P5)
Kragujevac 146 (P3)
Kranj 142 (M1)
Kranjska Gora 58, 142
 (L1)
Kras 45
Krk 45
Krujë 59
Kuçovë 146 (O7)
Kukës 83, 146 (P5)
Kumanovo 146 (P5)
Kusturica, Emir 121, 121

Lagos 44, 44, 140 (A10)
Lake Bled 9, 142 (M1)
Lake Como 9, 142 (J2)
Lake Maggiore 142 (J2)
Lake of Cirque de
 Sobavedo 8
lakes, largest 151
Lambretta 137
Landini, Taddeo 99
landscape 150-1
Landscape in the Mist 121
Larisa 146 (Q8)
Last Emperor 120
Last Supper 134
Last Tango in Paris 120
Latina 142 (L6)
law, Roman 22
Leaning Tower of Pisa
 105, 105
Lecce 143 (O7)
Ledda, Gavino 35
leisure 70-73
León 140 (C5)
Leonardo da Vinci 27, 94,
 134

Leone, Sergio 51
Lepanto, Battle of 25, 106
Leskovac 146 (P5)
Levi, Primo 119
life expectancy 152
Lingotto 134
Lipari islands 38, 39, 145
 (M9)
Lisbon 65, 70, 72, 85, 85,
 90, 90, 123, 140 (A9)
 World Fair 65
literature 119
Livanos, Stavros 135
Livno 143 (N4)
Livorno 142 (K4)
Ljubljana 58, 110, 110,
 142 (M1)
Lleida 141 (F6)
Logroño 140 (D5)
Lombard League 69, 69
Lombards 23
Lorca, Federica Garcia
 117, 119
Lorenzo the Magnificent
 134, 134
Lorraine, coalfields 57
Loyola, Saint Ignatius 66
Lucca 94
Lucia, Paco de (Paco
 Peña) 117, 117
Lugano 142 (J1)
Lushnjë 143 (O7)
Lykabettos 108

Macedonia 57, 81
 statistics 148
Machiavelli, Niccolò 27,
 94
McPherson, Elle 133
Madeira 141 (A1)
*Madonna and Child with
 saints 124*
Madrid 65, 75, 76, 88,
 88, 122-3, 140 (D7)
Mafia 59, 69, 77, 77, 91
Mafra 126
Magellan, Ferdinand 27
Magerit 88
Maggiore, Lake 142 (J2)
Mahón 79, 141 (H8)
Majorca 60, 78-79, 141
 (G8)
Málaga 75, 140 (C11)
Mallos de Riglos, Los 37,
 37
Malta 106, 106, 129, 145
 (M12)
 cross 106
 Knights of St John 25,
 106, 106
 statistics 148
Mantegna, Andrea 105,
 127

Mantua 104, 105, 105,
 127, 142 (K2)
Manzanares 140 (D9)
maquis 35
Maradona, Diego 76
Marbella 60, 60, 140
 (C11)
marble 53
 quarries 53, 53
Maribor 143 (M1)
Marinatos, Spyridon 129
Mark the Evangelist, Saint
 93
Martini, Simone 36
Mastroianni, Marcello
 120
meats, preserved 55
Medici, Cosimo I 134
Medici, Lorenzo the
 Magnificent 134, 134
Medici family 94, 134
Mediterranean Sea 40-41,
 40, 41
 coastal development
 41, 41
 flora and fauna 41
 pollution 40, 40, 41,
 41
 volcanoes 38, 38
Mediterraneo 121
megaliths 79
Meier, Richard 65
melon growing 51
meltemi 40
Memphis group 132
Mendini, Alessandro 132
Meninas, Las (Picasso)
 123
Meninas, Las (Velásquez)
 125
Messina 121, 145 (M9)
Mestre 142 (L2)
Metaxis, Joannis 28
Metéora monasteries 109,
 146 (P8)
Methodius, Saint 22, 22
Mezquita 86, 86
Michelangelo Buonarroti
 27, 53, 94, 97, 105, 134
migration 56-57
Míkonos 34, 60
Milan 27, 69, 142 (J2)
 fashion and design
 132, 132
Milan, AC 76
Milosevic, Slobodan 83,
 111
Minoans 16-17, 16
Minorca 78, 79, 79, 141
 (H8)
Minos 19
Minotaur 19, 19
Miró, Joan 123
Missoni 132, 133, 133

mistral 40
Mistras 127, 147 (Q10)
Modena 137, 142 (K3)
Mohammed V of
 Granada 126
Monaco 41
monasteries of Mount
 Athos 128, 128
Monchique, Serra de 44,
 140 (A10)
Monsanto 114-15
Montalbán, Manuel
 Váquez 119
Montalcino 142 (K4)
Montenegro 83
Monte Pellegrino 91
Monte San Savino 36
Monteverdi, Claudio 105,
 118
Monti del Gennargentu 35
Monza 142 (J2)
Moors 44, 86
Mostar 80, 82, 82, 143
 (N4)
mountaineering 43
mountains 42-43
 highest 151
Mount Athos 128, 128
Mount Parnassus 109
Mount Pentelicon 53
Mouskouri, Nana 116,
 116
Movida 88
Murcia 141 (E10)
museums 122-3
music:
 fado 72, 72, 73
 singing 116, 116
Muslims *see* Islam
Mussolini, Benito 28, 28,
 56, 77, 98, 120
Mycenae 122, 129, 147
 (Q10)
 mask 122
Mycenaeans 17
Mykonos 147 (R10)
Mysteries, Villa of the 95,
 95
myths and legends, Greek
 16, 19, 40

Nafpaktos 147 (P9)
Name of the Rose 119, 120
Naples 22, 39, 71, 76, 91,
 91, 95, 122, 126, 143
 (M7)
Napoleon Bonaparte 27,
 107
Nasrids 87
National Parks 42-43
 Abruzzo 43
 Aigües Tortes 15, 43,
 141 (F5)

Gran Paradiso 142 (I2), 151
Ordesa 37, *42*, 43, 141 (F5)
Stelvio 42-43, 142 (K1)
NATO 81, 82, 83, 111
navigators 26-27, *26*
Naxos 147 (R10)
Nazaré *54*, 140 (A8)
nefos 154, *154*
Nelson, Willie 116
Nevada, Sierra *15*, 140 (D10)
Niarchos, Stavros 108, 135, *135*
Niksic *80*, 143 (O5)
Nis 146 (P4)
Northern League 69
Novara 142 (J2)
Novi Sad 143 (O2)
Novo Mesto *58*, 143 (M2)

O'Brian, Patrick 79
obsidian 39
Octavian, Emperor 21
Odysseus *13*, *16*, 61
Odyssey 16
Ogorsko *82*
Ogygia *13*
Olhão 64, 140 (B10)
olive oil 52
olives, growing *47*, 52, *52*
Olympia 129, 146 (P10)
Olympic Games 18
  Barcelona 65, *89*
  Sarajevo 110
Olympus, Mount 146 (Q7)
  gods of 17
omphalos 109
Onassis, Aristotle 108, 135, *135*
opera 118
Oporto (Porto) 48, *48*, 140 (A6)
  wine 48
Oracle *13*
oranges, growing *50*
Órcia, valley of *36*
Ordesa National Park 37, *42*, 43, 141 (F5)
Orense 140 (B5)
Orfeo 105, 118
Oristano 142 (J8)
Orlando Furioso 105
Orosei, Golfo di *35*, 142 (J7)
Osijek 143 (O2)
Othello 93
Otok Hvar 45
Ottoman Empire 25, 27, 28, 80

Oviedo 140 (C4)
owl, Eurasian eagle *42*

Padania, Republic of 69
Padre Padrone 35
Padua 104, 105, 142 (K2)
paintings:
  catacomb *22*
  cave *11*
  Christian *22*
  tomb *20*
palaces 126
Palatine Hill *98*
Palazzo Contarini-Fasan *93*
Palermo 77, 91, *91*, 144 (L9)
Palio 115, *115*
Palma 78, 79, 141 (G8)
Pamplona 140 (E5)
Pancevo 143 (P3)
Panevéggio, Parco Naturale 43
Pantheon *100*
Paola, Sister *74*
Paracin 146 (P4)
Parco Naturale Panevéggio 43
Paredes, Marisa *121*
Parma 142 (K3)
Parnasus, Mount 109
Páros 53
Parthenon 108, *108*
Pasolini, Pier Paolo 120
pasta 136, *136*
Patra 147 (P9)
Patroclus *19*
patronage 134
Paul, Saint *106*
Pavarotti, Luciano 118
Pavelic, Ante 28
Pec 143 (P5)
Pedro I of Castile 126
Pellegrino, Monte 91
Peña, Paco (Paco de Lucia) 117, *117*
Penelope *16*
Pentelicon, Mount 53
Pérignon, Dom Pierre 48
Perugia 142 (L4)
Pesaro *118*
Pescara 142 (M5)
Peter, Saint 96
Peterlin, Anton 58
Phidias 108
Philip II of Macedonia 19
Philip II of Spain 27, 88, 124, 126, *126*
Philip, Prince, Duke of Edinburgh 61
philosophers, Greek 18
Piacenza 142 (J2)
Piaggio 137

Piano, Renzo 134
Picasso, Pablo 88, 123, *123*
Pico d'Aneto 8
Pietrasanta *53*
Pintoricchio 36
Piraeus 108
Pirandello, Luigi 119
Pirot 146 (Q4)
Pisa 94, 104, 105, *105*, 142 (K4)
Pitti Palace 94, 134
Pizarro, Francisco 27
Plato 18
Pliny the Elder 95
Pliny the Younger 95
Ploiesti 146 (S3)
Plovdiv 146 (R5)
Podgorica 143 (O5)
Poggio alle Mura, Villa *36*
pollution, of sea 40, *40*, 41, *41*, 92
Polo, Marco 25, 45, 136
Pombal, Marquês de, statue of *90*
Pompeii 39, 95, *95*, 122, 129, 143 (M7)
Pompey 99
Ponti, Gio 132
population 152
  urbanisation 154
  working, distribution 153
port (wine) 48
Porta, Giacomo della 99
Porto (Oporto) 48, *48*, 140 (A6)
Porto Marghera 92
Porto Torrès 142 (J7)
Portugal, statistics 149
Poseidon *17*, 108
Postino, Il (The Postman) 121, *121*
Postojna 142 (M2)
pottery *see* ceramics
Pozarevac 146 (P3)
Prato 142 (K4)
Pregl, Fritz 58
prickly pear *35*
Pristina 146 (P5)
Prizren 146 (P5)
Procida 64
Puccini, Giacomo 118
Puerto Bañus 60
Puglia 64, *64*
Pula 142 (L3)
pumice 39
Punic Wars 20
Pyrenees 8, 37, 42, 43, 61, 141 (F5)
Pyrgí 64, 147 (S9)
Pyrgos *115*, 147 (P10)
Pythagoras 18
Pythia 109

Quarteira 60
Quartesi family 134
Quinn, Anthony 117

Radford, Michael 121
Ragusa 107
Rainy Taxi 123
Ramazzotti, Eros 116, *116*
Rape of Proserpina 99
Raphael 27, 36, 97, 105
Ravenna 127, 142 (L3)
Reconquista 24-25, *24*, 27
Red Shirts 27
Reggio di Calabria 145 (M9)
relief 151
religion 66-67
  festivals 66, *66*, 67, 114
  see also Christianity; Islam; Jews
Remus 98
Renaissance 27
  High, art 124-5
Rethymno 147 (R12)
  lighthouse *41*
Rhodes 25, 106, 129, 147 (S11)
Rigoletto 118
Rijeka 142 (M2)
Rimini 60, 121, 142 (L3)
Risorgimento 27
rivers, longest 151
Rocio, El, pilgrimage of 67
Rodrigues, Amália 72
Roger II 23
Roman empire 20-23
  law 22
Romanies 57
Romano, Giulio 105, *105*
Rome 21, 27, 53, *71*, 76, 85, 98-103, 122, 136, 142 (L6)
Rome, Open City 120
Romulus 98
Romulus Augustulus, Emperor 23
Ross, Diana 116
Rossellini, Roberto 120
Rossini, Gioacchino 118
Rucellai family 134

Sabadell 141 (G6)
Sabbioneta *104*, 105, 142 (K3)
Sacromonte 87
St Veronica 125
St Vincent, Cape 44, *44*
Salamanca 127, *127*, 140 (C7)

Salazar, Antonio 28
Salerno 121, 143 (M7)
Salvatore, Gabriele 121
Salvi, Nicolò *102*
Samaria Gorge *10*
San Daniele del Friuli 142 (L1)
San Gennaro, catacomb paintings 22
San Marino, statistics 148
San Martino, Certosa di *91*
San Savino, Monte 36
San Sebastián 121, 127
San Vicenzo 39
Sant' Angelo, Castel *98*
Sant Antoni de Portmany 79
Santander 140 (D4)
Santarém 140 (A8)
Santiago de Compostela 37, 67, 140 (A5)
Santorini *see* Thíra
Saragossa 24, 141 (E6)
Sarajevo 80, 81, 110, *110*, 143 (O4)
Sardinia *15*, 35, *35*, 55, *55*, 136, 142 (J7)
Sassari 142 (J7)
Satyricon 120
Savona 142 (J3)
Schliemann, Heinrich 129
Schumacher, Michael *137*
Sciacca 69, 144 (L10)
Scipio l'Africano (The Defeat of Hannibal) 120
Scuole 123
seafarers 26, *26*
seals 41
seaweed 41, *41*
Second World War 28-29, *29*, 56, 80, 111
Segovia, aqueduct 21
Senta 143 (P2)
Serbia 83
Serbs 80-81, 82-83
Serra:
  do Caldeirão 44
  da Estrela 140 (B7)
  de Monchique 44, 140 (A10)
Setúbal 140 (A9)
Severa, Maria 72
sevillana 117
Seville 24, 67, 72-73, 86-87, *86*, *87*, 117, *126*, 140 (C10)
SFOR 82
Shakespeare, William 93
sheep farming 55, *55*
sheep shearing 55
shipowners, Greek 135
Shkoder 143 (O5)

Sibenik 143 (M4)
Sicily 19, *38*, 39, 61, 77
Siena 36, 43, 53, 94, *104*, 142 (K4)
Palio 115, *115*
Sierra:
    de Guara 37, 141 (E5)
    dels Encantants *15*
    Nevada *15*, 140 (Q7)
sierras, of Aragon 37, *37*
Sifnos *13*, 147 (R11)
Silves 44
singing 116, *116*
sirocco 40
Síros 34
Sisak 143 (N2)
Sistine Chapel 97, 105
Six Characters in Search of an Author 119
Siza, Álvaro 65
Skopje 111, *111*, 146 (P6)
Slatina 146 (R3)
slaves 27
Slovenia 58, *58*, 81
statistics 149, 152
Smederevo 143 (P3)
Smeralda, Costa 142 (J6)
Sobavedo, Cirque de, lake 8
social life 70-73
Socrates 18
Sophocles 18
Sorrento peninsula 91
Sottsass, Ettore *132*
Spain:
    languages 89
    statistics 148
Spanish Civil War 28, *28*, *29*, *29*, 56
Sparta 129, 147 (Q10)
Spezia, La 142 (J3)
spice trade 25
Split 143 (N4)
Srebrenica 81, 82
Stefan, Jozef 58
Stelvio National Park 42-43, 142 (K1)
Strada, La 120
strawberries 51
Stromboli:
    island 145 (M9)
    volcano 33, 38, *39*
Strozzi family 134
Subotica 143 (O1)
Swiss Guard 97, *97*
Syracuse 145 (M10)
syrtaki 117

Tacones Lejanos (High Heels) 121
tapas 72, 73, *73*
Taranto 143 (N7)
Tarasa 141 (F6)

Tarquinia 122
Tarragona 141 (F6)
taulas 79
Taviani brothers 35
Teatro Olympico *104*, 105
television, Italian 74, *74*
Teresa, Mother 66
Terni 142 (L5)
That Obscure Object of Desire 120
Theodorakis, Mikis 116, 117
Theresa of Avila, Saint 66
Thessaloníki 146 (Q7)
Thíra (Santorini) *34*, 38, 39, 129, *129*, 147 (R11)
    fresco *16*
Third of May 1808 125
Thucydides 18
Thyssen-Bornemisza collection 88, 123
Tiber, River 98
Tiberius, Emperor 21
Tiepolo, Giovanni Battista 124
tiles, *azulejos* 64, *64*
Tínos 147 (R10)
Tirana *59*, 111, *111*, 143 (O6)
Titans 17
Titian 124
Tito (Josep Broz) 29, *29*, 80, 83
Toledo 24, 140 (C8)
tomatoes:
    festival *51*
    growing *50*, 51
Tordesillas, Treaty of 26
Tornatore, Giuseppe 121
Tortosa 141 (F7)
Toscani, Oliviero 133
tourism 60-61
Trajan, Emperor 21, *21*, *102*
    Forum *102*
tramontana 40
Traviata, La 118
Trentino 43
Trento 142 (K1)
Trevi Fountain *102*
Treviso 142 (L2)
Trieste 121, 142 (L2)
Trogir 143 (N4)
Troisi, Massimo *121*
Trojan War 16, 17
trompe l'oeil 127, *127*
Troy 129
trulli houses 64, *64*
Tudjman, Franjo 81
tuna fishing *55*
Turandot 118
Turin 76, 121, 134, 137, 142 (I2)
Turner, Tina 116

Tuscany 33, 36, *36*, 61, 136
Tuzla 81, 143 (O3)
Tyrrhenian Sea 36, 38, 142 (L7)

Ubeda *150*
Udine 142 (L1)
Ulysses' Gaze 121
Underground 121, *121*
unemployment rates 153
United Nations 81, 82, *82*
Uranus 17
urbanisation 154
Urbino 104, *104*, 105, 142 (L4)

Val di Chiana 36
Valencia 114, 141 (E8)
    Huerta de 50
Valentino 132, 133, *133*
Vall d'Aran 8, 141 (F5)
Valladolid 121, 140 (C6)
Valle d'Aosta 142 (I2)
Valletta 64, *106*
Varlaam, monastery of *109*
Vasari, Giorgio 134
Vasco da Gama 26, *26*
Vatican 96-97, *96-97*, 122, *123*
vegetables 50-51
Velázquez, Diego Rodriguez de Silva *123*, 125, *125*
Venice 25, *25*, 27, *40*, 45, 69, 71, *91-93*, 92-93, *118*, *118*, 121, 122, 142 (L2)
    art 124, *124*
    Biennale 92
    Carnival 114, 115
    saving 92
    Scuole 123
    winged lion 92, 93
Venice, Gulf of 142 (L2)
Verdi, Giuseppe 118
Verona 121, 142 (K2)
Veronese, Paolo 124, *124*
Verrazzano, Castello di *49*
Versace, Gianni 132, 133
Vespa 138
Vesuvius, Mount 7, 33, 38-39, 91, *91*, 95
Vettii, House of the 95
Viano do Castelo 114, *114*
Viaréggio 36
Vicenza 142 (K2)
Vigo 54, 140 (A5)
Vilamoura 60, *61*, 140 (A11)
Vila Nova de Gaia 140 (A6)

villages 64
Visconti, Luchino 120
Visegrad 143 (O4)
Visigoths 23
    art *23*
Vita è Bella, La 121
viticulture 48-49
Vitoria-Gasteiz 140 (D5)
Vlorë 143 (O7)
Vojvodina 83
volcanoes 38-39, *38-39*
Vólos 146 (Q8)
Vukovar *81*, 143 (O2)
Vulcano 38, *38*, 39

William Tell 118
windmills *34*
winds 40
wine-making 48-9
Women on the Verge of a Nervous Breakdown 120
World Health Organization 50

Yugoslavia 83
    split 80-82
    statistics 149, 152

Z (film) 121
Zadar *45*, 143 (M3)
Zagreb 110, *110*, 143 (M2)
Zamora 140 (C6)
Zara 133
Zaragosa 37
Zenica 143 (N3)
Zeus 17, *17*
Zog I, King of Albania 59
Zrenjanin 143 (P2)

Acknowledgments

Abbreviations: t = top, m = middle, b = bottom, l = left, r = right.

FRONT COVER: *View of Oporto, Portugal*: STOCK IMAGE/P. Frilet.
BACK COVER: *The Mezquita, Codoba, Spain*: HOA QUI/Ph. Body

Pages: 4/5: DIAF/B. Morandi; 6/7: COSMOS/SPL/Geospace;
8t: HOA QUI/A. Félix; 8b: RAPHO/M. Yamashita; 9: FOTOGRAM-
STONE/T.Thompson; 10l: TOP/H. Champollion; 10/11: HOA
QUI/Ph. Body; 11b: THE BRIDGEMAN ART LIBRARY/Altamira,
Spain; 12/13: SCOPE/ILES IMAGES/Ph. Bleuzen; 12b: TOP/
P. Putelat; 13t: HOA QUI/W. Buss; 14/15: RAPHO/H. Silvester;
15t: COSMOS/R. Frerck; 15b: SCOPE/J. Guillard; 16tr and bl:
G. DAGLI ORTI/Musée du Louvre, Paris; 16/17: G. DAGLI ORTI;
17t: G. DAGLI ORTI/Doc. J. Vinchon, Paris; 17br: G. DAGLI
ORTI/National Archaeological Museum, Athens; 18t: G. DAGLI
ORTI/Musée du Louvre, Paris; 18bl: G. DAGLI ORTI/
Glyptotheque, Munich; 18/19, 19br: G. DAGLI ORTI/National
Archaeological Museum, Athens; 19tr: G. DAGLI ORTI/
Archaeological Museum, Madrid; 20t: G. DAGLI ORTI/Tarquinia,
Italy; 20m: G. DAGLI ORTI/Archaeological Museum, Seville;
20b: G. DAGLI ORTI/Musée du Louvre, Paris; 21tl: G. DAGLI
ORTI/Museum of Roman Civilisation, Rome; 21bl: G. DAGLI
ORTI; 21br: G. DAGLI ORTI/Museo Archeologico Nazionale,
Naples; 22l: G. DAGLI ORTI/Cathedral Library, Vercelli;
22m: G. DAGLI ORTI/Catacombs of San Gennaro, Naples;
22r: G. DAGLI ORTI/St Mark's Monastery, Dracevo; 23tl: G. DAGLI
ORTI/Chiesa S.Maria dell'Ammiraglio o Martorana, Palermo;
23tr: G. DAGLI ORTI/Archaeological Museum, Madrid; 23m:
G. DAGLI ORTI/Cathedral Museum, Monza; 23b: G. DAGLI
ORTI/Marciana Library, Venice; 24tl: G. DAGLI ORTI/
Archaeological Museum, Madrid; 24/25: J.-M. HUPE; 24b:
G. DAGLI ORTI/San Lorenzo del Escorial, Spain; 25tr: G. DAGLI
ORTI/Musée Condé, Chantilly; 25b: G. DAGLI ORTI/Estense
Library, Modena; 26l: G. DAGLI ORTI/Marciana Library, Venice;
26m: G. DAGLI ORTI/Academy of Sciences, Lisbon; 26r:
G. DAGLI ORTI/Museum of Ancient Art, Lisbon; 27bl: G. DAGLI
ORTI/Prado, Madrid; 27br: G. DAGLI ORTI/Museum of the
Risorgimento, Turin; 28ml: G. DAGLI ORTI/*La Domenica del
Corriere*; 28mr: coll. VIOLLET; 28bm: HARLINGUE-VIOLLET;
28/29: KEYSTONE; 29t and br: coll. VIOLLET; 29mr: ANA/J.P.
Paireault; 30/31: COSMOS/Steinmetz; 32/33: SCOPE/M. Gotin;
34t: DIAF/G. Simeone; 34m: TOP/M.-J. Jarry-J.-F. Tripelon;
34b: HOA QUI/B. Pérousse; 35t: HOA QUI/J.-L. Dugast;
35m: DIAF/G. Simeone; 35b: DIAF/B. Belly; 36t: ANA/G. Cozzi;
36m: ANA/S. Cellai; 36b: DIAF/G. Simeone; 37t: FOTOGRAM-
STONE/R. Frerck; 37m: DIAF/TPC/M. Busselle; 37b: DIAF/
MARCO POLO/Hidalgo-Lopesino; 38t: TOP/Th Foto Werbung/
Architect Ludovico Quaroni; 38bl: DIAF/P. Somelet; 38/39: HOA
QUI/J. Durieux - I &V; 39t: DIAF/J. Huber; 40t: CORBIS-SYGMA/
P. Vauthey; 40b: SCOPE/M. Gotin; 41bl: HOA QUI/B. Pérousse;
41br: PHOTOCEANS/A. Rosenfeld; 42bl: HOA QUI/A. Félix;
42br: DIAF/G. Simeone; 42/43t and 43br: P. SOMBARDIER;
44ml: DIAF/Pratt-Pries; 44b: COSMOS/R. Frerck; 45t: DIAF/
G. Simeone; 45m: COSMOS/C. Sattlberger/Anzenberger; 45b:
COSMOS/WOODFIN CAMP/J. Blair; 46/47: RAPHO/M. Setboun;
48tl: R. LANDIN; 48tr: FOTOGRAM-STONE/R. Frerck;
48/49: FOTOGRAM-STONE/K. Blaxland; 49t: COSMOS/AGE;
49m: HOA QUI/Serena; 49br: GIRAUDON-ALINARI/Bargello
Museum, Florence; 50tr: MAGNUM/F. Scianna; 50ml: ANA/
S. Gutierrez; 50/51: RAPHO/G. Gerster; 51m: GAMMA/Y. Gellie;
51b: COSMOS/INTERNATIONAL ST/R. Arakaki; 52t: TOP/D. de
Neve; 52m: BIOS/Klein - Hubert; 52bl: BIOS/E. de Pazzis;
52br: ANA/S. Gutierrez; 53tr: ANA/S. Amantini; 53ml: DIAF/
Pinheira; 53b: HOA QUI/S. Grandadam; 54t: BIOS/M. Gunther;
54m: HOA QUI/H. Lesetre; 54b: HOA QUI/P. Frilet; 55t: COSMOS/
P. Boulat; 55m: DIAF/B. Morandi; 55b: COSMOS/Anzenberger -
H. Wiesenhofer; 56t: AKG/L.W. Hine; 56b: CORBIS-SYGMA/
I. Lorenc; 57t: RAPHO/M. Gantier; 57m and b: COSMOS/
MATRIX/S. Leen; 58t and b: DIAF/G. Simeone; 58m: COSMOS/
M. Béziat; 59tl: RAPHO/NETWORK/R. Hutchings; 59tr: RAPHO/
M. Setboun; 59b: RAPHO/P. Box; 60t: RAPHO/F. Le Diascorn;
60bl: DIAF/C. Moirenc; 60/61: RAPHO/H. Donnezan; 61t: DIAF/
G. Simeone; 61b: COSMOS/Anzenberger/T. Anzenberger; 62/63:
RAPHO/M. Bertinetti; 64t: COSMOS/Focus/Hoyer/Snowdon;
64bl: ANA/J. du Sordet; 64br: ANA/P. Ward; 65t: GAMMA/
E. Vandeville/Architects Francisco Javier Sàenz de Oiza, Estanislao
Pérez Pita, Emilio Esteras Martin and José Luis Estebàn Penelas;
65mr: ARCHIPRESS/L. Boegly/Architect Frank Gehry;
65bl: DIAF/G. Simeone/Architect Jean Vassord; 66t: ANA/J. du
Sordet; 66/67: ANA/S. Gutierrez; 67tl: ANA/Henneghien;
67tr: COSMOS/A. Keler; 67br: COSMOS/P. Menzel; 68t: COSMOS/
S.P.L./S. Fraser; 68m and b: COSMOS/AURORA/J. B. Pinneo;
69t: COSMOS/G. Neri/G. Arici; 69m: ASK IMAGES/L. Şechi;

69b: RAPHO/NETWORK/B. Lewis; 70tr: HOA QUI/P. de Wilde;
70m: DIAF/D. Thierry; 70bl: ASK IMAGES/P. Lages; 70/71:
COSMOS/ASPECT/G. Hellier; 71tl: HOA QUI/P. Frilet; 71tr: ASK
IMAGES/M. Cristofori; 72t: VU/Navia; 72/73: COSMOS/VISUM/
T. Rautert; 73t: VU/Ch. Garcia Rodero; 73m: RAPHO/H. Donnezan;
73b: RAPHO/H. Donnezan; 74m: COSMOS/G. Neri/A. Rotoletti;
74bl: FARABOLAFOTO/Panzariello; 74br: COSMOS/G. Neri/
M. Galbiati; 75t: ANA/P. Ward; 75m: DIAF/B. Zémor; 75b: ANA/
R. Rowan; 76t: VANDYSTADT/M. Hewitt; 76mr: VANDYSTADT/
S. Bruty; 76bl: VANDYSTADT/ALLSPORT/D. Cannon;
77tl: GAMMA/M. Sestini; 77tr: GAMMA/Guerrini; 77b: GAMMA/
G. Martorana; 78tr: DIAF/TPC/J. Miller; 78m: DIAF/J.-D. Sudres;
78b: RAPHO/B. Wassman; 79t: RAPHO/G. Gerster; 79m: DIAF/
P. Somelet; 79b: DIAF/P. Somelet; 80t: CORBIS-SYGMA/
Chandler; 80b: COSMOS/Katz/S. Nicol; 81t and b: COSMOS/
E. Dagnino; 82tl: CORBIS-SYGMA/Y. Kontos; 82m: CORBIS-
SYGMA/Chandler; 82bl and br: COSMOS/E. Dagnino; 83t:
COSMOS/Katz/F. Webb; 83b: CORBIS-SYGMA/I. Uimonen;
84/85: DIAF/G. Simeone/Architect Calatrava; 86t: TOP/J. Ducange;
86m: DIAF/Y. Travert; 86bl: HOA QUI/Ph. Body; 86/87: DIAF/
G. Simeone; 87t: DIAF/J. Kerebel; 87m: COSMOS/M. Hilgert;
88tr: HOA QUI/W. Buss; 88m: HOA QUI/Ph. Roy; 88bl: DIAF/
D. Lérault; 88br: HOA QUI/W. Buss; 89tr: FOTOGRAM-STONE/
F. Herholdt; 89mm: VANDYSTADT/B. Asset; 89mr: FOTOGRAM-
STONE; 89b: Raimon CAMPRUBI i SALA; 90tr: ARCHIPRESS/
L. Boegly; 90m and br: DIAF/G. Simeone; 90bl: DIAF/
R. Mazin/with the authorisation of the Fundação das Casas de
Fronteira e Alorna; 91tr: Ferrante FERRANTI; 91bl: RAPHO/
K. Poulsen; 91br: ANA/S. Amantini; 92tl: RAPHO/G. Sioen;
92m: DIAF/ G. Simeone; 92/93: HOA QUI/ALTITUDE/Y. Arthus-
Bertrand; 93t: DIAF/G. Simeone; 93bm: HOA QUI/F. Thomas;
93br: SCOPE/M. Gotin; 94t: DIAF/G. Simeone; 94bl: COSMOS/
WESTLIGHT/J. Zuckerman; 94bm: RAPHO/G. Sioen;
95t: G. DAGLI ORTI; 95b: ANA/S. Amantini; 96tl: COSMOS/
Gorgoni; 96bl: CORBIS-SYGMA/F. Origlia; 96/97: SCALA/Vatican
Library, Rome; 97t: SCALA/Vatican; 97br: CORBIS-SYGMA/
F. Origlia; 98/103: HOA QUI/ALTITUDE/G. A. Rossi; 98t: HOA
QUI/Ch. Vaisse; 98m: RAPHO/F. Le Diascorn/Architects Romano
- Lapadula; 98b: HOA QUI/W. Buss; 99tl: DIAF/J.-P. Langeland;
99m: DIAF/J. Huber; 99mr: HOA QUI/B. Morandi; 99b: HOA
QUI/W. Buss; 100t: DIAF/B. Morandi; 100ml: TOP/
H. Champollion; 100b: DIAF/P. Somelet; 101tl: ASK IMAGES/
K. A. de Gendre; 101tr: RAPHO/W. Buss; 101m: IMAGE BANK/
F. Ruggeri; 101b: RAPHO/L. Goldman; 102tl: DIAF/G. Simeone;
102tr: G. DAGLI ORTI/Church of San Luigi dei Francesi, Rome;
102ml: RAPHO/H. Bruhat; 102mr and b: DIAF/G. Simeone;
103t: RAPHO/Réga; 103m: TOP/H. Champollion; 103b: DIAF/
G. Simeone; 104tr: G. DAGLI ORTI/Palazzo Ducale, Urbino;
104m: SCALA; 104b: DIAF/P. Somelet; 105m: G. DAGLI ORTI/
Palazzo del Tè, Mantua; 105bl: DIAF/P. Somelet; 105br: ASK
IMAGES/M. Cristofori; 106tl: HOA QUI/Ph. Renault;
106tr: PHOTOCEANS/A. Rosenfeld; 106m: ANA/J. du Sordet;
106b: HOA QUI/W. Buss; 107m: RAPHO/M. Yamashita;
107b: DIAF/J.-P. Garcin; 108t: DIAF/C. Moirenc; 108m: RAPHO/
B. Wassman; 108b: RAPHO/G. Sioen; 109tr: G. DAGLI ORTI;
109bl and bm: COSMOS/WESTLIGHT/J. Zuckerman;
109br: COSMOS/A. Tsiaras; 110tl: CORBIS-SYGMA/J. Peck;
110m: COSMOS/G. Neri/G. Arici; 110b: DIAF/Pratt-Pries;
111t: COSMOS/MATRIX/S. Leen; 111ml: HOA QUI/Ph. Roy;
111mr: Igor Jovanov/Rex Features; 112/113: J.-M. HUPÉ;
114tr: RAPHO/G. Sioen; 114mr: RAPHO/F. Le Diascorn;
114b: HOA QUI/Ph. Bourseiller; 115tl: HOA QUI/R. Manin;
115r: RAPHO/B. Wassman; 115bl: DIAF/G. Simeone; 116tr: KIPA/
J.-F. Rault; 116mr: FARABOLAFOTO/Piro; 116bl: KIPA/D. Lefranc;
116bm: KIPA; 117ml: GAMMA/Ph. Renault; 117m: VU/C. Garcia
Rodero; 117b: GAMMA/F. Guenet; 118tl: G. DAGLI ORTI;
118bl: CORBIS-SYGMA/Collection SEGALINI; 118br: COSMOS/
G. Neri/G. Arici; 119tr: CORBIS-SYGMA/S. Bassouls;
119ml: KIPA/Gaudenti; 119mr: COSMOS/G. Neri/E. Ferorelli;
119b: KIPA/CATS/The Name of the Rose, 1986, J.-J. Annaud;
120tl: COSMOS/G. Neri; 120bl: FARABOLAFOTO/The Defeat of
Hannibal, 1938, C. Gallone; 120br: ANA/M. Durazzo/Otto e
mezzo (8¹/₂), F. Fellini and M. Mastroianni; 121ml: KIPA
Coll./High Heels, 1991, P. Almodóvar, with V. Abril and M.
Paredes, prod. Ciby 2000; 121mr: KIPA Coll./Il Postino, 1994,
with M.Troisi, prod. Cecchi Gori Group Tiger and Blue Dahlia;
121b: KIPA Coll./L. Riztovski/Underground, 1995, E. Kusturica,
Productions nocturnes; 122tl: SCOPE/Ch. Bowman/Architects
(transformation 1974) Joaquin Ros de Ramis and Alejandro
Bonaterra; 122m: G. DAGLI ORTI/National Archaeological
Museum, Athens; 122/123/124/125: L. Boegly/Architect

Frank Gehry; 123tl: G. DAGLI ORTI/Picasso Museum, Barcelona
© Estate of Picasso, Paris 2000; 123br: SCALA/Museo Pio-
Clementino, Vatican; 124t: GIRAUDON/Galleria dell'Accademia,
Venice; 124bl: GIRAUDON-ALINARI/Palazzo Labia, Venice;
124br: GIRAUDON-ALINARI/Galleria Sabauda, Turin;
125tr: G. DAGLI ORTI/Museum of Santa Cruz, Toledo; 125bl and
br: G. DAGLI ORTI/Prado, Madrid; 126tl: DIAF/G. Simeone;
126m: TOP/Ch. Sappa; 126b: ANA/P. Horree; 127tr: G. DAGLI
ORTI/Mistra, Greece; 127bl: G. DAGLI ORTI/Clerecia, Salamanca,
Spain; 127br: G. DAGLI ORTI/Palazzo Ducale, Mantua;
128tr, m and b: CORBIS-SYGMA/A. Keler; 129m: CORBIS-
SYGMA/M. Attar; 129bl: G. DAGLI ORTI; 129br: HOA QUI/
Ph. Renault; 130/131: COSMOS/Steinmetz; 132tr: ARCHIPRESS/
L. Boegly; 132bl: COSMOS/G. Neri/L. Carra; 132br: COSMOS/
G. Neri; 133ml: COSMOS/G. Neri/U. Battaglia; 133r: CORBIS-
SYGMA/Mali Grazia Neri; 133b: COSMOS/G. Neri/C. Lannutti;
134tl: G. DAGLI ORTI/Chapel of the Palazzo Medici-Riccardi,
Florence; 134m: CORBIS-SYGMA/Origlia/Pizzoli;
134b: COSMOS/G. Neri/Cerchioli; 135l: CORBIS-SYGMA/
KEYSTONE; 135m: RAPHO/G. Sioen; 135r: CORBIS-SYGMA/
R. Galella; 136tl: TOP/H. Amiard; 136m: TOP/NETWORK/
Ch. Pillitz; 136b: COSMOS/G. Neri/L. Vitale;
137t: FARABOLAFOTO; 137bl: COSMOS/Steinmetz;
137br: VANDYSTADT/J.-M. Loubat; 138/139: DIAF/Pratt-Pries;
150: COSMOS/P. Boulat; 151l: HOA QUI/Ch. Sappa;
151r: SCOPE/J. Guillard; 153: DIAF/J.-P. Garcin; 154: CORBIS-
SYGMA/J.-P. Amet.

Printing and binding: Printer Industria Gráfica S.A., Barcelona
Colour Separations: Station Graphique, Ivry-sur-Seine
Paper: Perigord-Condat, France

617-004-01